Abbreviations

1 absolute, absolutely	2 adminis-trate, ion	3 advertise	4 America, n	5 amount	6 and	7 approximate, approxi-mately	8 April	9 associate	10 August
11 avenue	12 average	13 boulevard	14 bureau	15 capital, capitol	16 catalog	17 certify, certificate	18 child	19 children	20 Christmas
21 company	22 corporation	23 credit	24 day	25 December	26 department	27 discount	28 doctor	29 East	30 envelope
31 establish	32 February	33 federal	34 feet, foot	35 figure	36 Friday	37 government	38 inch	39 independent	40 intelligent, intelligently, intelligence
41 invoice	42 January	43 July	44 June	45 junior	46 magazine	47 manufacture	48 March	49 maximum	50 May
51 memorandum	52 merchandise	53 mile	54 minimum, minute	55 miscel-laneous	56 Monday	57 month	58 mortgage	59 North	60 November
61 number	62 October	63 ounce	64 page	65 paid	66 pair	67 parcel post	68 percent	69 place	70 popular
71 post office	72 pound	73 president	74 question	75 railroad	76 railway	77 represent, represent-ative	78 room	79 Saturday	80 second, secretary
81 senior	82 September	83 signature	84 South	85 square	86 street	87 subscribe, subscription	88 Sunday	89 superin-tendent	90 telephone
91 Thursday	92 total	93 Tuesday	94 vice-president	95 volume	96 warehouse	97 Wednesday	98 week	99 West	100 year
101	102	103	104	105	106	107	108	109	110

PRINCIPLES OF *Speedwriting*®

PREMIER EDITION

Glencoe Publishing Company
Encino, California

Send all inquiries to:
Glencoe Publishing Company
17337 Ventura Boulevard
Encino, CA 91316

Printed in the United States of America

Library of Congress Catalog Card Number: 76-41048

ISBN 0-02-679790-9

12 13 14 15 16 89 88 87 86

NOTICE

You are now studying a course in *"Speedwriting"* which identifies the best known and, in our opinion, the most efficient system of ABC shorthand. It is known throughout the United States and abroad under the distinguishing trademark and service mark *"Speedwriting."*

PREFACE

Speedwriting Shorthand is truly *the* shorthand of the modern age . . . the choice of modern men and women who seek employment in today's world of business. Yet, although *Speedwriting* is as up to date as the space capsule to the moon, it has a long and venerable history stretching back over two generations. This *Premier Edition* of *Speedwriting* Shorthand represents the culmination of more than forty years of research, testing, and practical use in the business office.

The original *Speedwriting* Shorthand came into being in the early 20's because Emma Dearborn, then one of the country's foremost shorthand teachers, was dissatisfied with the symbol systems she was teaching. She recognized that these systems had been invented as far back as the eighteenth century – long before the invention of the typewriter and long before that wonderful new employee called the *secretary* came into existence. She also knew that signs and symbols were devised specifically for parliamentary reporting, but they took much too much time to learn and were difficult to read back, especially for office dictation. It was Emma Dearborn's inspiration to create a shorthand system using the familiar ABC's, thereby enabling students to easily finish their training in a mere fraction of the time the old shorthands had required and to achieve top performance on the job.

Since the inception of this brilliant new shorthand, *Speedwriting* has been studied by nearly one million men and women, who have employed it with success in every major firm in every major industry from coast to coast.

Today *Speedwriting* Shorthand is taught at business schools in almost all cities in the United States and Canada and in many countries around the world.

INDEX

Lesson 1

What Is Speedwriting Shorthand?

Speedwriting is a system of shorthand in which letters of the alphabet and marks of punctuation are written to represent the sounds that make up our language. It is a scientific system composed of rules that can be employed for the writing of all words in the English language. Every word, whether used in business, law, medicine, engineering, or the arts, falls under a *Speedwriting* Shorthand principle. In this course, you will be trained to apply these principles as easily and naturally as you now write longhand.

Let's Look At the Alphabet

Since *Speedwriting* Shorthand uses letters of the alphabet to represent sounds, let's examine some of the features of the alphabet. As you know, the alphabet is divided into two types of letters called vowels and consonants. The letters we call vowels are: *a*, *e*, *i*, *o*, and *u*. All other letters are called consonants.

About Consonants

The sound of "b" in the words *book, bill,* or *rib* always has the same sound. This is true of most consonants—each represents just one sound. A few consonants, however, have more than one sound.

For example, the letter *s* has the sound of "s" in such words as *say, base,* and *less*; but it has the sound of "z" in words like *rise, visit,* and *does.* The letter *g* in *get, leg,* and *stag* has what we call a hard sound; but it has the soft sound of "j" in *rage, edge,* and *college.* And what of the letter *c* in *city, citizen,* and *face*? In these words, you hear the sound of "s."

How will this be important to you in learning *Speedwriting* Shorthand? Since shorthand is based on sound, you will completely disregard the spelling of words and concern yourself only with the sounds that you hear. This is true of all shorthand systems—symbol as well as *Speedwriting* Shorthand.

Make sure that you understand what has been covered to this point by testing yourself. In the following words, what letter would you use to represent the sound that has been underscored?

Example: **rage** j

1. race ______ **2. manage** ______

3. cell ______ **4. city** ______

5. bag ______ **6. judge** ______

7. season ______ **8. citizen** ______

Answers:

1. s 2. j 3. s 4. s 5. g 6. j 7. z 8. s

About Vowels

All vowels (*a, e, i, o, u*) have more than one sound. In *Speedwriting* Shorthand, we divide all vowel sounds into two major types – long and short. When the sound of a vowel is the same as its alphabetic name, we call it a long vowel. In other words, a long vowel is one that is pronounced as follows:

a as in **ape** and **make**

e as in **eat** and **seal**

i as in **ice** and **file**

o as in **oat** and **hope**

u as in **unit** and **fuse**

The vowel sound in the words *do, too,* or *tool* is so similar to the one heard in *due* and *tube* that we treat it as a long "u" sound.

These are all of the sounds of long vowels. A vowel having any other sound is referred to as a short vowel.

Pronounce the following groups of words to help you become familiar with the differences in the sounds of long and short vowels:

SHORT VOWELS		LONG VOWELS
at tap tall	→	ate tape tale
etch sell	→	each seal
is fill	→	ice file
on hop	→	own hope
us fun but	→	use fume boot

Now, test your understanding of what you have just learned by putting L after those words that contain a long-vowel sound and S after those that contain a short-vowel sound.

Example: **made** L

1. mat S	2. fell S
3. cost S	4. lit S
5. coast L	6. mean L
7. seat L	8. sun S
9. set S	10. soon L
11. talk S	12. took L or S
13. tail L	14. fool L

Answers:

1. S	2. S	3. S	4. S	5. L	6. L	7. L
8. S	9. S	10. L	11. S	12. S	13. L	14. L

A Word About Writing Shorthand

Because *Speedwriting* Shorthand is based on precise, clearly defined rules, you will find it an easy system to learn. And, since you will be using your natural penmanship to a large extent, you will also find it is an easy system to write.

Let's talk for a moment about how to use your natural penmanship to maximum advantage. Observe the handwriting in the following sentence:

I shall pay my bill in June.

Now, in the sentence below, notice how the amount of writing has been cut down considerably by simply eliminating all non-essential strokes:

i shall pay my bill in june.

What shortcuts have we employed?

1. No capital letters. In *Speedwriting* Shorthand, we do not use capitals except as applied to certain principles that you will learn.
2. No unnecessary strokes on the first and last letters of each word.
3. No crossing of *t*'s or dotting of *i*'s or *j*'s.

Understand that you are not expected to radically alter your normal handwriting; but to help yourself build extra speed in shorthand, you should concentrate on streamlining your letters as illustrated in these examples.

Practice streamlining your handwriting by copying the following words in your shorthand pad, using the shortcuts listed above.

baby flag gay iron joy key toy

jury title treat file pig buff

Finally, you should learn to write a streamlined *Speedwriting* *m* and *w*. Since these are the most time-consuming letters to write, we recommend the use of  for *m*. What we are doing is simply writing a longhand *m* without any up and down movement of the pen, like this: .

Similarly, we are going to write  for *w*. Like the *m*, we have just streamlined the longhand *w*  .

In your shorthand pad, practice writing the streamlined  and  by substituting them for the longhand *m* and *w* in the following words.

Initial, Medial, and Final Sounds

There are three positions that a sound may have in a word. It may be the first sound; it may be the last sound; or it may be somewhere between the first and last sound. There is a definite name that is given to each of these positions.

Initial refers to the sound at the beginning of a word. For example: The "i" in the word *item* or the "b" in the word *book* is an initial sound.

Final refers to the sound at the very end of a word. For example: The "o" in *radio* or the "d" in *bad* is a final sound.

Medial refers to any sound that occurs between the first and last sound in a word. For example: The "a" in the word *made* or the "ol" in *hold* are medial sounds.

You are now ready to study your first rule in *Speedwriting* Shorthand.

RULE 1 | **Write what you hear, omitting all medial short vowels.**

Let's examine this rule carefully to see what it means. "Write what you hear" tells you that words will be written according to sound, not spelling. The word *pay,* for example, is made up of two sounds, "p" + "a." The *y* is silent. Therefore, when written according to sound, **pay** is *pa* . Two sounds are heard in the word *low,* "l" and "o." The *w* is silent so write **low** *lo* . In the word *eat* you hear the sounds "e" and "t" so write **eat** *el* . Similarly, the word *do* contains the two sounds "d" + "u" so write **do** *du* . Since words are to be written according to sound, you will write the word **a** *a* , the word **I** *i* , **you** *u* , and **owe** *o* .

Study these examples:

aim	*am*	**high**	*hi*
ate	*al*	**know**	*no*
lay	*la*	**own**	*on*
say	*sa*	**few**	*fu*
me	*me*	**knew**	*nu*
see	*se*	**who**	*hu*

You write:

1. tie ___ti___	**2. way** ___va___
3. due ___du___	**4. weigh** ___va___
5. fee ___fe___	**6. new** ___nu___
7. so ___so___	**8. aid** ___ad___
9. view ___vu___	**10. may** ___ma___
11. no ___no___	**12. die** ___di___

Confirmation:

1. li 2. wa 3. du 4. wa 5. fe

6. mu 7. so 8. ad 9. vu 10. ma

11. mo 12. di

Consider the word *base*. It contains three pronounced sounds: "b" + "a" + "s." Therefore, you write **base** bas . Similarly, *file* contains the sounds "f," "i," and "l." Thus, write **file** fil .

Study the following words:

mail	mal	**hope**	hop
lease	les	**seal**	sel
robe	rob	**sign**	sin
deep	dep	**rule**	rul

You write:

1. safe saf____ **2. tape** tap____

3. wife wf____ **4. goal** gol____

5. tool tul____ **6. yield** yeld____

Confirmation:

1. saf 2. tap 3. wf 4. gol 5. tul

6. yeld

Now turn your attention to the second part of Rule 1:

"Write what you hear, omitting all medial short vowels." You know that medial means middle, so the rule simply tells you that a short vowel will not be written if it occurs anywhere in the middle of a word. In other words, it is only at the beginning or at the end of a word that a short vowel is to be written.

Compare the words *seal* and *sell*. You have already written **seal** *sel*. What of the word *sell?* In this word, the *e* has a short-vowel sound; and it occurs in the middle of the word. According to the rule, you are to drop this medial short vowel and write **sell** *sl*. For the same reason **bill** is *bl* and **lamp** *lmp*.

Study these examples:

some	*sm*	**map**	*mp*
sum	*sm*	**said**	*sd*
head	*hd*	**met**	*mt*
built	*blt*	**get**	*gt*
men	*mn*	**won**	*wn*
none	*nn*	**half**	*hf*
give	*gv*	**red (read)**	*rd*
yet	*yt*	**set**	*st*
build	*bld*	**far**	*fr*

What about a word such as *when?* In the "wh" combination sound the *h* is almost silent, so it will be dropped. Accordingly, you write the word **when** *wn* and **what** *wt*.

You write:

1. **done** ____________ 2. **tell** ____________

3. **bid** ____________ 4. **run** ____________

5. **felt** ____________ 6. **got** ____________

7. **did** ____________ 8. **son, sun** ____________

9. **big** ____________ 10. **bus** ____________

11. **job** ____________ 12. **lot** ____________

13. **let** ____________ 14. **fill** ____________

15. **yes** ____________ 16. **gas** ____________

Confirmation:

1. dn 2. ll 3. bd 4. rn 5. fll
6. gl 7. dd 8. sn 9. bg 10. bs
11. jb 12. ll 13. ll 14. fl 15. ys
16. gs

The examples you have seen so far have all been one-syllable words. The omission of medial short vowels also applies to words that contain more than one syllable. For example, the word *metal* contains more than one short vowel. Applying the rule to drop all medial short vowels, you write **metal** mll ; **happen** hpn .

As you study these words, observe that all medial short vowels have been eliminated from the outline: **ballot** bll ; **middle** mdl ; **panel** pnl ; **senate** snl ; **model** mdl .

You write:

1. bulletin bltn 2. limit lmt

3. written rtn 4. level lvl

Confirmation:

1. bltn 2. lmt 3. rtn 4. lvl

You have now covered some words that contain long vowels and some that contain short vowels. There are, of course, many words that contain both long and short vowels. For example: *value, item, ready.* To write these words, simply apply the rule that tells you to write long vowels and omit medial short vowels.

value	vlu	**policy**	plse
item	itm	**follow**	flo
ready	rde	**money**	mne
memo	mmo	**unit**	unt
happy	hpe	**fellow**	flo

Remember, it is to medial short-vowel sounds only that this rule refers. Short vowels at the beginning or end of a word will be written.

dilemma	dlma	**ahead**	ahd
off	of	**add**	ad
often	ofn	**edit**	edt
us	us	**pajama**	pjma
egg	eg	**if**	if

Part of this rule, "Write what you hear," requires further explanation. As you will recall, certain letters have more than one sound. In the word *edge,* for example, the *g* has the sound of "j"; therefore, to be consistent with the rule to "Write what you hear," write the word **edge** ej . In the same way, because the *c* in the word *face* has the sound of "s," write **face** fas .

Study the following words to see how spelling is ignored completely and each word is written according to <u>sound</u>.

visit	vzt	**age**	aj
deposit	dpzt	**knowledge**	nlj
citizen	stzn	**damage**	dmj
type	tip	**nice**	nis
judge	jj	**civilian**	svln

You write:

1. **race** ra 2. **manage** mj

3. **says** saz 4. **office** ofs

5. **my** m 6. **message** mj

7. **civil** svl 8. **wage** waj

Confirmation:

1. ras 2. mj 3. sz 4. ofs

5. m 6. msj 7. svl 8. waj

Read the following sentence, paying particular attention to the sounds of the underscored words.

If you have no use for the book, I know someone who can use it.

As you can see, the word *use* has more than one pronunciation. Since you are writing words according to their sounds, you will write *us* in the first part of the sentence and *uz* in the second.

Study these words:

enough	*enf*	**mill**	*ml*
gauge	*gaj*	**tube**	*tub*
passage	*psj*	**top**	*tp*
snow	*sno*	**asset**	*ast*
debt	*dt*	**hot**	*ht*
budget	*bjt*	**settle**	*stl*
heavy	*hve*	**body**	*bde*
win	*◡n*	**revenue**	*rvnu*
leaf	*lef*	**solicit**	*slst*
film	*flm*	**ribbon**	*rbn*
women	*◡m*	**role**	*rol*
fit	*ft*	**twin**	*t◡n*
gallon	*gln*	**dozen**	*dzn*

You have now completed Rule 1. Test your understanding of what you have learned by writing the following words. As you do so, remember:

1. Write all pronounced consonants and all long vowels.
2. Write short vowels only at the beginning or end of a word.
3. Disregard spelling and write words according to sound.

You write:

1. bad bd
2. offset ofsl
3. bottom bls
4. yellow ylo
5. huge huj
6. meal rel
7. piece pes
8. gone gn
9. away a-a
10. league leg
11. does dz
12. led ld

Confirmation:

1. bd 2. ofsl 3. bls 4. ylo
5. huj 6. rel 7. pes 8. gn
9. a-a 10. leg 11. dz 12. ld

Our language contains certain sounds such as "ch," "sh," and "th" that result from the blending together of two letters. In this and later lessons, you will learn how to represent these combination sounds. But first a reminder: In the section dealing with the writing of shorthand, you were told that capital letters are not used in *Speedwriting* Shorthand as in longhand. Instead, *Speedwriting* Shorthand uses capital letters to represent certain specific sounds. Be extremely careful, therefore, never to write a capital letter except as an application of rules you will learn in your course of study.

RULE 2 | Write capital *C* for the sound of "ch."

What does this rule tell you? It simply states that whenever the sound of "ch" is heard in a word, it is represented by writing a capital *C*. Thus, the word **cheap** is written *Cep*, the word **much** *mC*. Notice, in writing the *C* in **much**, that it is joined to the *m* *mC*. Similarly, **watch** *wC*.

Study the following words:

chief	*Cef*	**teach**	*teC*
attach	*atC*	**match**	*mC*
each	*eC*	**chop**	*Cp*

You write:

1. rich *rC* ______ **2. touch** *tC* ______

3. reach *reC* ______ **4. patch** *pC* ______

5. which *wC* ______ **6. such** *sC* ______

Confirmation:

1. *rC* **2.** *tC* **3.** *reC* **4.** *pC*

5. *wC* **6.** *sC*

As was stated in the introduction, *Speedwriting* Shorthand makes use of the alphabet and marks of punctuation to represent sounds. (By a mark of punctuation, we mean any character that is found on the keyboard of a typewriter.) The next rule refers to one of these marks of punctuation – the underscore.

RULE 3 | **When "ing" or "thing" is added to a word, underscore the last sound of the outline.**

You know that **reach** is written reC . If the ending "ing" is added to form the word *reaching,* the C will be underscored in compliance with the rule. Thus, **reaching** reC̲ . The word *mailing* is composed of the word *mail* + *ing*. Following the rule, **mailing** is written ml̲ .

Study these words:

following	fl̲o̲	**selling**	sl̲
giving	gv̲	**getting**	gt̲
telling	tl̲	**doing**	du̲
building	bld̲	**typing**	tp̲
using	uz̲	**adding**	ad̲
attaching	atC̲	**living**	lv̲

Read the following words:

1.	se	**2.**	no	**3.**	hop
4.	pa	**5.**	fl	**6.**	bl
7.	rn	**8.**	vzt	**9.**	wa
10.	fil	**11.**	tec	**12.**	tc

Confirmation:

1. seeing 2. knowing 3. hoping 4. paying 5. filling 6. billing 7. running 8. visiting 9. weighing 10. filing 11. teaching 12. touching

The rule also states that the underscore is used to indicate that the sound of "thing" has been added to a word. *Something,* for example, is made up of *some* + *thing.* Since you know that **some** is written sm, you will write **something** sm. What of the word *nothing?* The word **no** is written no. Since the *o* in *nothing* has a short vowel sound and you have learned to omit medial short vowels from an outline, you will write **nothing** n.

Brief Forms

Throughout this course, the word outline will be used to mean the *Speedwriting* Shorthand representation of a word. Thus, the outline for the word **pay** is pa and the outline for the word **my** is mi.

Although every word in the English language can be written according to a *Speedwriting* Shorthand rule, certain words are used so often in our daily speech that we adopt special outlines for them so that they can be written in the shortest time possible. All shorthands do this. In *Speedwriting* we call such outlines Brief Forms. Fortunately, the list of Brief Forms in *Speedwriting* Shorthand is not very long; but the words of which the list is composed will be vital to your success in taking dictation. Since they are not written according to rule, you must study and practice them until you know them thoroughly. Here is the first list of Brief Forms. Others will be given in later lessons.

is, his	s	**the**	.
that	la	**to, it**	t
for	f	**will, well**	l
can	c	**we**	e
in, not	n	**are, our, hour**	r

Notice that two or three words are sometimes represented by the same Brief Form. You will find that, when read in context, only one of the meanings will make proper sense so there is no need for this to disturb you. Also notice that the Brief Form for the word *the* is the mark of punctuation that is usually put at the end of a longhand sentence. Since you will have to indicate the end of a sentence in your shorthand notes, you will do so by using a backward slant like this \ in place of the period.

Pay the bill. I will pay the bill.

pa . bl\ i l pa . bl\

Standard Abbreviations

Certain abbreviations that are used in the business world and in our daily lives are so common that they come to mind automatically. In *Speedwriting,* we are going to make use of some of these popular abbreviations. Here are a few. You will study others in later lessons.

company co **president** P **vice-president** VP

and & (This is called an ampersand.)

Reading Exercises

Your goal during the initial stages of your course in *Speedwriting* Shorthand is not only to learn the rules and their application, but also to acquire the ability to read *Speedwriting* outlines fluently and rapidly. This skill can be acquired only through practice, and we urge you to read and reread each of the *Speedwriting* Reading Exercises that you will find in every lesson until you can read them as easily as longhand.

In writing these Exercises, we have indicated paragraphs, punctuation, and proper names in the following manner.

1. Paragraphs: The end of a paragraph is indicated by doubling the last mark of punctuation. For example: \\ ??
2. Punctuation marks: Indicated by encircling them within the sentence. For example: (,) (;)
3. Proper names: Indicated by placing a wavy line (~) under the word or words that are proper names. For example: **Bill** and **May** bl + ma.

If you have difficulty in reading a particular outline, do not puzzle too long over it. Instead, read on to the end of the sentence to see whether this will give you a clue to the outline that caused you trouble. If you still cannot read the outline, refer to the Key that follows each Reading Exercise.

Reading Exercises

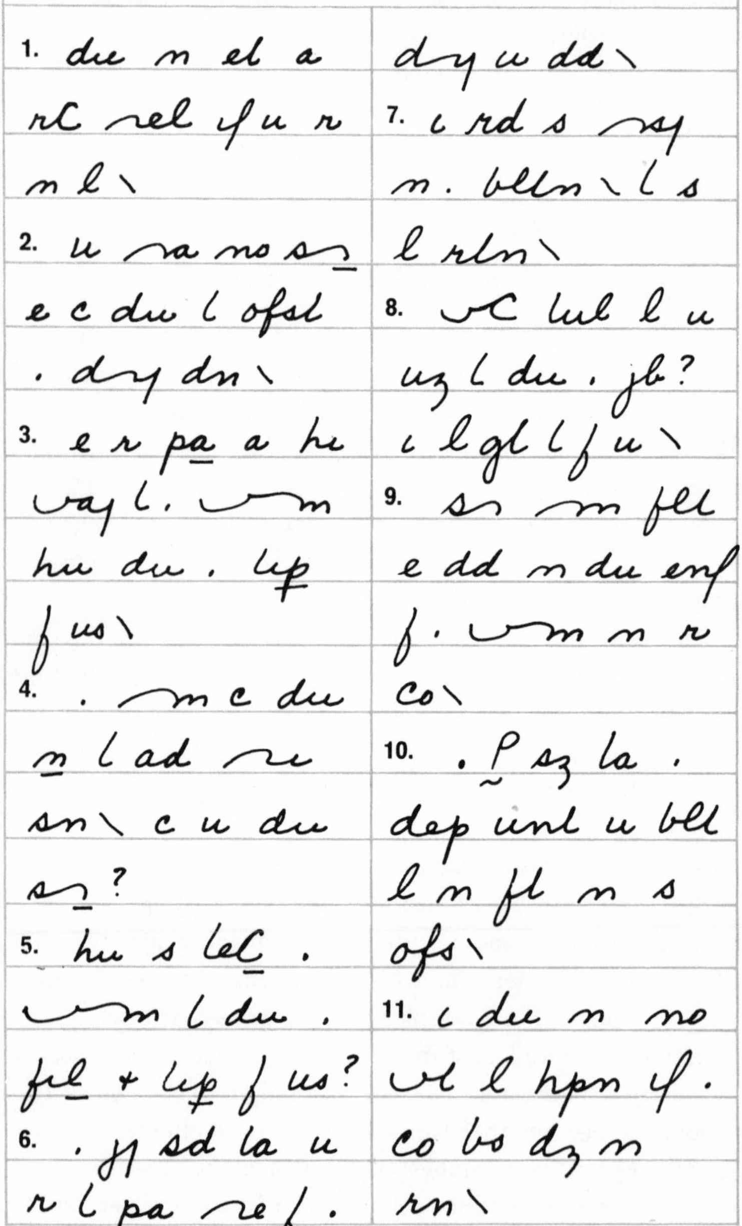

12. e no la a
fu m du n
se vC vlu n
. va u r du
. jb \

13. m Cefa
s l ad l m
nly so la i c
gl ahd n. co \

14. . m hu
on. bld l ll
u vn u c sn
a nu les \

15. i dd n se
a bl f. ylo
rob \ l u sl
ll se?

16. m vf & i
r hop l se u
vn e r vzt
r sn \

17. u c reC r
co f u l flo
. p la e r
alC \

18. dd u sa la
u r rde l sn
a nu plse?

19. . sll bas u
r bld s n bq
enf f. hve
lp \

20. e hop l sll
r dl vn e
se u \ f vC
ls du e o
sC a hu
s?

21. c rd . mo
n vC u sd
la u l my
. ofs un . P̃
s ava \
22. s blf .
vC dd n yl
rel re \ un
l dz c l pa
vl s du \
23. dpzl . me
u o re n .
saf + ll . VP̃
l gv l l re \
24. l u ll re
yf c c gl a Cep
vC f nu sn?
25. c c gl a
nl fel l
nC . unl n
nu ofs? yf u
du n sl sC
a fel c l se
yf . mn c bld
l \
26. . P̃ s hpe l
sa lã r nu gs
gay s sl̲ l \
27. e r bl̲ u f
. ylo lap e r
ral̲ l u \
28. c l alC a
rd rbn l .
rob \

Key To Lesson 1

1. Do not eat a rich meal if you are not well.
2. You may know something we can do to offset the damage done.
3. We are[2] paying a high wage to the women who do the typing for us.
4. The men can do nothing to aid my son. Can you[4] do something?
5. Who is teaching the women to do the filing and typing for us?
6. The judge said that you are to pay[6] me for the damage you did.
7. I read his message in the bulletin. It is well written.
8. Which tool will you use to[8] do the job? I will get it for you.
9. Some men felt we did not do enough for the women in our company.
10. The[10] President says that the deep unit you built will not fit in his office.
11. I do not know what will happen if the[12] company bus does not run.
12. We know that a few men do not see much value in the way you are doing the job.[14]
13. My chief aim is to add to my knowledge so that I can get ahead in the company.
14. The men who own the building[16] will tell you when you can sign a new lease.
15. I did not see a bill for the yellow robe. Will you mail it to me?[18]
16. My wife and I are hoping to see you when we are visiting our son.
17. You can reach our company if you will[20] follow the map that we are attaching.

18. Did you say that you are ready to sign a new policy?
19. The metal[22] base you are building is not big enough for the heavy lamp.
20. We hope to settle our debt when we see you. For which[24] item do we owe such a huge sum?
21. I read the memo in which you said that you will manage the office when the President[26] is away.
22. His bill for the watch did not yet reach me. When it does, I will pay what is due.
23. Deposit[28] the money you owe me in the safe and tell the Vice-President to give it to me.
24. Will you tell me if I can[30] get a cheap watch for my son?
25. Can I get a metal file to match the unit in my office? If you do not sell[32] such a file, I will see if the men can build it.
26. The President is happy to say that our new gas gauge is selling[34] well.
27. We are billing you for the yellow tape we are mailing to you.
28. I will attach a red ribbon[36] to the robe.
(362 words)

Writing Assignment – Lesson 1

1. I will edit the film and mail it to the President.

i l edl . fl & ml l . P,

2. The company will pay you well for doing the filing.

. co l pa u l f du . fl,

3. If the memo which you are typing is ready, I will sign it.

f . mo c u r tp s rde,
i l sin l,

4. We are hoping a message will follow telling us when the new watch will reach us.

e r hop a mj l flo tl us
n . nu vC l reC us

5. We are happy to see that his son is doing the job well.

e r hpe l se la s sn s du . jb
l,

6. I did not see the men deposit the money in the office safe.

i dd n se . mn dpol . me n
. ofs saf.

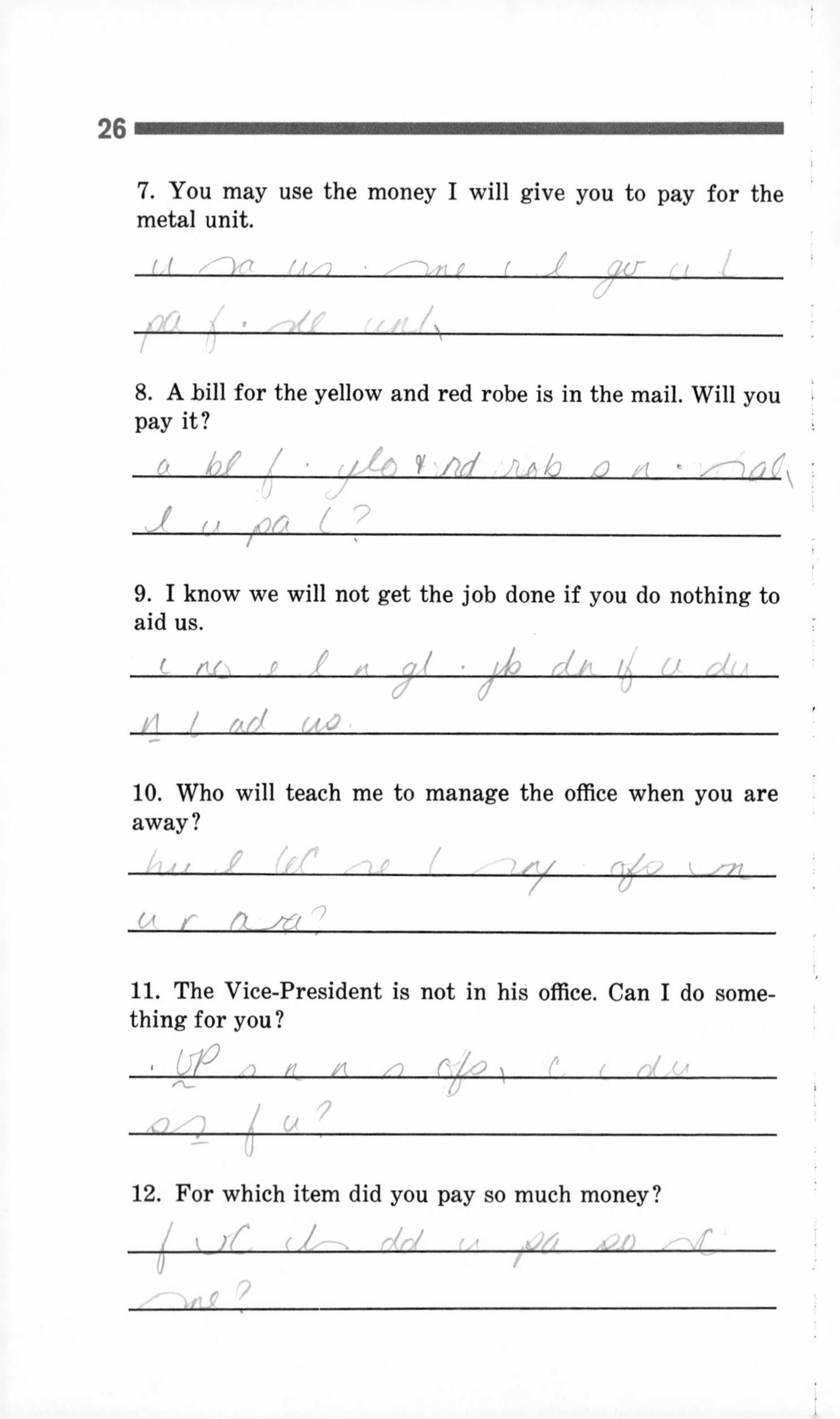

7. You may use the money I will give you to pay for the metal unit.

8. A bill for the yellow and red robe is in the mail. Will you pay it?

9. I know we will not get the job done if you do nothing to aid us.

10. Who will teach me to manage the office when you are away?

11. The Vice-President is not in his office. Can I do something for you?

12. For which item did you pay so much money?

Lesson 2

In Lesson 1 you learned to write an underscore to indicate that the sound of "ing" or "thing" has been added to a word. You are now going to learn to write another mark of punctuation to represent a different sound.

RULE 4	**For the medial and final sound of "nt" or "ment" write a hyphen (-).**

Let's start with the sound of "nt" heard at the end of the words *agent* and *want*. The word **age** is *aj* . If the sound of "nt" is now added to form the word *agent,* simply add a hyphen (-) and write **agent** *aj-* . The word *want* is made up of the sounds "w" + "nt," so write **want** *w-*.

Study these words:

sent	*s-*	**event**	*ev-*
paint	*pa-*	**resident**	*rzd-*
went	*w-*	**evident**	*evd-*

The rule tells you to write a hyphen for the medial and final sound of "nt." In other words, you will also write a hyphen for the sound of "nt" in the middle of a word such as **rental** *r-l* .

What is the sound at the end of the words *doesn't* and *don't?* Do you recognize it as the same sound heard in *went?* Since it is the same sound of "nt," apply the rule to these contractions and write **doesn't** *dz-* ; **don't** *do-* .

You write:

1. won't wo- **2. rent** r-

3. didn't dd- **4. hunt** h-

5. dental d-l **6. bent** b-

Confirmation:

1. *wo-* 2. *r-* 3. *dd-*

4. *h-* 5. *d-l* 6. *b-*

There are many words that end in the sound of "nt" to which "ing" is added. For example: *hunting* and *wanting.* When writing these words in *Speedwriting* Shorthand, the hyphen will be handled just as if it were a letter of the alphabet, and the rule to underscore for "ing" will be applied. Thus, **hunting** *h=* ; **renting** *r=* ; **painting** *pa=* .

The second part of this rule tells you that the hyphen is also written for the medial or final syllable "ment." You know that **pay** is *pa* ; in the word *payment* you simply add a hyphen for the syllable "ment": **payment** *pa-* . **Regiment** is *rj-* ; **regimental** *rj-l* ; **judgment** *jj-* .

You write:

1. settlement sll- **2. management** mj-

Confirmation:

1.  2. 

What of the word *meant*? This rule tells you to write a hyphen for the medial and final sound of "ment" but it does not say initial. Therefore, the word **meant** is written 

It is important in writing the hyphen to use a short stroke in order to save time and to facilitate the reading of your notes.

Read the following sentences:

1. 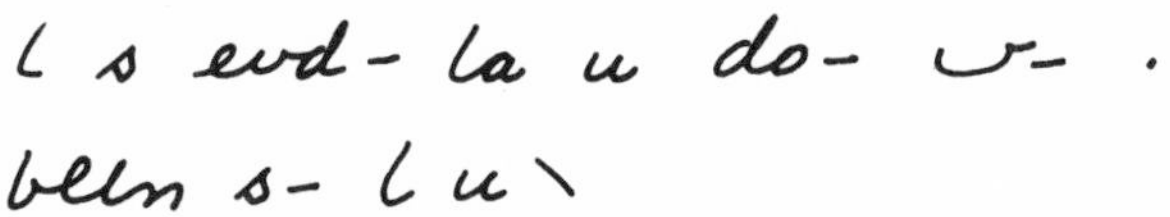

2. 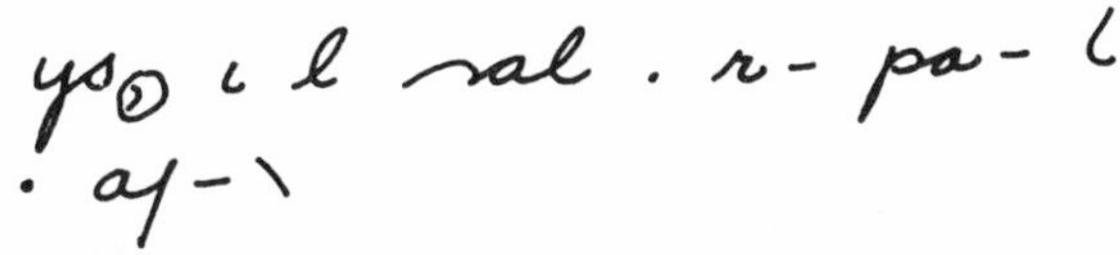

3. 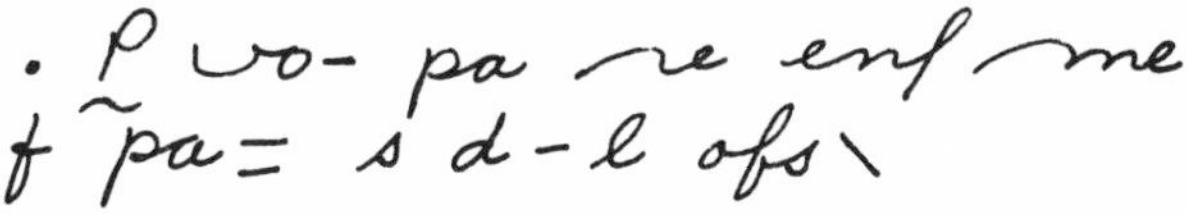

Key:

1. It is evident that you don't want the bulletin sent to you.
2. Yes, I will mail the rent payment to the agent.
3. The President won't pay me enough money for painting his dental office.

RULE 5	**Add s to form the plural of a shorthand outline that ends in a letter of the alphabet; when an outline ends in a mark of punctuation, form the plural by repeating the mark of punctuation.**

The word **net** is written *nt*. This rule instructs you to add *s* to the outline to indicate the plural. Thus, **nets** *nts*. Since **piece** is written *pes*, you will write **pieces** *pess*.

Study these examples:

units	*unts*	**offices**	*ofss*
faces	*fass*	**lots**	*lts*
maps	*mps*	**debts**	*dts*
hopes	*hops*	**assets**	*asts*

Some plurals have the sound of "z"; for example, *items* and *jobs*. Through long years of usage, you are accustomed to writing *s* for all plurals regardless of sound. You are going to take advantage of this established habit by doing the same in *Speedwriting* Shorthand, so you will add *s* to your outline for either plural sound. Thus, **items** *itms*; **jobs** *jbs*; **dues** *dus*; **citizens** *stzns*

You write:

1. policies *plses*	**2. ribbons** *rbns*
3. bills *bls*	**4. fees** *fes*
5. files *fls*	**6. bulletins** *bltns*
7. models *mdls*	**8. tools** *tuls*
9. rules *ruls*	**10. mills** *mls*
11. ways *was*	**12. seals** *sels*

Confirmation:

1. plses	2. rbns	3. bls
4. fes	5. fls	6. bllns
7. ⌒dls	8. luls	9. ruls
10. ⌒ls	11. ⌣as	12. sels

Although the rule refers to the formation of plurals, you are going to use the same rule to indicate possessives, contractions, and the addition of *s* to verbs.

Study these examples:

pays	pas	**follows**	flos
gives	gvs	**reaches**	reCs
women's	⌣⌒ns	**men's**	⌒ns
what's	⌣ls	**types**	lps
gets	gls	**tells**	lls
touches	lCs	**sells**	sls

In all of the examples given for this rule, you will notice that the pronunciation of the basic word remains unchanged with the addition of *s*. Since this is not true of *says* and *does*, you will recall that these words are written **says** sz and **does** dz .

The second part of the rule refers to *Speedwriting* outlines that end in a mark of punctuation. For example, **want** ⌣— . The rule states that in such cases you are to repeat the mark of punctuation to indicate the addition of *s* to the word, so **wants** ⌣— — . As you know, the outline for the word **paint** is pa- . To write *paints* you simply add another hyphen: **paints** pa-- . Consider the word *buildings*. Since the outline for the word **building** is bld̲ , you add another underscore to your outline: **buildings** bld̳ . Similarly, **payment** is pa- and **payments** pa-- .

Study these examples:

ceilings	sel̳	**wrappings**	rp̳
agents	aj--	**billings**	bl̳

You write:

1. judgments jj--

2. settlements sll--

3. events ev--

4. mailings sal̳

5. rents r--

6. residents rzd--

Confirmation:

1. jj--   2. sll--   3. ev--

4. mal̳   5. r--   6. rzd--

In Lesson 1, reference was made to the combination sounds of "ch," "sh," and "th." You have already learned to write C for the sound of "ch." The next rule deals with the sound of "sh." Here again, you are going to make use of a capital letter to represent a sound.

RULE 6 | For the sound of "sh" write capital S .

In the word *show* you hear the sound of "sh." Applying the rule that you are to write S for this sound, **show** is written So . The sound of "sh" is heard in the word *rush*. Following the rule, you write **rush** rS .

Study the following words:

should	Sd	**shows**	Sos
wish	vS	**issue**	iSu
showing	So̲	**finish**	fnS
sufficient	sfS-	**shopping**	Sp̲
efficient	efS-	**issuing**	iSu̲
fishing	fS̲	**shape**	Sap

You write:

1. wishes vSs ____ **2. issues** iSus ____

3. bushel bSl ____ **4. shoes** Sus ____

5. mesh mS ____ **6. polishing** plS̲ ____

Confirmation:

1. vSs 2. iSus 3. bSl

4. Sus 5. mS 6. plS̲

Remember, the rule tells you to write S for the sound of "sh." You have learned to disregard spelling and to write what you hear. Notice that we did exactly that in the words *sufficient* and *issues* in the above word list.

You have now learned two combination sounds: "ch" and "sh." Fix them firmly in your mind by writing the following words. Remember, C for the sound of "ch" and S for the sound of "sh."

You write:

1. chop Cp	2. shop Sp
3. sheep Sep	4. cheap Cep
5. shell Sl	6. chill Cl
7. push pS	8. patch pC

Confirmation:

1. Cp	2. Sp	3. Sep
4. Cep	5. Sl	6. Cl
7. pS	8. pC	

Brief Forms

firm	F	this	th
letter	L	on	o
would	d	have, very, of	v

Abbreviations

catalog cal

Dictation Hints

In writing numbers, you simply write the figure as you do in longhand. Thus:

5 men 5 ⌒n **15 maps** 15 ⌒ps **someone** s⌒1

99 women 99 ∪⌒n **3,764 policies** 3764 plses

Word Combinations and Development

In *Speedwriting* Shorthand, as in longhand, you are going to build words from the simple to the more complex by starting with a word that is already familiar and adding to it. For example, notice how many words can be built from just the one word **for,** which as you know is written f

for	f	**form**	f⌒
forms	f⌒s	**formal**	f⌒l
formula	f⌒la	**forget**	fgt
forgotten	fgtn	**forgive**	fgv
force	fs	**forces**	fss
efforts	efts	**afford**	afd
effort	eft	**affording**	afd̲
fortune	fCn	**fortunate**	fCnt

You can see from this illustration that, whenever a word contains the sound of "for," you will write f for that sound. In the same way, notice how words can be built from the word **can,** which as you have already learned is written *c* .

cancel	*csl*	**canvas**	*cvs*
cannot	*cn*		

Also, since you know that **in** is *n* , you will write **involve** *nvlv* and **inform** *nfs* .

Study the following to see how words are formed by applying rules to Brief Form outlines or by simply adding other sounds to the basic words.

its	*ts*	**isn't**	*s-*
it's	*ts*	**that's**	*las*
accompany	*aco*	**ours**	*rs*
willing	_l_	**hours**	*rs*
into	*nt*	**having**	_v_
president's	*ps*	**haven't**	*v-*
companies	*cos*	**letters**	*Ls*
letterhead	*Lhd*	**firms**	*Fs*
catalogs	*cals*	**wouldn't**	*d-*

In the above examples, you can see how new words are built from Brief Forms or standard abbreviations; but any two words can be joined together in the same way to form another word. For example: **somewhat** *svl* , **somebody** *sbde* .

Reading Exercises

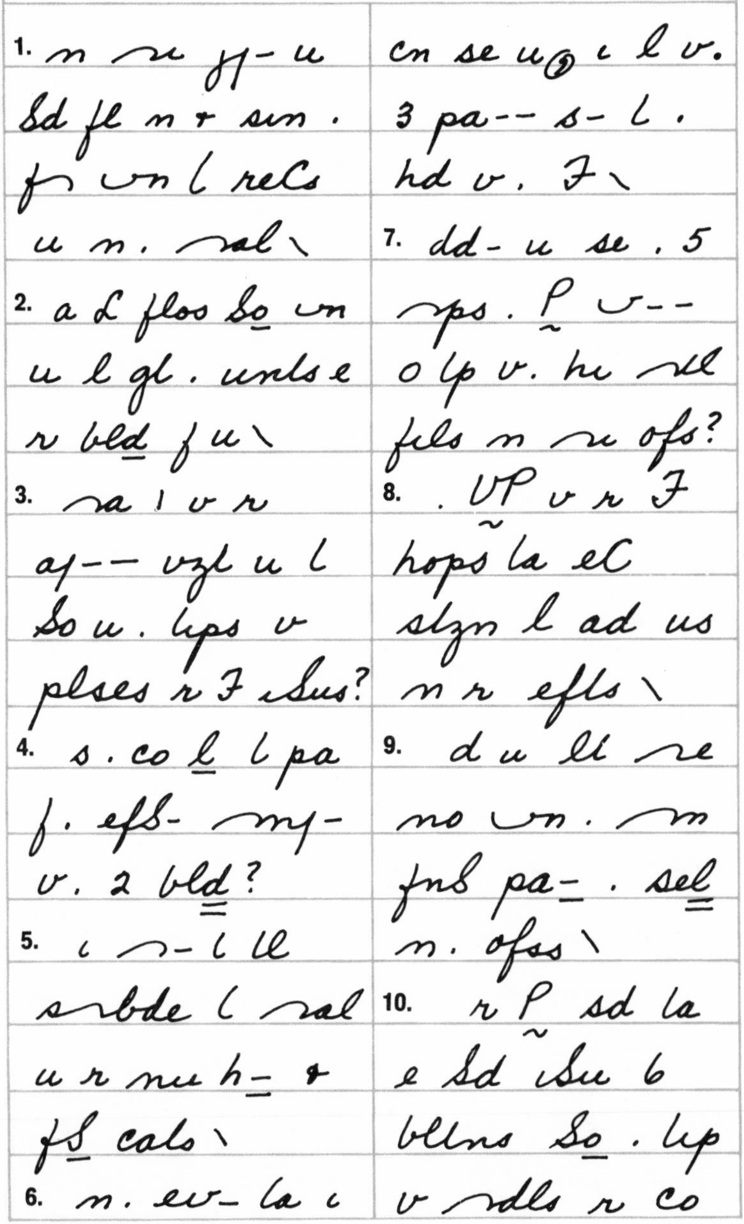

s bld\

11. i no i v s-
~u pa-- n
sll- v ~u
d-l bl\

12. lh s l nf~
u la. d~ u
~- s rde + e
r ~al l\

13. e v s- u /
v r nu cals\
f u Sd se s~
u ~- n lh
cal? ~o- u ll
~e no so la
i ~a r8 l l
u\

14. i do- no f
i l v sf8-
~me f. pa- v
~u dls\

15. l s v evd- la
u v fgln la
pa- s du f.
r-l v. ofs\

16. f u ~-
~e l du so?
i l v / v r
~m So u s~
v. pess la e
hopl sl\

17. e ~8 l gl
s~/ l du. lp
v. Ls n r co\
f u ~- sC a
jt? fl n.
f~s la e r
alC\

18. v- u ofn
sd la . P̃ vSs
se l lip s Ls
+ pa s bls?

19. ds- fgl la i
v- l aco u
vn u vzl .
ofs\

20. dz- . Sp sl
ms + v ms
Sus?

21. ll . af- la
i cn afd l
pa sC hi r-
fr ofss\

22. if e du n
gl . pa - - ⑨
u l fs us l
csl lh plse\

Key To Lesson 2

1. In my judgment you should fill in and sign the form when it reaches you in the mail.
2. A letter follows showing when[2] you will get the units we are building for you.
3. May one of our agents visit you to show you the types of[4] policies our firm issues?
4. Is the company willing to pay for the efficient management of the two buildings?[6]
5. I meant to tell somebody to mail you our new hunting and fishing catalogs.
6. In the event that I cannot[8] see you, I will have the three payments sent to the head of the firm.
7. Didn't you see the five maps the President wants[10] on top of the high metal files in my office?
8. The Vice-President of our firm hopes that each citizen will aid us[12] in our efforts.
9. Would you let me know when the men finish painting the ceilings in the offices.
10. Our President[14] said that we should issue six bulletins showing the type of models our company is building.
11. I know I[16] have sent my payments in settlement of my dental bill.
12. This is to inform you that the item you want is ready[18] and we are mailing it.
13. We have sent you one of our new catalogs. If you should see something you want in this[20] catalog, won't you let me know so that I may rush it to you.
14. I don't know if I will have sufficient money[22] for the payment of my debts.
15. It is very evident that you have forgotten that payment is due for the rental[24] of the office.

16. If you want me to do so, I will have one of our men show you some of the pieces that we[26] hope to sell.

17. We wish to get someone to do the typing of the letters in our company. If you want such a[28] job, fill in the forms that we are attaching.

18. Haven't you often said that the President wishes me to type his[30] letters and pay his bills?

19. Don't forget that I want to accompany you when you visit the office.

20. Doesn't the[32] shop sell men's and women's shoes?

21. Tell the agent that I cannot afford to pay such high rent for our offices.

22. If[34] we do not get the payments, you will force us to cancel this policy. *(352 words)*

YOUR HOMEWORK MAKES A BIG DIFFERENCE

Speedwriting shorthand graduates repeatedly and enthusiastically look back and point to the definite role homework played in their success. It can be of the same distinct importance in *your* success, too.

You know it takes study—diligent study—to master any subject. And shorthand, your key to an interesting job and high salary, is no exception to this rule. If you study diligently, you will learn more easily. If you study in the right way, you will progress more rapidly toward the desirable goal of happiness, which you have set for yourself.

Here are some helpful hints on how to study in "just the right way"—the way that brings *results:*

First, be sure in your own mind that the *meaning* of each rule is crystal-clear. Think about it. It is the very foundation of your study.

Then go on to the words listed under the rule. These are typical examples of how the rule is applied. Examine each one carefully. Can you see how the rule is applied to produce the shorthand outline? It is imperative that you do in every case.

Now, move to the brief forms and abbreviations. Call on the wonderful human power to *memorize* and fix each outline in your mind. Write each brief form and abbreviation several times to help you memorize it. Remember, they are the very backbone of the dictation you will be taking in the future.

Now complete your assignment by reading – and rereading – the shorthand plates which appear in the lesson. It is the practice you get now that will help you when you are ready to transcribe from your own shorthand notes!

Make sure that you write your name on all homework, especially the Writing Assignment.

Writing Assignment – Lesson 2

1. We wish you would mail us one of the catalogs that shows the items you are selling.

e vS u d ral us 1 v . cals la

Sos . ilos u r sl.

2. This letter is to inform you that we want you to mail us the payment for the bulletins we sent.

th s l nf u la e v- u l

ral us . pa- f . bllns e s-.

3. It is evident that the firm cannot afford to pay such high rent for its offices.

l s evd- la . f cn afd l pa sC

hi r- f ls ofss.

4. Somebody said that the models are selling very well.

sbde sd la . mdls r sl v l.

5. You should have one of the policies that our company issues.

u Sd v 1 v . plcs la r co

Sus.

6. Not getting the job done would force me to cancel my visit.

n gl- · jb dn d fo re l csl
re vzl,

7. May we have one of our agents visit you to show you our new tools.

ra e u 1 u r aj-- vzl u l
So u r nu tuls?

8. The pieces you want are on top of the unit in my office.

· pss u w- r o tp u · unl
n re ofs,

9. Won't you let us show you the types of men's and women's shoes we sell.

wo- u ll us So u · tips u
mns & wmns Sus e sl,

10. Did I tell you that I would not visit the President of the company?

dd i tl u ta i d n vzl · P u
· co?

Lesson 3

The letter *c* is a letter that has no sound of its own. In the word *cat* it has the sound of "k"; in the word *city* it has the sound of "s." An analysis of the English language shows that in words that have the sound of "k," this sound is represented by the letter *c* over 90 percent of the time. You need only think of words such as *car, cut, college, coal, coffee, locate, physical, fact,* and *attic* to realize the validity of this figure. Since *k* is one of the most difficult and time-consuming letters to write, and since *c* is the easiest and quickest, we represent the sound of "k" in *Speedwriting* by writing *c* as stated in the next rule.

RULE 7 | For the sound of "k" write c .

Study the following examples:

could	cd	cabinet	cbnt
checking	<u>Cc</u>	college	clj
copy	cpe	can't	c-
car	cr	back, book	bc
package	pcj	lack	lc
key	ce	desk	dsc
looking	<u>lc</u>	skill	scl
sick	sc	check	Cc
cases	cass	talking	<u>lc</u>
cash	cS	cause	cz

You write:

1. medical ______	2. oak ______
3. pick ______	4. case ______
5. booklet ______	6. cotton ______
7. took ______	8. books ______
9. risk ______	10. tickets ______
11. look ______	12. cashing ______
13. cottage ______	14. milk ______
15. walk ______	16. camp ______

Confirmation:

1. rdcl 2. oc 3. pc 4. cas
5. bcll 6. cln 7. lc 8. bcs
9. rsc 10. lcls 11. lc 12. cg
13. cf 14. rlc 15. vc 16. cp

Read the following sentences:

1. l u Cc l se f. m cd gl . pcj v bcs\
2. wn u r lc l. P sa la l lc . ce l . oc dsc\

Key:

1. **Will you check to see if the men could get the package of books.**
2. **When you are talking to the President, say that I took the key to the oak desk.**

You have learned that the last letter or mark of punctuation of an outline is underscored to indicate the addition of "ing" or "thing." You are now going to learn to use a mark of punctuation to indicate that the sound of "ed" has been added to a word.

RULE 8 | **When "ed" is added to a word to form the past tense, overscore the last letter or mark of punctuation of the outline.**

For example, the word **file** is written fl ; and when this rule is applied to the word *filed*, you simply overscore the l in the outline and write **filed** f$\bar{l}$. In the same way, the word **reach**, as you know, is written reC ; and **reached** re$\bar{C}$. The word **issue** is iSu ; the word **issued** iS$\bar{u}$.

Study these words:

used	u$\bar{z}$	added	a$\bar{d}$
filled	f$\bar{l}$	typed	t$\bar{p}$
signed	si$\bar{n}$	limited	l$\bar{t}$
mailed	ma$\bar{l}$	finished	fn$\bar{S}$
damaged	d$\bar{j}$	listened	ls$\bar{n}$

1. attached al$\bar{C}$ 2. involved nvl$\bar{v}$
3. checked C$\bar{c}$ 4. billed b$\bar{l}$
5. happened hp$\bar{n}$ 6. delayed dl$\bar{a}$
7. showed S$\bar{o}$ 8. talked t$\bar{c}$

Confirmation:

1. al$\bar{C}$ 2. nvl$\bar{v}$ 3. C$\bar{c}$ 4. b$\bar{l}$

5. hp$\bar{n}$ 6. dl$\bar{a}$ 7. S$\bar{o}$ 8. t$\bar{c}$

Do you recall that you wrote the word **hunting** *h=* ? In other words, you treated the hyphen as though it were a letter of the alphabet; and it was underscored to indicate the addition of "ing." Similarly, when an outline ends in a hyphen and "ed" is added to the word, you will overscore the hyphen.

painted	*pa=*	**rented**	*r=*
invented	*nv=*	**wanted**	*w=*

You have now had two rules—one dealing with the underscore and one dealing with the overscore. To help separate these rules in your mind, think of the *g* in *ing* ; its downward stroke points to the underscore that represents "ing." And think of the *d* in *ed* ; its upward stroke points to the overscore that represents "ed."

Read the following sentences:

1.
2.
3.

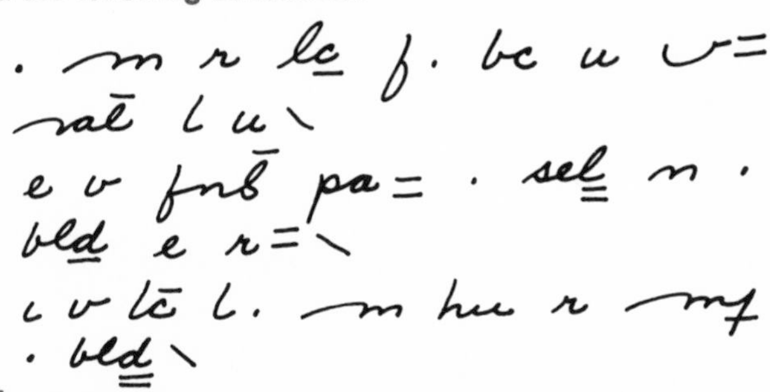

Key:

1. **The men are looking for the book you wanted mailed to you.**
2. **We have finished painting the ceilings in the building we rented.**
3. **I have talked to the men who are managing the buildings.**

You have already learned to write the combination sounds of "sh," "ch," and "wh" in previous lessons. Now you are going to learn another combination sound.

RULE 9 | **For the medial and final sound of "ow" write**  **.**

Let's illustrate this rule with the word *how*. This word is composed of two sounds, "h" + "ow." Since you are learning to write  for the sound of "ow," the word **how** will be written  . Similarly, the word *town* contains the sound of "ow" so **town** is written  .

Listen to the sound as you say the words *doubt* and *house*. These words also contain the sound of "ow," so **doubt** is  and **house**  .

Study these illustrations:

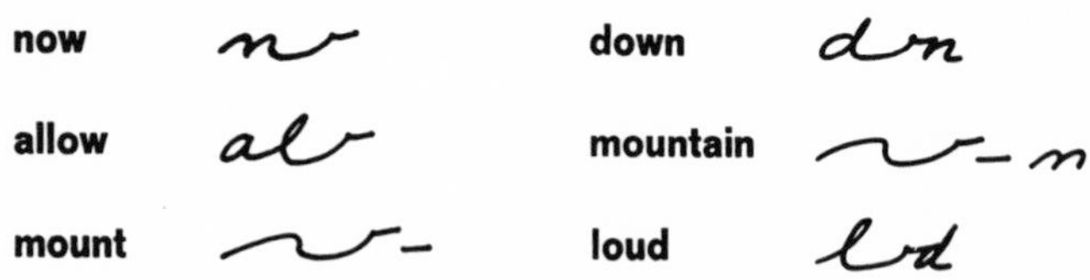

Brief Forms

help	hp	**why**	y
like	lc	**ask**	sc
during	du	**buy, by, be, been, but**	b

Abbreviations

day	d	**week**	

month	mo	**year**	y

Additional Words

days	ds	**before**	bf
today	td	**informs**	nfms
today's	tds	**informed**	nfm̄
accompanied	acō	**being**	b̲
asking	sc̲	**buying**	b̲
asked	sc̄	**canceled**	csl̄
helps	hps	**months**	mos
helping	hp̲	**weeks**	wks
helped	hp̄	**years**	ys
mechanical	mcl		

Dictation Hints

Indicate complimentary closings and salutations as follows:

Dear Sir:	ds	**Sincerely yours,**	su
My dear Sir:	mds	**Very truly yours,**	vtu
Gentlemen:	/	**Yours truly,**	ut
Dear Madam:	dm	**Yours very truly,**	uvt
Cordially yours,	cu	**Respectfully yours,**	ru

Reading Exercises

1. l u al— r aj—
l So u y. plses
e cSu r v sC
vlu\

2. yfec b v hpl
u(o) vo—u vzl
r ofs —nu r
dnln\

3. —n lc l. P(o) l
u sa la. alC̄ cpe
v. les s l b sm̄
& nal̄ bc l us\

4. na e no y u
v n b l se us
du. no\

5. . hd v r F cSū
a Cc l pa f. pcj
v ndcl bcs la u
nal̄ l r co\

6. . P sd la. bl
ej v. lrp dj̄.
fn8 o. lp v s oc
dsc\ c n b dn?

7. e d lc l hp u(o)
b e c—v. —m
Cc eC pes n.
5 cass\

8. c fgl l ll u la
c lc. ce l. cbnl\
yfu vSlvl(o)
ll re no\

9. c d n pc lh
lp v lrpf nu
dsc\ c du n lc
. Sap v l\

10. n r L e sc̄
r aj— l vzl u
1 d du lh —k\

11. fu r a rzd- v lh ln(?) r Sp l b hpe l hp u b cS Ccs f u \

12. ds: c dd- nola n ndcl bl d b sohu(?) b c hop c c pa ss ol lh ro \ cu

13. nds: c no c lc scl n (?) b c d lc l gl a jb n lh co vnc v fnS clj \\ ra c sc fu l v ss f re \ ru

14. ds: fu r so sc la u cn lcl re ld(?) l u v a rsj s- l re \ ul

15. j: c v Cc l se vl hpn l. bcll u s- \\ c nola l reC n dsc \ c v sc. P l lc f l \ su

16. ds: n bjl s so lre lh y la c dvl v nC la c c b. cr u So re \\ l u ll re no hr nC c d v l gv f a dn pa- \ uvl

17. nds: u v bl re f 3 lcls la v

n yl reC ~re\\
l u Cc l se h~
Ch hpn \ cu
18. ds: c ub lc
f a nu h~s\
du u v s~
n Ln la u c
So re?? f u v
n n~ ~ra c
sc la u ll re
no ~n u du\
s
19. ~ds: Ch s l
nf u la e v
n~ fnS .
cbnl la u v=
us l bld +
e r n~ rde
l pa- l\\ ll

re no f u
~S Ch cbnl l b
pa= l ~C .
dsc n . ofs\
ul
20. ds: d- u lc
lv a ~~-n
cy la cd b uz
f h= + fS? e v
sC a cy la e r
l l r-b . ~o\\
d u lcl sel?
ul

Key To Lesson 3

1. Will you allow our agent to show you why the policies we issue are of such value.
2. If we can be of[2] help to you, won't you visit our office when you are downtown.
3. When talking to the President, will you say that the attached copy of the lease is to be signed and mailed back to us.
4. May we know why you have not been to see us during the[6] month.
5. The head of our firm issued a check to pay for the package of medical books that you mailed to our[8] company.
6. The President said that the bottom edge of the lamp damaged the finish on the top of his oak desk.[10] Can nothing be done?
7. We would like to help you, but we can't have the women check each piece in the five cases.
8. I forgot[12] to tell you that I took the key to the cabinet. If you wish to have it, let me know.
9. I would not pick this[14] type of lamp for my desk. I do not like the shape of it.
10. In our letter we asked our agent to visit you one[16] day during this week.
11. If you are a resident of this town, our shop will be happy to help you by cashing checks[18] for you. *(181 words)*
12. Dear Sir: I didn't know that my medical bill would be so high, but I hope I can pay something on it this month.[2] Cordially yours, *(22 words)*
13. My dear Sir: I know I lack skill now, but I would like to get a job in this company when I have finished college.[2] *¶ May I ask if you will have something for me. Respectfully yours, *(32 words)*
14. Dear Madam: If you are so sick that you cannot talk to me today, will you have a message sent to me. Yours truly,[2] *(20 words)*

*¶ refers to new paragraph.

15. Gentlemen: I have checked to see what happened to the booklet you sent. ¶ I know that it reached my desk. I have asked[2] the President to look for it. Sincerely yours, *(28 words)*

16. Dear Sir: My budget is so limited this year that I doubt very much that I can buy the car you showed me. ¶ Will[2] you let me know how much I would have to give for a down payment. Yours very truly, *(35 words)*

17. My dear Sir: You have billed me for three tickets that have not yet reached me. ¶ Will you check to see how this happened. Cordially[2] yours, *(21 words)*

18. Dear Sir: I have been looking for a new house. Do you have something in town that you can show me? ¶ If you have nothing[2] now, may I ask that you let me know when you do. Sincerely, *(30 words)*

19. My dear Sir: This is to inform you that we have now finished the cabinet that you wanted us to build, and we[2] are now ready to paint it. ¶ Let me know if you wish this cabinet to be painted to match the desk in the office.[4] Yours truly, *(42 words)*

20. Dear Sir: Wouldn't you like to have a mountain cottage that could be used for hunting and fishing? We have such a cottage[2] that we are willing to rent by the month. (¶) Would you like to see it? Yours truly, *(34 words)*

Name............................Class..........Date................

Writing Assignment – Lesson 3

1. The letter I typed is now on the President's desk. I have asked that it be signed today.

· L c tpo n n · Po dsc, c v sc̄

la c b sin̄ td,

2. I will be talking to my son one day during the week, and I will ask for the college catalogs that you wanted.

c l b tc l m sn 1 d du · wk

& c l sc f · clj cals la u w̄,

3. How much would I have to pay if I rented a car by the year?

h m C d c v l pa f c r̄ a

cr b · y?

4. My budget is so limited this month that I know I will not have sufficient money to buy the oak cabinet you showed me in the catalog.

m bj s so lt th ms la c no

c l n v sfs- mne l b · ok cbnt

la u Sō m n · cal,

5. The agent took me to see a new house in town, but I doubt that I will buy it.

6. I have been asked to inform you that a check will be issued when the package reaches us.

7. Why didn't you tell the men to help me when I packed the medical books in the cases?

8. We are buying a cottage that is on top of a high mountain. My wife and I hope you will visit us often.

Lesson 4

You know that you write *c* for the sound of "ch" and *s* for the sound of "sh." This is how you will write another combination sound.

RULE 10 | For the sound of "th" write *t*.

This rule states that whenever the sound of "th" is heard in a word, you are to write *t* for that sound. **Them** is written *tm*; the word **method** *mtd*; and **health** *hlt*.

You write:

1. then *tn* ________ **2. thus** *ts* ________

3. though *to* ________ **4. death** *dt* ________

5. methods *mtds* ________ **6. than** *tn* ________

Confirmation:

1. *tn* 2. *ts* 3. *to* 4. *dt* 5. *mtds* 6. *tn*

As you pronounce the following words, notice that the initial sound in each word is produced by a blending together of two sounds: *bred, cry, drive, from, grant, profit, truck.* It is to this combination sound of an initial letter combined with "r" that the next rule applies.

RULE 11	To indicate the sound of an initial letter that is combined with "r" write a hyphen on the initial letter of the outline.

Thus, at the beginning of a word you write for "br," for "cr," for "dr," for "fr," for "gr," for "pr," and for "tr."

You know that **bed** is written . How would you write *bred?* Since represents the initial sound of "br," the word **bred** is written . In the same way, you write **beef** and **brief** .

You write:

1. brown ______ **2. brought** ______

Confirmation:

1. 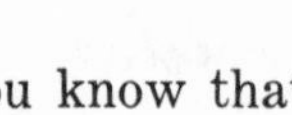 2. 

You know that **cash** is written . Therefore, **crash** is .

You write:

1. cry ci **2. critical** ctcl

Confirmation:

1. ci **2.** ctcl

Applying this same principle, you can see why **grow** is written go ; **drop** dp ; **profit** pfl ; **try** ti .

Study the following words:

bridge	bj	**privilege**	pvlj
broad	bd	**print**	p-
broke	boc	**proud**	pd
crashed	cs̄	**proof**	puf
crop	cp	**promise**	ps
dry	di	**traffic**	tfc
free	fe	**true**	tu
group	gup	**travel**	tvl
granted	g=	**trees**	tes
gray	ga	**tried**	tī
profits	pfls	**trying**	ti_

You write:

1. from f **2. criticism** ctsz

3. drug ________ 4. front ________

5. growth ________ 6. present ________

7. growing ________ 8. truck ________

9. trip ________ 10. grant ________

Confirmation:

1. fn 2. dlzn 3. dg 4. f- 5. gol

6. pz- 7. go 8. tc 9. tp 10. g-

As you say the following words, notice the sound formed by the initial letter pronounced with "r": *arm, air, iron, orphan, urge*. Since the rule tells you that this type of combination sound is indicated by writing a hyphen on the first letter, you will simply write **arm** an ; **air** a ; **iron** in ; **orphan** ofn ; **urge** uj .

You write:

1. urban ________ 2. argue ________

3. arguments ________ 4. article ________

5. irons ________ 6. or ________

7. original ________ 8. urgent ________

9. army ________ 10. art ________

Confirmation:

1. ubn 2. agu 3. agu-- 4. alcl 5. ins

6. o 7. ojnl 8. uj- 9. ane 10. al

What of the word *earn?* There is no practical way to attach a hyphen to an *e* written in this manner: e . Therefore, write E in this instance because it lends itself more easily to the attaching of an initial hyphen. For the sound of initial "er" write E . The word **earn** will be written En and **earth** El . Notice that the word **urge** is written uj although the initial sound is identical with that at the beginning of the word *earn.* This is done as an aid to transcribing.

Note the sound at the beginning of the words *through* and *throw.* You know that you write l for the sound of "th." Since "thr" combines this sound with "r," follow the rule and write an initial hyphen on the *t* for the sound of "thr": **through** Tu ; **throw** To ; and **thrill** Tl .

Similarly, for the sound of "shr" in the word *shred,* the initial hyphen is added to S ; the word **shred** is written Sd and **shrubs** Sbs .

Read the following sentences:

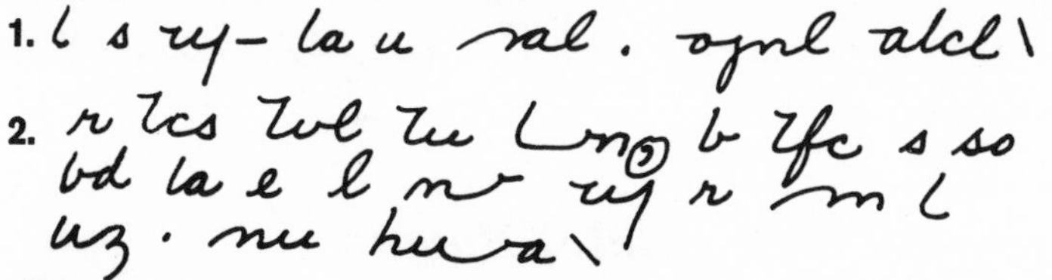

Key:

1. **It is urgent that you mail the original article.**
2. **Our trucks travel through town, but traffic is so bad that we will now urge our men to use the new highway.**

RULE 12 | For the final sound of "lee" write l .

You know that **rapid** is written rpd. To write **rapidly** you simply add *l.* Thus, **rapidly** rpdl. Similarly, **bad** is *bd* ; **badly** *bdl*. The word **family** is written *fml*.

You write:

1. efficiently *efs-l* **2. evidently** *evd-l*

3. readily *rdl* **4. highly** *hil*

5. easily *ezl* **6. truly** *Tul*

7. early *El* **8. valley** *vl*

Confirmation:

1. *efs-l* 2. *evd-l* 3. *rdl* 4. *hil*
5. *ezl* 6. *Tul* 7. *El* 8. *vl*

Applying the rule to write *l* for the final sound of "ly," **originally** will be written *ojnl* , the same as **original** *ojnl* . When you are reading your notes, the context will tell you which form of the word to use. So, too, with words such as **chill** *Cl* **chilly** *Cl* ; and **hill** *hl* **hilly** *hl* .

Brief Forms

your	*u*	**price**	*ps*
great	*g*	**woman**	*wm-*
man	*m-*	**was, as**	*z*
there, their	*T*	**with, were**	*w*

Abbreviations

credit	*cr*	**discount**	*dis*

Additional Words

priced	ps̄	daily	dl
prices	pss	yearly	yl
credited	cr̄	greatly	gl
credits	crs	likely	lcl
there's	Ts	monthly	⌒ol
therefore	Tf	weekly	⌣kl
thereby	Tb	within	⌣n
therein	Tn	yours	us
thereof	Tv	forth	ft

Reading Exercises

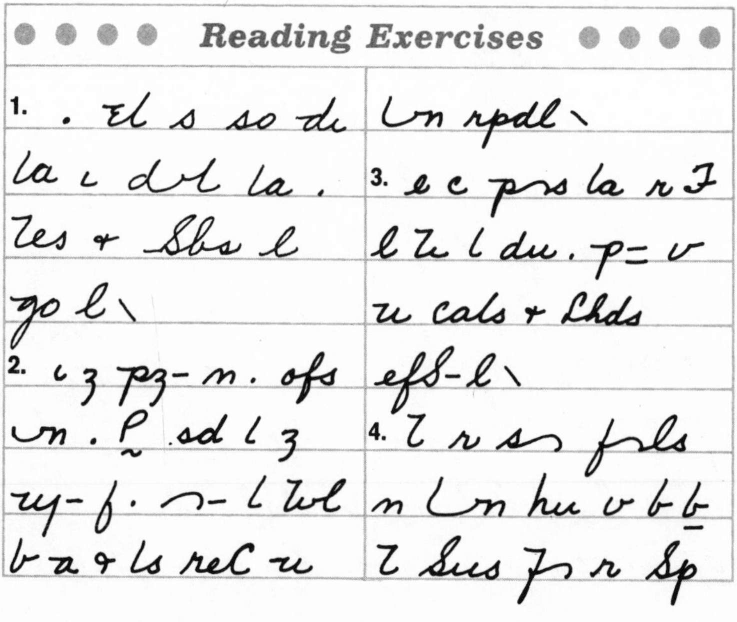

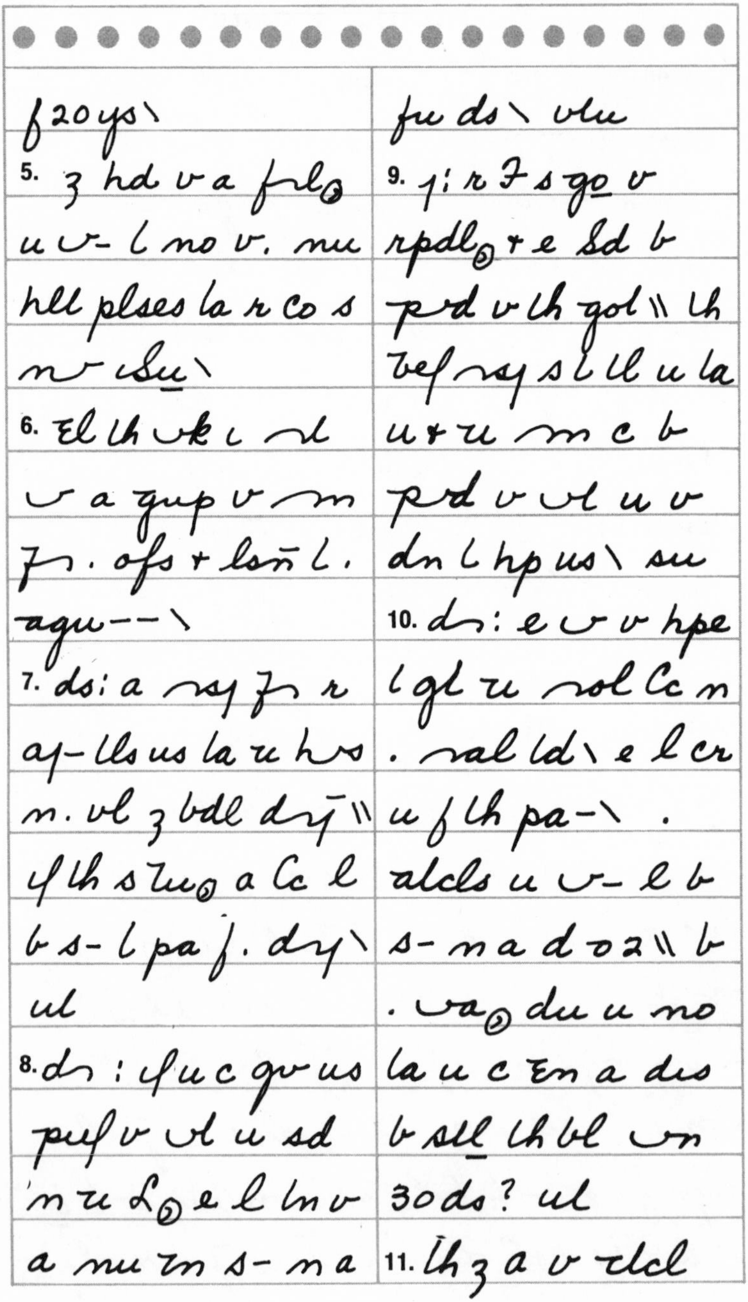

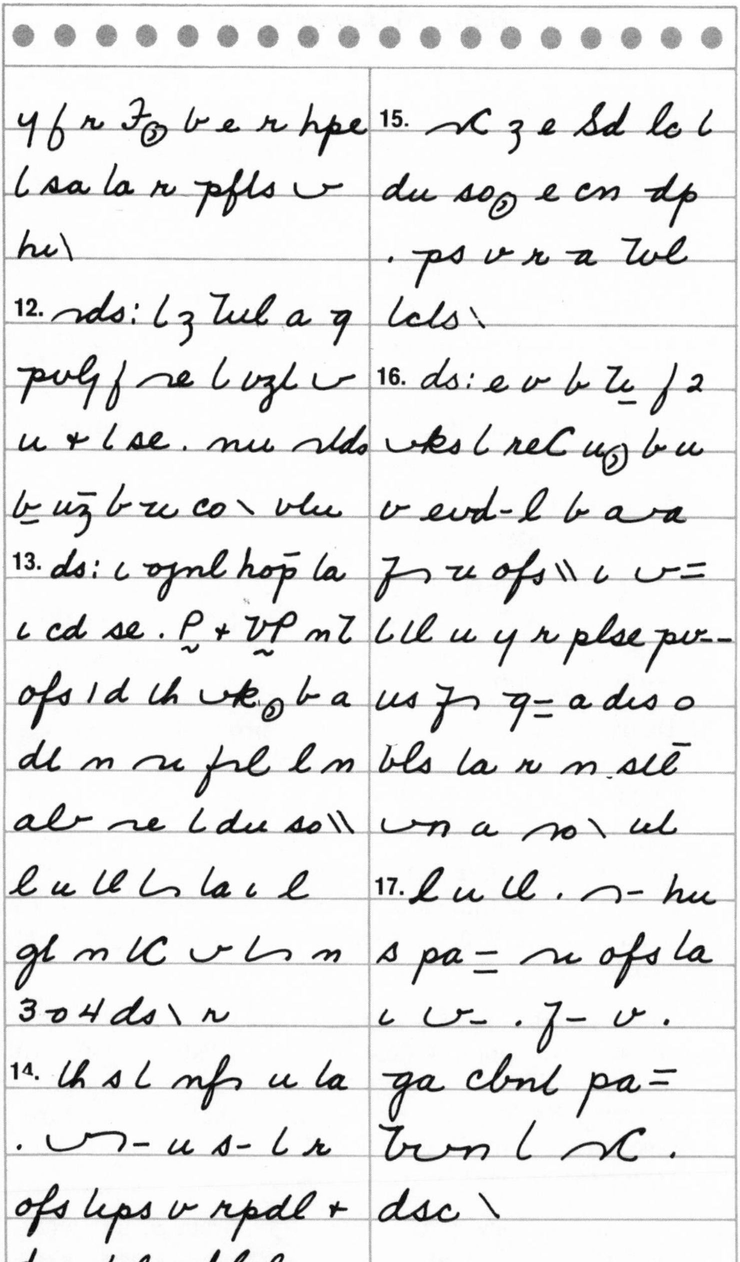

Key to Lesson 4

1. The earth is so dry that I doubt that the trees and shrubs will grow well.
2. I was present in the office[2] when the President said it was urgent for the man to travel by air and thus reach your town rapidly.
3. We[4] can promise that our firm will try to do the printing of your catalogs and letterheads efficiently.
4. There are[6] some families in town who have been buying their shoes from our shop for 20 years.
5. As head of a family, you[8] want to know of the new health policies that our company is now issuing.
6. Early this week I met with a[10] group of men from the office and listened to the arguments. *(115 words)*
7. Dear Sir: A message from our agent tells us that your house in the valley was badly damaged. (¶) If this is true, a[2] check will be sent to pay for the damage. Yours truly, *(29 words)*
8. Dear Madam: If you can give us proof of what you said in your letter, we will then have a new iron sent in a[2] few days. Very truly yours, *(25 words)*
9. Gentlemen: Our firm is growing very rapidly, and we should be proud of this growth. (¶) This brief message is to tell[2] you that you and your men can be proud of what you have done to help us. Sincerely yours, *(35 words)*
10. Dear Madam: We were very happy to get your monthly check in the mail today. We will credit you for this payment.[2] The articles you want will be sent in a day or two. (¶) By the way, do you know that you can earn a discount[4] by settling this bill within 30 days? Yours truly, *(50 words)*
11. This was a very critical year for our firm, but we are happy to say that our profits were high. *(21 words)*

12. My dear Sir: It was truly a great privilege for me to visit with you and to see the new methods being[2] used by your company. Very truly yours, *(27 words)*

13. Dear Sir: I originally hoped that I could see the President and Vice-President in their office one day[2] this week, but a death in my family will not allow me to do so. (¶) Will you tell them that I will get in touch[4] with them in three or four days. Respectfully, *(47 words)*

14. This is to inform you that the woman you sent to our office types very rapidly and does the filing[2] efficiently. *(22 words)*

15. Much as we should like to do so, we cannot drop the price of our air travel tickets. *(15 words)*

16. Dear Sir: We have been trying for two weeks to reach you, but you have evidently been away from your office. (¶) I[2] wanted to tell you why our policy prevents us from granting a discount on bills that are not settled within[4] a month. Yours truly, *(42 words)*

17. Will you tell the man who is painting my office that I want the front of the gray cabinet painted brown to match[2] the desk. *(21 words)*

More Help For The Student

HOW TO USE YOUR NOTEBOOK EFFICIENTLY

Have you stopped to think about how you are using your notebook? Whether you're slowing yourself down by not using it properly? Well, it's a fact: Proper use of your notebook will decidedly improve your dictation and transcription efficiency! Check the list of hints below. Be sure you are following each one carefully.

1. Use a standard 6- by 9-inch steno pad that has a line printed down the middle of the page dividing it into two columns.
2. Write in columns rather than across the whole page.
3. As you begin writing, use the thumb and index finger of your left hand to slowly move the sheet upward. This minimizes arm movement and brings the page into position for flipping, so that you can begin writing on the next page with no loss of time.
4. Form the habit of starting each day's dictation by writing the date at the *bottom* of the page.
5. Place a rubber band around the cover of your pad and slip your finished notes under it, so that you can immediately open your pad at the proper place for taking dictation.
6. Always draw a diagonal line through each letter as soon as it has been transcribed.
7. Indicate the end of a letter by drawing a horizontal line before starting the next letter.
8. Edit your notes carefully before you transcribe them.

Name..............................Class..........Date................

Writing Assignment—Lesson 4

1. Is there something we can do to help you?

o l o . e c du l hp u?

2. Were you on the truck when it crashed into the bridge?

u u o . Tc un l c-S n l . brj?

3. It is a great privilege to print your articles in our monthly bulletin.

l o a g pvlj l p- u alcls
n r -ol bltn.

4. We have now credited you for the check that reached us early in the week.

e v n- cr u f . Cc la reC
us El n . wk.

5. This brief message is to tell you how urgent it is for us to get the brown and gray paint we asked to have sent to our shop.

th bef msj o l l u h-
uj- l o f us l gl . brn +
ga pa- e sc l v o- l r Sp.

6. As the head of the family, you can readily see the value of our health policies.

3· hd v· fmlo u c rdl se·
vlu v r hlt plses.

7. How much discount would you grant on the original price if we were to pay cash within ten days?

h r mC dis d u g- o· ojnl
prs f e w l pa cS wn 10 ds?

8. You can promise them that by using our methods each item will sell rapidly.

u c prs h la b uz r mtds
eC ilm l sl rpl.

9. When you have finished typing the letters, will you then file the copies away?

wn u v fnS tip· ltrs l u tn
fil· cpes awa?

10. Why didn't the man and woman tell you their son is now in the army?

y ddn· mn + wmn tl u t
sn s nw n· arme?

Lesson 5

You have learned to write the long-vowel sounds in such words as **mail** *~al* ; **seal** *sel* ; **type** *tp* ; **hope** *hop* ; **rule** *rul* . Notice that these are all one-syllable words. The following rule deals with long-vowel sounds that occur in words of more than one syllable.

RULE 13	Omit all medial long vowels in words of more than one syllable.

In other words, a long vowel in the middle of a word will be written in a one-syllable word only. For example, you know that the outline for the word **tail** is *tal* . The word *retail,* however, has more than one syllable; and the rule in this lesson tells you to omit this medial long vowel. Therefore, **retail** is written *rtl* . Look at the word *league.* It is a one-syllable word so you write the long "e" in your outline: **league** *leg* . On the other hand, the word *legal* is a word of more than one syllable, so omit the medial long vowel and write **legal** *lgl* . As a further example, the words *deep* and *deeply* both contain the sound of "e" but you write this vowel only in the word that has one syllable. Thus, **deep** *dep* **deeply** *dpl* .

Study the following words:

recently	rs-l	**taken**	tcn
machine	Sn	**decide**	dsd
alone	aln	**prevailing**	pvl_
radio	rdo	**proceed**	psd
chosen	Czn	**schedule**	scdl
obtaining	obtn_	**music**	zc
appeal	apl	**producing**	pds_
reason	rzn	**reduce**	rds
presented	pz=	**prevent**	pv-
hotel	htl	**ordeal**	odl
season	szn	**local**	lcl
provided	pvd̄	**gasoline**	gsln
region	rjn	**aluminum**	almn

The word **title** is written *ttl* . Notice that for clarity in reading the double *t* is crossed in the outline.

Read these sentences:

1. l se no rzn y. Sns cn b s-

2. . rsj sd la u v b Czn l teC mzc n r lcl clj th szn

3. e rs-l dsd̄ l obtn nu mSns f r rtl Sps

Key:

1. I see no reason why the machines cannot be sent.
2. The message said that you have been chosen to teach music in our local college this season.
3. We recently decided to obtain new machines for our retail shops.

You write:

1. recent rs-	2. coupon cpn
3. remain rmn	4. refuse rfz
5. campaign cmpn	6. proposed ppz̄
7. revised rvz̄	8. widely vdl
9. patient pS-	10. recognized rcgnz̄
11. proposal ppzl	12. regional rjnl
13. area aa	14. areas aas

Confirmation:

1. rs- 2. cpn 3. rmn 4. rfz

5. cmpn 6. ppz̄ 7. rvz̄ 8. vdl

9. pS- 10. rcgnz̄ 11. ppzl 12. rjnl

13. aa 14. aas

Let's summarize what has been covered in this and other rules regarding the writing or omission of long and short vowels.

1. Write vowels—long or short—at the beginning and end of a word. Examples: **each** *eC* ; **value** *vlu* ; **add** *ad* ; **data** *dla* ; **yellow** *ylo* ; **review** *rvu* .

2. Omit all medial short vowels. Examples: **bit** *bl* ; **rug** *rg* ; **bulletin** *blln* ; **ahead** *ahd* .

3. Write medial long vowels in words of one syllable. Examples: **reach** *reC* ; **shape** *Sap* ; **tool** *lul* .

4. Omit all medial long vowels in words of more than one syllable. Examples: **suppose** *spz* ; **aside** *asd* ; **retain** *rln* .

You write:

1. base ____________	**2. basic** ____________
3. basis ____________	**4. lease** ____________
5. release ____________	**6. brief** ____________
7. briefly ____________	**8. belief** ____________
9. relief ____________	**10. broke** ____________
11. broken ____________	**12. safe** ____________
13. safely ____________	**14. tails** ____________
15. retails ____________	**16. details** ____________
17. mail ____________	**18. airmail** ____________

Confirmation:

1. *bas* **2.** *bsc* **3.** *bss* **4.** *les*

5. rls 6. tef 7. tfl 8. blf

9. rlf 10. toc 11. tcn 12. saf

13. sfl 14. lals 15. rlls 16. dlls

17. ~al 18. a~l

There are a few simple exceptions to this rule which you need to understand in order to apply it correctly.

First, when "ing" or "ed" is added to an outline that contains a long vowel, this vowel is not dropped from the outline. Thus: **hoping** hop ; **teaching** teC ; **filed** fil .

Second, when the outline of a root word ends in a vowel, that vowel is retained when a suffix is added to it. For example: **high** hi ; **highly** hil ; **highway** hiwa ; **true** tu ; **truly** tul ; **pay** pa ; **payroll** parl ; **payment** pa- ; **renew** rnu ; **renewal** rnul .

Notice in these examples that the pronunciation of the root word remained unchanged when the suffix was added. But you must remember that in such words as **ready** rde ; **readily** rdl ; and **happy** hpe ; **happily** hpl , the pronunciation of the basic word changes when the suffix is added, and therefore the vowel is not retained.

Finally, when a long vowel is followed by a mark of punctuation, retain the vowel. For example: **moment** ~o- ; **truant** tu-

Another sound that is common in our language is the sound of "oi" that is heard in such words as *boy, choice,* and *loyal.*

RULE 14 | For the sound of "oi" write y .

Study these words:

oil	yl	**appointments**	apy---
boys	bys	**avoid**	avyd
points	py--	**choice**	Cys
join	jyn	**noise**	nyz
***disappoint**	dsapy-	**toys**	tys

*Remember: when a prefix is added to an outline that begins with a vowel, this vowel is retained.

You write:

1. voice vyc	**2. disappointment** dsapy--
3. soil syl	**4. appointed** apy=
5. point py-	**6. joint** jy-
7. appointment apy--	**8. loyal** lyl

Confirmation:

1. vys	2. dsapy--	3. syl
4. apy=	5. py-	6. jy-
7. apy--	8. lyl	

Brief Forms

feel, fail	fl	**field**	fld

those	los	**busy**	bz
she, shall, ship	S		

Abbreviations

doctor	dr	**number**	no
secretary, second	sec		

Additional Words

doctor's	drs	**ships**	Ss
secretarial	secl	**shipment**	S-
secretaries	secs	**fails**	fls
feeling	fl̲	**failed**	fl̄
feels	fls	**failing**	fl̲
fields	flds	**numbers**	nos
shipped	S̄	**numbered**	nō
shipping	S̲	**inside**	nsd
shipments	S--	**indeed**	ndd

Dictation Hints

The months of the year are written as follows:

January	ja	**February**	fb

March	mr	**August**	ag
April	ap	**September**	sp
May	ma	**October**	oc
June	jn	**November**	nv
July	jl	**December**	dc

Reading Exercises

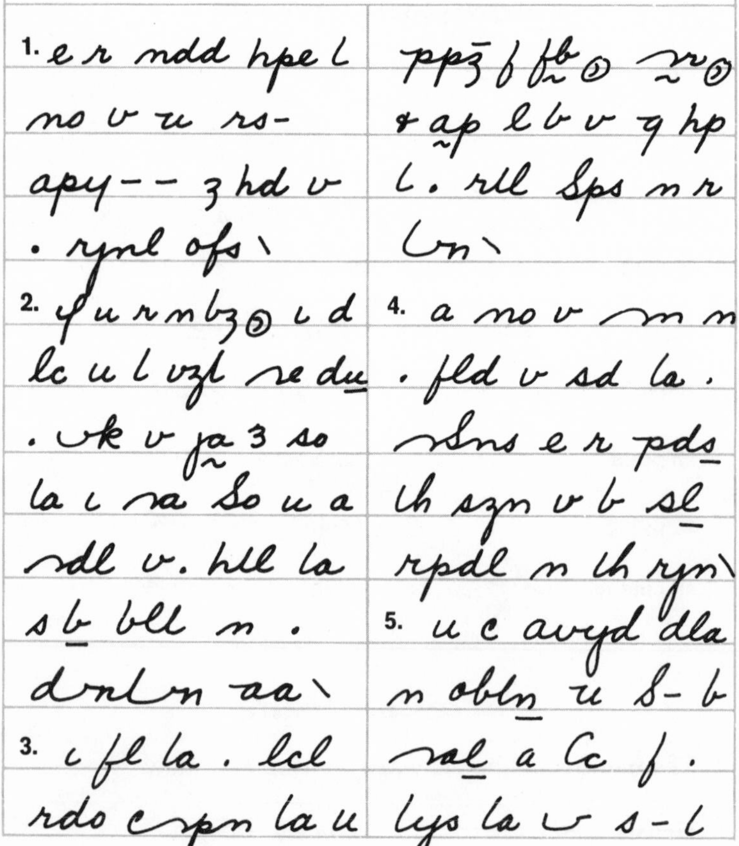

u o ~a b\
6. i fl l se y u
cn rds . ps u
r gt f yl +
gsln\
7. l s r plse l
pvd jbs f los
~m hu v obtn
T rls Fs . a~
fss\
8. e fl u v no
lgl bss f sc us
l pa f . dy dn
l . nsd v u
hs n jn\
9. e S S r r rvz
cal l u f u l
fl n . alC cpn
+ sal l bc l
us\ . cal Sd
reC u b nv 20\
10. i l no d l
b a a F ~u
dsc du u scdl
vzl o dc 9 b i
l sc ~u sec
l v u lcn l se
r nu ofss\
11. a q no v r
Sns v b Tcn
rs-l\ f lh rzn
i ppz la u apl
l. ~m + sc l
l jyn u n a
cpn l rds
. dy\
12. ds: . ~s-
u s- l us o

aq 12 s n~ sec
l r P \ S s v
efS- o. jb +
lyl l r F \\ l s
~u blf la◯ y
S dsds l r~m
~ us◯ S l b a
q asl l. co \ ul

13. dr: ~a e no
y u rfz l pa u
bl f. bys Sus
la ~ S o jn9 \
e bē u n jl◯
aq◯ + sp b dd
n gl u Cc \\ y
e du n v l b
oc 10◯ e l v
no Cys b l sc
f lgl ad l
obln pa- \ e no
u v- l avyd
th + l Y ~al
us vl s du \
vlu

14. ds: v u
dsd l b. h~s
c Sō u rs-l
n. vl ??. dr
hu ons l s
n~ rde l sl \
y c cd se u
bfl n s ofs◯ c
no e cd sll.
dlls \ s

15. ds: e r hpe
l nfs w la e
c n~ pvd.
al m~ cass

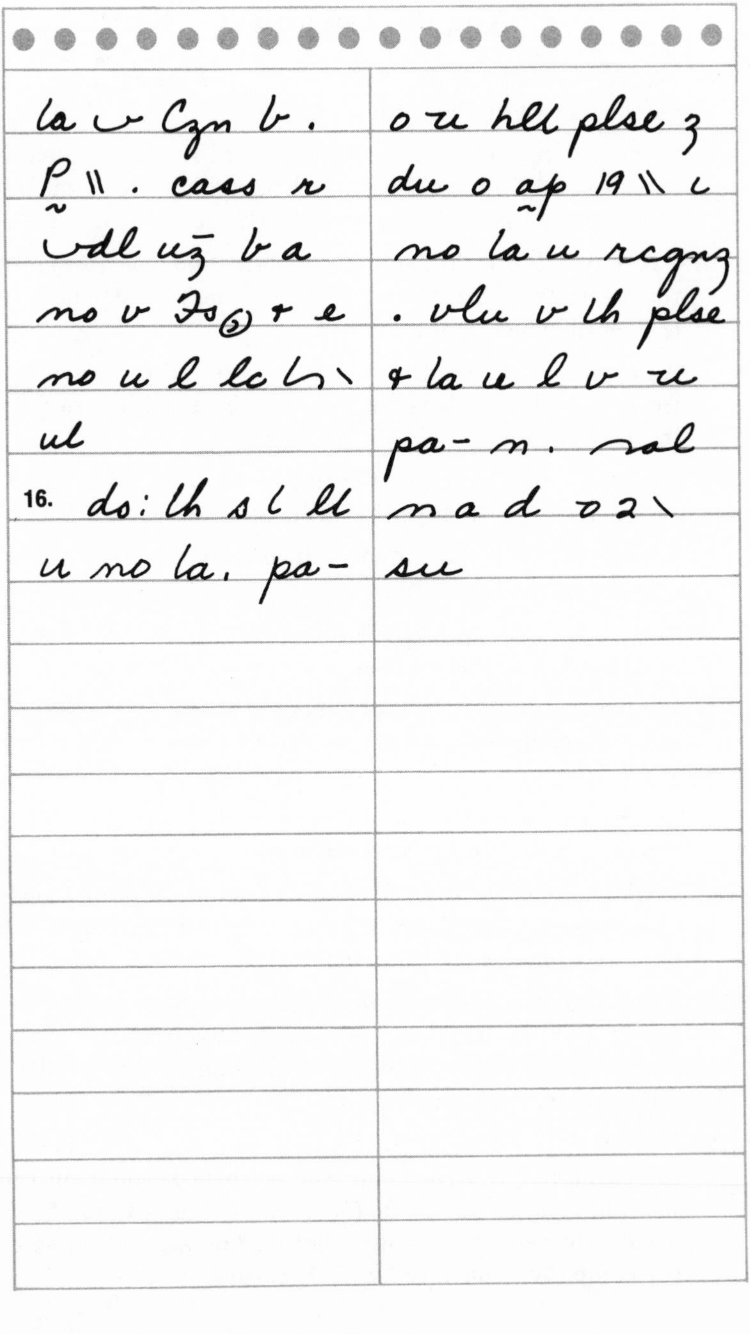
la v Czn b.
P\\. cass r
vdl uz b a
no v Fs + e
no u l lc ls\
ul
16. do: lh s l ll
u no la, pa-
o u hll plse z
du o ap 19\\ c
no la u rcgnz
. vlu v lh plse
+ la u l v u
pa-n. sal
n a d o2\
su

Key to Lesson 5

1. We are indeed happy to know of your recent appointment as head of the regional office.
2. If you are not[2] busy, I would like you to visit me during the week of January 3 so that I may show you a model[4] of the hotel that is being built in the downtown area.
3. I feel that the local radio campaign[6] that you proposed for February, March, and April will be of great help to the retail shops in our town.
4. A number[8] of men in the field have said that the machines we are producing this season have been selling rapidly in[10] this region.
5. You can avoid delay in obtaining your shipment by mailing a check for the toys that were sent to[12] you on May 6.
6. I fail to see why you cannot reduce the price you are getting for oil and gasoline.
7. It is[14] our policy to provide jobs for those men who have obtained their release from the armed forces.
8. We feel you have no[16] legal basis for asking us to pay for the damage done to the inside of your house in June.
9. We shall ship our[18] revised catalog to you if you will fill in the attached coupon and mail it back to us. The catalog should[20] reach you by November 20.
10. I will no doubt be away from my desk during your scheduled visit on December[22] 9, but I will ask my secretary to have you taken to see our new offices.
11. A great number of[24] our machines have been broken recently. For this reason, I propose that you appeal to the men and ask them[26] to join you in a campaign to reduce the damage. *(269 words)*
12. Dear Sir: The woman you sent to us on August 12 is now secretary to our President. She is very[2] efficient on the job and loyal to our firm. (¶) It is my belief that, if she decides to remain with us, she[4] will be a great asset to the company. Yours truly, *(50 words)*

13. Dear Madam: May we know why you refuse to pay your bill for the boy's shoes that were shipped on June 9. We billed you in[2] July, August, and September but did not get your check. (¶) If we do not have it by October 10, we will have[4] no choice but to ask for legal aid to obtain payment. We know you want to avoid this and will therefore mail us[6] what is due. Very truly yours, *(62 words)*

14. My dear Sir: Have you decided to buy the house I showed you recently in the valley? (¶) The doctor who owns it[2] is now ready to sell. If I could see you briefly in his office, I know we could settle the details. Sincerely,[4] *(40 words)*

15. My dear Sir: We are happy to inform you that we can now provide the aluminum cases that were chosen[2] by the President. (¶) The cases are widely used by a number of firms, and we know you will like them. Yours[4] truly, *(41 words)*

16. Dear Sir: This is to let you know that the payment on your health policy was due on April 19. (¶) I know[2] that you recognize the value of this policy and that you will have your payment in the mail in a[4] day or two. Sincerely yours, *(42 words)*

YOU'LL DO BETTER WITH A PEN THAN WITH A PENCIL

1. Experience has proved that a reliable, free-flowing pen – either ball point pen or fountain pen – is a more efficient writing instrument than a pencil.

2. Pen-written notes are more legible because they do not smudge. They can also be read more easily under artificial light.

3. Writing with a pen requires less effort . . . and this results in a minimum of fatigue.

   A pencil point eventually becomes blunt, thus requiring more effort to write.

   You will grip a pencil more tightly and press harder when you write. This increases fatigue and slows the rate of writing.

4. You can write at a maximum rate of speed for longer periods of time.

5. Remove the cap so that your pen will be as light as possible.

6. Choose a fine, firm pen point, so that you'll feel comfortable when taking dictation.

Writing Assignment–Lesson 5

1. As far as I know, the woman did not give the reason she did not join our group in July.

2. We have decided to reduce the price of our gasoline and oil in February or March.

3. Why didn't your airmail letter of June 9 give the details of your recent proposal?

4. If what my secretary said is true, then you have broken a number of appointments this month. In view of this, I feel I have no choice but to refuse to see you.

5. We have chosen your hotel for a showing of those toys we will release in October to the local retail shops in town.

6. Your firm can avoid delay in getting shipment by mailing a check for the boys' shoes we shipped on April 15.

7. We should not fail to give those men who are in the field a voice in deciding what items we should produce this season.

BRIEF FORM and STANDARD ABBREVIATION REVIEW

Lessons 1 through 5

1. Dear Sir: During my talk with your secretary early this week, I was informed that you were not[2] feeling well and would not be in the office for a number of months. (¶) If there is some way in which I can be of help, I hope you[4] will not fail to get in touch with me. Yours truly, *(48 words)*

2. My dear Sir: We know that this is a very busy season of the year in your shop. You have no doubt forgotten[2] that payment is due for the shipment that was sent on January 4. Your check should have been mailed by the second of the[4] month, but as you know, it did not reach us. (¶) This letter is to ask that your check be sent within a few days.[6] Yours very truly, *(63 words)*

3. Dear Sir: The President of our firm said that a great number of men in the field have written to his office to[2] ask why it is not our policy to grant a discount to those who buy from our company on credit. (¶) We have[4] not yet decided what to do and would like to have some help from you. Yours truly, *(54 words)*

4. Dear Sir: The President and Vice-President of our firm are looking for two new secretaries for their offices.[2] Do you know of a man and woman in this area who could fill the jobs? (¶) If so, will you have them get in touch[4] with us. Cordially yours, *(44 words)*

5. Dear Doctor: Will you have your secretary let me know the day and hour of my appointment with you. (¶) I shall be away[2] on a trip for a few weeks and would like to see you before October 15. Sincerely yours, *(38 words)*

–REVIEW–

Lessons 1 through 5

1. If you know of two or three local boys who would be willing to help us during the busy season, would you ask[2] them to drop in to see us. *(25 words)*

2. I do not wish to argue with what you say, but I know that what you have proposed will do nothing to check the present[2] high prices being asked for this article. *(28 words)*

3. Dear Sir: It is my basic belief that each man and woman should have a voice in the choice of our new Vice-President.[2] (¶) Isn't this the policy followed in your firm? Yours truly, *(31 words)*

4. Dear Sir: We have decided to try your new method of packaging. (¶) As you know, a number of our radios were[2] broken during shipment on our trucks, and we feel that something should now be done to prevent or reduce such damage.[4] Yours very truly, *(43 words)*

5. Gentlemen: It is evident that you have forgotten the payment that is due for the ten dozen catalogs[2] which were sent on May 13. (¶) We are hoping that your check will reach us in the mail by June 15. Cordially yours,[4] *(40 words)*

6. My dear Sir: Our management is truly proud that you have chosen our hotel for the regional showing of the[2] machines you produce. (¶) It will be a privilege to have you with us. Sincerely yours, *(35 words)*

7. Dear Sir: I want to show my family the gray house in the valley that your agent talked of when we met. (¶) Is it[2] very far from town? Can we reach the house by bus, or should I use my car to get there? Yours truly, *(37 words)*

Lesson 6

Before learning the next rule, let's review one that you have been using since Lesson 1—the rule that states, "Write what you hear, omitting all medial short vowels." It is according to this rule that the following words are written: **rage** *raj* ; **seal** *sel* ; **twice** *Lis* ; **cheap** *Cep* ; **shape** *Sap* ; **coal** *col* .

In these outlines you wrote all long vowels and all pronounced consonants. You are now going to learn about a group of words that contain a sound that is quite different from any of the sounds heard in the examples just given. You can hear the sounds referred to as you pronounce the following words. As you do so, notice that each word ends in the sound of a long vowel + "t": *rate, meet, write, vote, shoot, mute.*

It is to these final sounds of "ate, eet, ite, ote, ute" that this next rule refers.

RULE 15	**For the final sound of a long vowel and "t," omit the t and end the outline with the long vowel.**

Let's examine the word *rate*. This word is made up of the sound of "r" + "ate." Since the rule tells you to write *a* for this final sound of "ate," you write **rate** *ra* . Similarly, the word **date** is written *da* and **wait** *wa* .

You write:

1. fate fa　　　**2. gate** ga

Confirmation:

1. *fa*　　　**2.** *ga*

Look at another example: the word *meet* contains the final sound of "eet," and since the rule tells you to write *e* for this final sound, you write **meet** *me* ; **sheet** *She* ; and **heat** *he* .

You write:

1. neat ne　　　**2. seat** se

Confirmation:

1. *ne*　　　**2.** *se*

What of the word *write?* Again referring to the rule, you write *i* for the final sound of "ite," therefore, **write** is written *ri* ; **sight** *si* ; and **light** *li* .

You write:

1. night ni　　　**2. white** wi

Confirmation:

1. *ni*　　　**2.** *wi*

In the same way, you write *o* for the final sound of "ote," so **vote** is *vo* and **wrote** *ro* .

You write:

1. coat ___co___ **2. boat** ___bo___

Confirmation:

1. *co* **2.** *bo*

Finally, you write *u* for the final sound of "ute." Since this is the sound at the end of the words *suit* and *shoot*, you write **suit** *su* and **shoot** *Su* .

Study these examples:

late	*la*	**receipt**	*rse*
beat	*be*	**mute**	*mu*
hesitate	*hzla*	**indicate**	*ndca*
eliminate	*elma*	**route**	*ru*
boot	*bu*	**locate**	*lca*
wheat	*we*	**promote**	*pro*

You write:

1. delight ___dli___ **2. cheat** ___Ce___

3. devote ___dvo___ **4. fruit** ___fu___

5. height ___hi___ **6. lute** ___lu___

7. repeat ___rpe___ **8. invite** ___nvi___

9. **might** ~~ri~~ ______ 10. **weight** va ______

11. **write** ri ______ 12. **freight** fa ______

Confirmation

1. dli	2. Ce	3. dvo
4. fu	5. hi	6. li
7. rpe	8. nvr	9. mi
10. va	11. ri	12. fa

Let's pause for a moment to consider something that will be important in the application of this and future rules; namely, the meaning of the term "root word." In its simplest form, "root word" is defined as a word to which a prefix or suffix can be added. For example, *light* is the root word of *lights, lighting,* and *lightly*. See how you build your outlines by adding suffixes and prefixes to a root word: **light** li ; **lights** lis ; **lighting** li ; **lightly** lil. Note that the basic outline of li for **light** is maintained in all these words. From **indicate** ndca you derive **indicates** ndcas ; **indicating** ndca ; and **indicated** ndcā .

See how the outline for the root word has been retained in each of the following examples: **meetings** me ; **eliminated** elmnā ; **nightly** nil ; **voting** vo ; **treats** Tes ; **treated** Tē ; **treatment** Te— .

Remember, the rule states that you are to write *a* for the sound of "ate" at the end of a word. That is, you are to drop *t* after a long vowel. The word *fat* does not contain a long vowel so this rule does not apply: **fat** fl . Similarly, since the word *seat* contains the final sound of "eet," you write **seat** se ; but you write **set** sl . Don't forget that *t* is dropped at the end of a word only when it follows a long vowel.

You can test your understanding of what you have learned by writing the following words.

You write:

1. cheat Ce	2. cheap Cep
3. chief Cef	4. wife wif
5. white wi	6. wit wt
7. tight ti	8. type tip
9. tile til	10. lit lt
11. wrote ro	12. role rol
13. bit bt	14. bright Bi
15. beat be	16. beak bec

Confirmation:

1. Ce	2. Cep	3. Cef
4. wif	5. wi	6. wt
7. ti	8. tip	9. til
10. lt	11. ro	12. rol
13. bt	14. Bi	15. be
16. bec		

You have already learned that a final vowel is retained in the root word when a suffix is added to it. Notice in the following words how this same rule is applied.

Study these words:

lately	lal	receipts	rses
rates	ras	calculated	clclā
awaiting	ava	designated	dzgnā
dates	das	dated	dā
meets	res	invited	nvī
typewriting	tpri	voted	vō
devoted	dvō	routes	rus

You write:

1. located ________ 2. related ________
3. waiting ________ 4. meeting ________
5. suits ________ 6. sheets ________
7. devoting ________ 8. writing ________

Confirmation:

1. lcā 2. rlā 3. va 4. re
5. sus 6. Ses 7. dvo 8. ri

It is important to realize that, except for the addition of a suffix, this rule is to be applied at the end of a word only. The rule will not be applied when the long vowel and *t* is a medial sound. For example: **vital** vtl ; **futile** ftl ; **title** ttl .

Now that you have learned the rule that has just been presented, you will have no difficulty with the next rule because it simply states that you are going to treat words that end in a long vowel + "v" in the same way as those ending in a long vowel + "t."

RULE 16	**For the final sound of a long vowel and "v," drop the v and end the outline with the long vowel.**

Let's illustrate this rule with the word *gave*. The rule tells you to drop *v* when it follows a long vowel; therefore, write **gave** *ga*. Similarly, you write *e* for the sound "eve" that is heard in the word *leave*; and write **leave** *le*. The word *drive* ends in the sound of "ive"; thus, **drive** is written *di*; **drove** *do*; **groove** *gu*.

Study these examples:

arrived	*arī*	**arrival**	*aril*
achieve	*aCe*	**achievement**	*aCe-*
receive	*rse*	**leaving**	*le̲*

You write:

1. arrive ari **2. received** rse
3. pave pa **4. driving** di

5. dive ___di___ 6. wove ___⌣o___

7. believe ___ble___ 8. arrives ___aris___

9. achieved ___aCē___ 10. receiving ___rse̲___

Confirmation:

1. ari 2. rsē 3. pa 4. di̲

5. di 6. ⌣o 7. ble 8. aris

9. aCē 10. rse̲

RULE 17 | For the sound of "kw" (qu) write q.

The sound of "kw" is always associated with the letter *q* in longhand and, as you can see, you are going to take advantage of this association in this rule.

Study these examples:

quite	qi	equipped	eqp̄
quickly	qcl	quote	qo
equal	eql	frequently	Fq-l
acquainted	aqa=	quit	ql

Note that in the outline for the word *acquainted* you are using the rule that instructed you to write the long vowel if it is followed by a sound that is represented by a mark of punctuation.

You write:

1. quoted ___qō___ 2. adequate ___adql___

3. acquaint aqa- 4. equipment eqp-

5. quoting qo̲ 6. quick qc

7. frequent Fq- 8. equals eqls

Confirmation:

1. qō 2. adql 3. aqa- 4. eqp-

5. qo̲ 6. qc 7. Fq- 8. eqls

Brief Forms

charge	Cg	purchase	pC
keep	cp	too	lo
an, at	a	am, many	⌒
he, had, him	h		

Abbreviations

percent	pc	amount	a-l

Additional Words

analysis	alss	purchases	pCs
anticipate	alspa	purchased	pC̄
anticipated	alspā	purchasing	pC̲

keeps	cps	**amounts**	ants
keeping	cp	**amounted**	ant
charges	Cgs	**amounting**	ant
charged	Cg	**percentage**	pcj

Dictation Hints

Salutations containing proper names are written as follows:

My dear Mr. Gray: md M ga:
Dear Mrs. Price: d ms ps:
Dear Doctor: ddr:
Dear Bill: dbl:

Note: When Mr. or Mrs. appears within the body of a letter, the form M and ms will also be used. Example: **. . . a letter from Mr. Brown.**

a L f M brn.

Phrasing

The joining of words is known as phrasing, and such phrasing can be an aid to speed building. For example, the joining of **you can** uc or **I will** il is faster to write and therefore advisable. However, excessive phrasing (the joining of more than two words) is to be avoided because it results in outlines that are usually difficult to read. In the matter of phrasing, it is best to be guided by your own personal experience. If the joining of words comes naturally to you, by all means follow through with it; but if you find it unnatural, you would be wise to avoid it.

In the Exercises that follow, some phrasing has been done in such words as **you can** uc ; **to reach** lreC ; **it will** ll . Keep this in mind as you read your *Speedwriting* Shorthand plates.

Reading Exercises

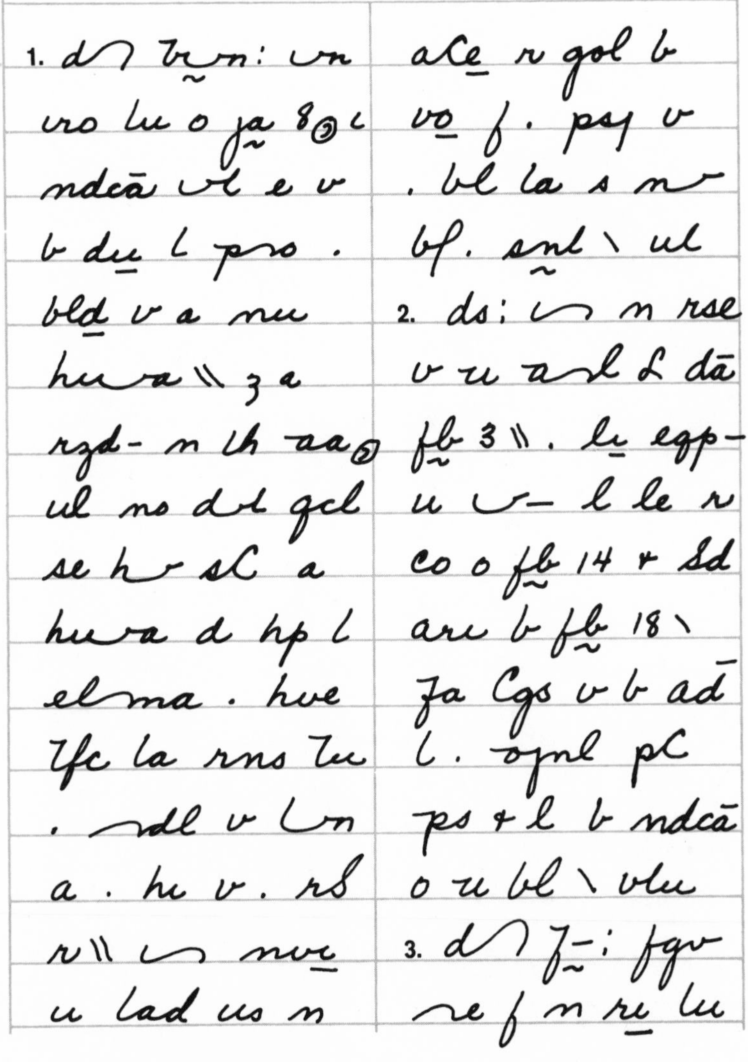

bf th la da\ uno
la e h a apy--
o jl 29 + i ti
breC u lsa la
iz lo sc lcp l\
idd lc l s-,
n u ofs + h
ga -e s p-s
la h d rpe -u
-sj lu\\ if u
r fe o ag 4
id b v hpe l
de u lse. bld
w lcā f u
nu ofss\.
r- b gō s
eql l vl u
r nv pa\ s
4. -ds: . alC̄

Se Sd b ad l.
cal u rsē El
th -o\\ l Sos
. - nu ds
er sl + ndcas
. ras lb Cq̄ f
r lpre eqp-\
ul
5. ds: u Cc f.
alcls pC̄ o
-a 7 arū o
ag 19\ uc 7/
rdl se y e Cn
cr u v. 10 pc
ds la s al
f pa- vn 30
ds\\ th s a
plse ev flō
f -ys\ c

6. d) bj: zu no(.)
ev 7g- re f r
m n. fld sola
e sa aga-ls
v r nu sdlo\
ible ud pfl gl
7s sC a re + la
ud b gu dle v
vl ud se\\ sa
i alspa v u jyn
us o. nu v
sp 10\ vlu

7. d) ga: w rse
u bl da ag7(.) b
bf sal u pa-(.)
id lc u l Cc.
arl u sa s du\\
vn u af-z n
u Spo gl6(.)

h sd la 7 d b no
Cqf S-(;) + yl uv
evd-l ad sC Cgs
l. arl v. ojnl
pC\\ sa uno.
rzn f lh? ul

8. drs bi: er n
rse v u Cc + r
hpe lno la r le(-)
va sus + Cos r
sl so gcl n u
Sp\\ 1v r m
l b n u aa o
sp 3(.) + ul sc
h lso u a cpe
v r nu cal\
ul

Key to Lesson 6

1. Dear Mr. Brown: When I wrote to you on January 8, I indicated what we have been doing to promote[2] the building of a new highway. (¶) As a resident in this area, you will no doubt quickly see[4] how such a highway would help to eliminate the heavy traffic that runs through the middle of town at the height of the[6] rush hour. (¶) I am inviting you to aid us in achieving our goal by voting for the passage of the bill that[8] is now before the Senate. Yours truly, *(87 words)*

2. Dear Sir: I am in receipt of your airmail letter dated February 3. (¶) The lighting equipment you want[2] will leave our company on February 14 and should arrive by February 18. Freight charges[4] have been added to the original purchase price and will be indicated on your bill. Very truly yours, *(60 words)*

3. Dear Mr. Front: Forgive me for not writing to you before this late date. I know that we had an appointment on[2] July 29, and I tried to reach you to say that I was too sick to keep it. I did talk to someone[4] in your office, and he gave me his promise that he would repeat my message to you. (¶) If you are free on August 4,[6] I would be very happy to drive you to see the building I have located for your new offices. The rent[8] being quoted is equal to what you are now paying. Sincerely, *(92 words)*

4. My dear Sir: The attached sheet should be added to the catalog you received early this month. (¶) It shows the[2] many new items we are selling and indicates the rates to be charged for our typewriting equipment. Yours truly,[4] *(40 words)*

5. Dear Sir: Your check for the articles purchased on May 7 arrived on August 19. You can, therefore, readily[2] see why we cannot credit you with the 10 percent discount that is allowed for payment within 30 days.[4] (¶) This is a policy we have followed for many years. Cordially, *(52 words)*

6. Dear Mr. Bridge: As you know, we have frequent meetings for our men in the field so that we may acquaint them with our[2] new models. I believe you would profit greatly from such a meeting and that you would be quite delighted with what[4] you would see. (¶) May I anticipate having you join us on the night of September 10. Very truly yours,[6] *(60 words)*

7. Dear Mr. Gray: I have received your bill dated August 7, but before mailing my payment, I would like you[2] to check the amount you say is due. (¶) When your agent was in my shop on July 6, he said that there would be no charge for[4] shipment; and yet you have evidently added such charges to the amount of the original purchase.[6] (¶) May I know the reason for this? Yours truly, *(68 words)*

8. Dear Mrs. Bright: We are in receipt of your check and are happy to know that our light-weight suits and coats are selling[2] so quickly in your shop. (¶) One of our men will be in your area on September 3, and I will ask him to[4] show you a copy of our new catalog. Yours truly, *(50 words)*

CONGRATULATIONS! NOW START BUILDING SPEED

You've successfully completed the "first lap" in your race toward secretaryship. What a feeling of pride and confidence it must give you to get your "second wind," fully realizing that success in mastering *Speedwriting* shorthand principles depends simply on your intelligent concentration and your devotion to the career goal of your choice!

Now you're ready to enter into the most exciting, most stimulating phase of your career training – *building speed.* And this you can do only by learning to *automatize* your shorthand – to write automatically. Repetitive dictation, scientifically designed to promote unthinking responses, is the avenue which lies before you now to insure that you achieve this goal. Now you will be adding true vocational value to your shorthand skills.

Dictation Tapes are the secret! Thousands of successful students before you have proved the value of these tapes, which are correlated with the lessons in your theory books. They give you practice in writing familiar words, reinforcing the principles you learn. And continuous repetition of words, phrases, and sentences at ever-increasing rates of speed will gradually lead you to the point at which the *thinking* process stops and *automatic* writing takes over. This is your goal . . . and the open door to a happy secretarial career.

Name............................Class..........Date................

Writing Assignment—Lesson 6

1. I have received the letter in which you indicated that the white sheets I purchased will arrive at an early date.

i v rsē · l n wc u ndca la
· wi Ses i pcō l arv a a
El da.

2. A 2-percent charge for shipment should be added to the prices quoted for our coats and suits.

a 2·pc cg f S- Sd b ad l
· pss gō f r cos + sus.

3. The man wrote to say that he had frequently used our equipment.

· m- ro l sa la h h fq-l
uz r eqp-

4. Tell him that I believe we can keep our rates at the present low level.

Ul h la i bl e c cp r ras a
· pz- lo lvl.

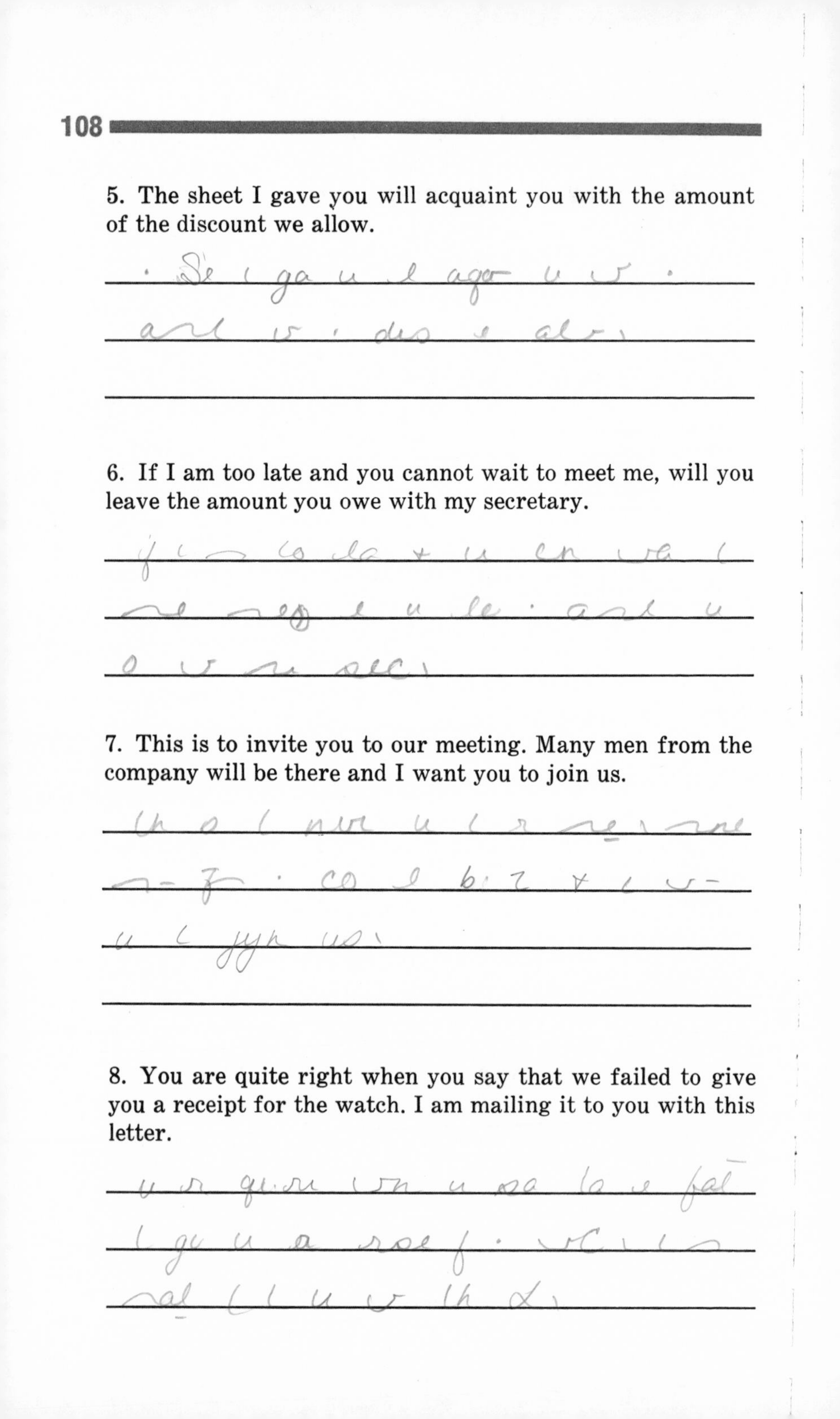

5. The sheet I gave you will acquaint you with the amount of the discount we allow.

6. If I am too late and you cannot wait to meet me, will you leave the amount you owe with my secretary.

7. This is to invite you to our meeting. Many men from the company will be there and I want you to join us.

8. You are quite right when you say that we failed to give you a receipt for the watch. I am mailing it to you with this letter.

BRIEF FORMS AND STANDARD ABBREVIATIONS

am	m	during	du
amount	amt	fail	fl
an	a	feel	fl
and	+	field	fld
are	r	firm	F
as	z	for	f
ask	sc	great	g
at	a	had	h
be	b	have	v
been	b	he	h
busy	bz	help	hp
but	b	him	h
buy	b	his	s
by	b	hour	r
can	c	in	n
catalog	cal	is	s
charge	Cg	it	t
company	co	keep	cp
credit	cr	letter	L
day	d	like	lc
discount	dis	man	m-
doctor	dr	many	m

month
not
of
on
our
percent
president
price
purchase
second
secretary
shall
she
ship
that
the
those
there
their
this
to
too
very
vice-president
was
we
week
well
were
why
will
with
woman
would
year
your

Lesson 7

RULE 18 | Write *ol* **for "old."**

This is a rule that requires very little explanation. It simply tells you that whenever the sound of "old" occurs in a word, you are to write *ol*. Thus, the words **old** *ol* ; **sold** *sol* ; **told** *tol* ; **holding** *hol* .

Study these examples:

golden	*goln*	**hold**	*hol*
cold	*col*	**household**	*hshol*
fold	*fol*	**gold**	*gol*

RULE 19 | For the sound of medial and final "tiv" write *v* **.**

Study these examples:

effective	efcv	**defective**	dfcv
relatively	rlvl	**tentative**	t-v
active	acv	**positive**	pzv

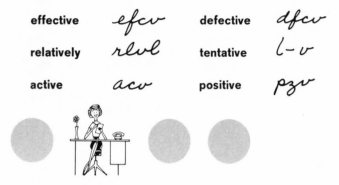

In Lesson 4 you learned how to handle "combination-r" sounds at the beginning of words such as **bright** bi ; **cry** ci ; and **from** fm . These sounds are often heard also in the middle of words such as *fabric, afraid,* and *program.* It is to these medial "combination-r" sounds that this next rule refers.

RULE 20	**To express a medial "combination-r" sound, capitalize the letter that precedes r and omit the r from the outline.**

In other words, in the <u>middle</u> of a word write B for "br"; C for "cr"; D for "dr"; F for "fr"; G for "gr"; P for "pr."

Study the following words to see how these "combination-r" sounds are written at the beginning and middle of a word.

brick	bc	⟶	**fabric**	fBc
crease	ces	⟶	**increase**	nCs
drama	dra	⟶	**melodrama**	mlDra

fresh	Fs	→	**refresh**	rFs
gram	g	→	**program**	pg
print	p-	→	**reprint**	rp-

Study these words:

abroad	aBd	**afraid**	aFd
telegram	tlg	**decrease**	dCs
prescribed	psCb̄	**agreement**	age-
refrain	rFn	**approach**	aPC

You write:

1. increasing nCs̲ **2. programs** pgs

3. degree dge **4. increases** nCss

5. agrees ages **6. agreements** age--

7. regret rgl **8. agreed** agē

Confirmation:

1. nCs̲ 2. pgs 3. dge 4. nCss

5. ages 6. age-- 7. rgl 8. agē

As you wrote these words, you were surely aware of the fact that these capital letters in the middle of the word can be written fluently and without difficulty. However, in such words as *electric* or *patron* you need to write a medial capital *T* in order to conform with this rule. Written in the usual way, this capital would be cumbersome, time consuming, and awkward. Therefore, this medial "tr" will be written as follows:

electric  patronize 

patronage 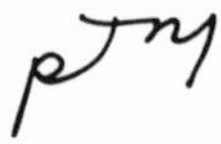 attractive 

You write:

1. electrical  2. introduce 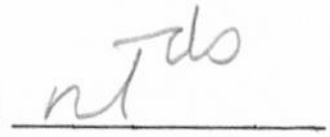

Confirmation:

1.  2. 

Read the following sentences:

1. 
2. 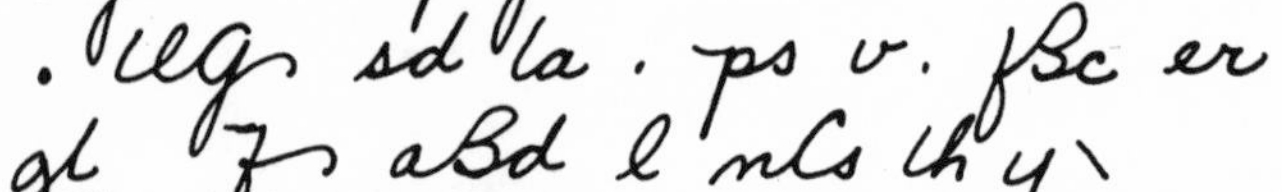
3. 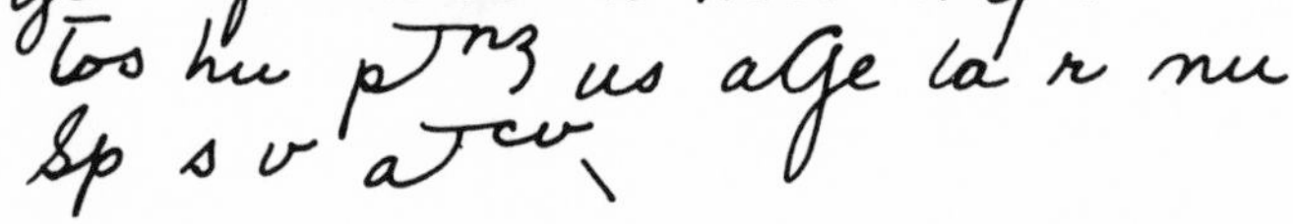

Key:

1. We are afraid that you will regret that you did not agree to his program.
2. The telegram said that the price of the fabric we are getting from abroad will increase this year.
3. Those who patronize us agree that our new shop is very attractive.

Brief Forms

they  easy 

kind	ci	held	hl
given	gv	line	li
appreciate	ap	little	ll
put, up	p	go, good	g
fine, find	fi		

Abbreviations

room	r⌒	telephone	tel
department	dpt		

Additional Words

goes	gs	lines	lis
going	$\underline{g}$	lining	$\underline{li}$
ago	ag	appreciates	aps
final	fil	appreciated	$\overline{ap}$
finally	fil	appreciative	apv
finding	$\underline{fi}$	departments	dpts
kinds	cis	rooms	r⌒s
kindly	cil	goods	gs

Reading Exercises

1. drs q-: r fr le
v aTcv cln fBcs
s vdl sol n a
q ~ Sps n Lm\
~ vm hu v
pC Ls v lol us
la ly r dlt l fr
. fBcs so ez l tm\\
cble la vn uv
Tl Ls ul b gc
l age\ ul
pa dpzt\ vn u
ga us lh dpzt e
sd la. vC d b
hl f 2 vks\\ lh s
l nf u la fu
du n pc p. vC
vn a d o 2 el
fl Ze lsl u vC
+ rln. dpzt\ d
u cl ll us nc
vl u v- us l
du\ ul

2. ds: e ap.
pTM uv gv us
lal + e hop ul
g o pTnz r Sp
f ~ ys\ s

3. drs sl: ev
b hol a gol vC
o vC u

4. ds: v. aC
v. nu y ~ vS
lll u hv vC ~
ap. hp uv gv
us du. ol y\
cfl la r pG
d n v b so

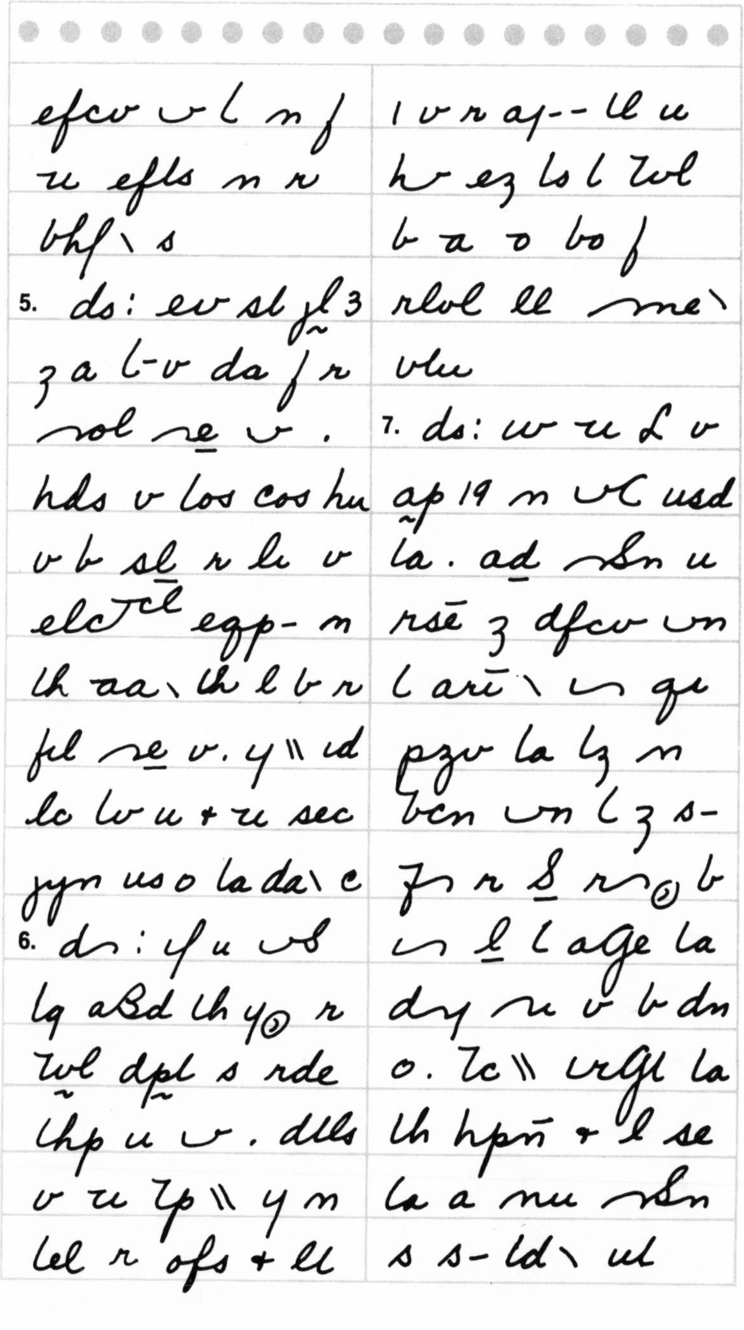

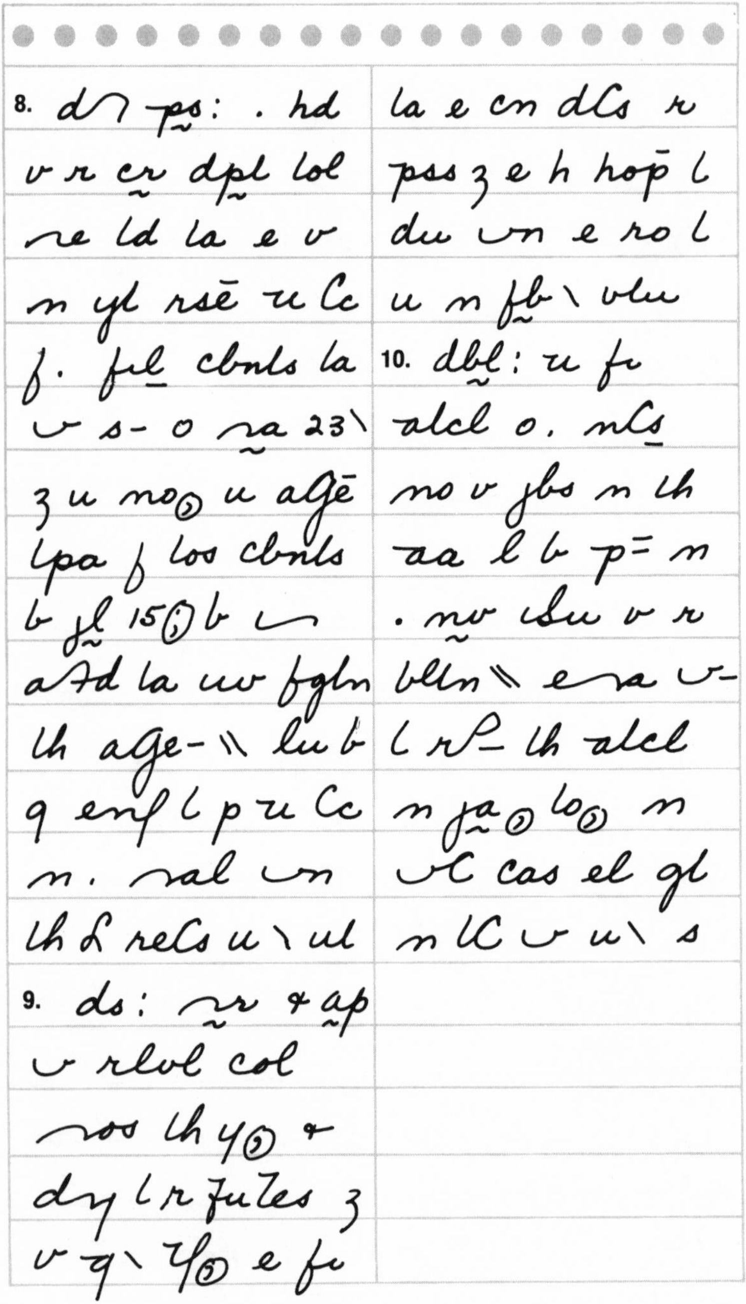
8.
9.
10.

Key To Lesson 7

1. Dear Mrs. Grant: Our fine line of attractive cotton fabrics is widely sold in a great many shops in town. Many[2] women who have purchased them have told us that they are delighted to find the fabrics so easy to iron.[4] (¶) I believe that when you have tried them you will be quick to agree. Yours truly, *(53 words)*

2. Dear Sir: We appreciate the patronage you have given us lately, and we hope you will go on patronizing[2] our shop for many years. Sincerely, *(27 words)*

3. Dear Mrs. Smith: We have been holding a gold watch on which you put a deposit. When you gave us this deposit,[2] we said that the watch would be held for two weeks. (¶) This is to inform you that, if you do not pick up the watch within[4] a day or two, we will feel free to sell your watch and retain the deposit. (¶) Would you kindly let us know what you[6] want us to do. Yours truly, *(65 words)*

4. My dear Sir: With the approach of the new year, I wish to tell you how much I appreciate the help you have given[2] us during the old year. I feel that our program would not have been so effective were it not for your efforts[4] in our behalf. Sincerely, *(45 words)*

5. Dear Sir: We have set July 3 as a tentative date for our monthly meeting with the heads of those companies[2] who have been selling our line of electrical equipment in this area. This will be our final meeting[4] of the year. (¶) I would like to have you and your secretary join us on that date. Cordially, *(56 words)*

6. Dear Madam: If you wish to go abroad this year, our Travel Department is ready to help you with the details[2] of your trip. (¶) Why not telephone our office and let one of our agents tell you how easy it is to travel[4] by air or boat for relatively little money. Very truly yours, *(54 words)*

7. Dear Sir: I have your letter of April 19 in which you said that the adding machine you received was defective[2] when it arrived. I am quite positive that it was not broken when it was sent from our shipping room, but I[4] am willing to agree that damage might have been done on the truck. (¶) I regret that this happened and will see that a[6] new machine is sent today. Yours truly, *(67 words)*

8. Dear Mr. Price: The head of our Credit Department told me today that we have not yet received your check for the[2] filing cabinets that were sent on May 23. As you know, you agreed to pay for those cabinets by July[4] 15; but I am afraid that you have forgotten this agreement. (¶) Will you be good enough to put your check[6] in the mail when this letter reaches you. Yours truly, *(69 words)*

9. Dear Sir: March and April were relatively cold months this year, and damage to our fruit trees was very great. Therefore,[2] we find that we cannot decrease our prices as we had hoped to do when we wrote to you in February. Very[4] truly yours, *(42 words)*

10. Dear Bill: Your fine article on the increasing number of jobs in this area will be printed in the[2] November issue of our bulletin. (¶) We may want to reprint this article in January, too, in which case[4] we will get in touch with you. Sincerely, *(47 words)*

Name............................Class..........Date................

Writing Assignment—Lesson 7

1. They have told me that the program you were kind enough to set up is very effective.

ly v tld m la . pg- u w
ci enf l sl p s v efcv.

2. Our President agrees that a reprint of your fine article should be given to each shop in which our fabrics are sold.

r P agrs la a rP- v u fi
alcl Sd b gv l eC Sp n
wC r fBcs r sld.

3. You will find it is easy to increase your profits by introducing our attractive line of fine gold watches.

u l fi l s ez l nCes u pfts
b nTds r aTcv ln v fi gol
wCs.

4. I would appreciate your telephoning my office to set up a tentative appointment with the head of our department.

i d aPSa u tel u ofs l sl
p a t-v apy-- w . hd v
r dpt.

5. I am going abroad this week for a meeting that is to be held on July 28.

i m go aBd th wk f a me la

o l b hld o jl 28.

6. With the busy season approaching, we should increase the number of men in our shipping room.

w . bz szn aPCq e Sd nCes

. no v mn n r S rm.

7. We regret to inform you that there will be a little delay in shipping the household items you purchased on June 17.

e rgt l nfm u la l l b a ltl

dla n S . hshol itms u pC o

jn 17.

8. Our shop can put a new lining in your old coat for relatively little money.

r Sp c pt a nu ln n u ol col

f rltvl ll mne.

Lesson 8

RULE 21	**For the medial and final sound of "ake" write c .**

make	mc	**lake**	lc
making	<u>mc</u>	**break**	bc
sake	sc	**take**	tc

This is a simple rule if you remember that it applies only to the sound of "ake." It does <u>not</u> apply to the sounds in one-syllable words such as **seek** sec ; **broke** boc ; **hike** hic .

You write:

1. makes mcs______ **2. taking** <u>tc</u>______

3. takes tcs______ **4. brake** bc______

Confirmation:

1. mcs **2.** <u>tc</u> **3.** tcs **4.** bc

RULE 22 | **For the sound of medial or final "shun," vowel plus "shun," and "nshun" write j.**

The sound of "shun" to which this rule refers may be spelled in various ways in longhand and may also have slight variations in pronunciation. For example: *nation, fashion, discussion, physician, occasion.* It is to the sounds in these words that this rule applies.

Let's start with the word *addition.* You know that **add** is ad. Thus, for the word **addition**, you simply write adj; and the word **provisions** is pvjs. Since the rule states that *j* is also written for the medial sound of "shun," you apply this rule to the words **national** njl; and **occasionally** ocjl.

Study these examples:

solution	slj	**division**	dvj
position	pzj	**election**	elcj
production	pdcj	**nation**	nj
vacation	vcj	**protection**	ptcj
qualifications	qlfcjs	**introduction**	n‾dcj
decisions	dsjs	**education**	edcj
television	tlvj	**relation**	rlj
actions	acjs	**deduction**	ddcj
session	sj	**location**	lcj
occasion	ocj	**fashion**	fj

You write:

1. **additional** adjl 2. **professional** pffl

3. **motion** mj 4. **discussion** dscj

5. **reduction** rdcj 6. **requisition** rqzj

7. **section** scj 8. **dedication** ddcj

9. **locations** lcjs 10. **promotion** pmj

11. **selection** slcj 12. **invitation** nvtj

Confirmation:

1. adjl 2. pffl 3. mj 4. dscj
5. rdcj 6. rqzj 7. scj 8. ddcj
9. lcjs 10. pmj 11. slcj 12. nvtj

This rule also instructs you to write *j* for the entire sound of "nshun." Thus, **attention** atj ; **prevention** pvj ; **mention** mj .

You write:

1. **mentioned** mj̄ 2. **intention** ntj

3. **dimensions** dmjs 4. **mentions** mjs

Confirmation:

1. mj̄ 2. ntj 3. dmjs 4. mjs

What of a word such as *reaction?* You previously learned that the first and last letter of a root word do not change when a prefix or suffix is added. Therefore, you retain this initial vowel from the root word and write **reaction**

The next rule is very similar to the one in which you learned to attach a hyphen to the initial letter of a word to indicate that it is immediately followed by the sound of "r." For example: **front** ; **bright** ; **true** . The rule in this lesson simply explains what's to be done to indicate that the initial letter of a word is combined in sound with the "l" that follows it as in such words as *album, blue, closely,* and *flood.*

RULE 23	**When the initial letter of a word is combined with the sound of "l," indicate the resulting sound by writing a dash (—) on the initial letter of the outline.**

You can see how similar this rule is to the one you have previously learned. In the word *album* the initial letter is pronounced with "l," and the rule states that this sound of "al" is indicated by writing a dash on the *a* ( ). Thus, **album** is written . The dash is distinguished from the hyphen by its length, so you can see why the initial stroke on the word *album* is longer than the hyphen used to indicate the sound "ar" at the beginning of the word **arm** . To avoid any confusion, be sure to form the habit of making your dash at least twice as long as the hyphen.

Let's look at the word *blue.* The first letter of this word is combined with "l," and for the resulting sound of "bl," you write *b* . Therefore, **blue** *bu* . What of the word *closely?* Since you write *c* for the initial sound of "cl," **closely** *is written* *csl* .

You will recall that in writing the word *earth* you use this *E* because it is easier to attach an initial hyphen *E* . For the same reason, you will use this same form of *E* when you indicate the sound of initial "el" *E* . Thus, **else** *Es* . Now see how the rule has been applied to the following words.

Study these examples:

black	*bc*	**ill**	*l*
clients	*cu --*	**plan**	*pn*
club	*cb*	**play**	*pa*
element	*E-*	**slow**	*so*
flight	*fi*	**slight**	*si*
flood	*fd*	**ultimate**	*ulml*
glad	*gd*		

You write:

1. alibi abi	**2. blood** bd
3. clothing co	**4. elm** Em
5. fleet fe	**6. gladly** gdl
7. plant p-	**8. slip** sp
9. pleasant pz-	**10. plates** pas

11. classroom crm **12. clinic** cnc

Confirmation:

1. —abc 2. —bd 3. —col 4. —Em

5. —fe 6. —gdl 7. —p— 8. —sp

9. —pz— 10. —pas 11. —crm 12. —cnc

Before continuing, let's pause for a moment to call your attention to a fact that is essential to your understanding of the rules governing the use of the initial hyphen and dash. To illustrate, let's consider the words *arm* and *album*. Notice that in these words the sounds of the first two letters are blended together into a single sound. On the other hand, in the words *arise* and *alone*, there is not the combination of two sounds into one. You must bear in mind, therefore, that it is only when the initial letter is combined with the sound of "l" or "r" that these two rules are applied. In view of this, you can understand why **arise** is written arz and **election** elc .

RULE 24	**When the medial sound of "combination-l" occurs in a word, omit the l and write the letter that precedes it.**

Following this rule, **problems** is written pbms ; **obliged** obj ; **include** ncd ; **legislation** ljsj

You write:

1. apply apa **2. obligation** obgj

3. duplicate dpca **4. inflation** nfj

5. application apcj
6. legislative lgsv
7. supplement sp-
8. supply spi
9. reply rpi
10. inclusion ncj

Confirmation:

1. api 2. obgj 3. dpca 4. nfj
5. apcj 6. lgsv 7. sp- 8. spi
9. rpi 10. ncj

Brief Forms

about	ab	**order**	O
has	as	**please**	-p
over	O	**customer**	K
came, come, committee	k		

Abbreviations

child	ch	**avenue**	ave
children	chn	**boulevard**	blvd
street	st	**place**	pl

Dictation Hints

To express an even amount of dollars or cents write:

dollar, dollars d **cents** c

Examples: **$5** 5d ; **$1** 1d ; **45 cents** 45c ; **$2** 2d .

To express an uneven amount of money write:
$33.62 $33^{\underline{62}}$; **$98.75** $98^{\underline{75}}$; **$7.29** $7^{\underline{29}}$.

Additional Words

become	bk	**oversight**	Osi
becomes	bks	**overlooked**	Olc̄
became	bk	**pleased**	—p̄
becoming	bk̲	**pleasing**	—p̲
coming	k̲	**placing**	pl̲
comes	ks	**placement**	pl—
income	nk	**places**	pls
welcome	lk	**placed**	pl̄
welcomed	lk̄	**replaced**	rpl̄
committees	ks	**replacement**	rpl—
ordered	Ō	**child's**	chs
ordering	O̲	**children's**	chns
orders	Ōs	**cancellation**	csly
customers	Ks	**information**	nfy
overdue	Odu	**relationship**	rlys

Reading Exercises

1. d) pl: i rgl la
n obj l ll u la l
l b a — si dla n
spe . chns — col
u O \ z i nj O.
lel sn v . eqp-
nr — p-z bdl
dy b. hve fd n
lh sc/ + pdcj as b
v lt n rs- vks \\
er rc pujs lrpl
lh eqp- n a fu ds
+ Sd lnb n a pzj
lrc 8-lr Ks \\ id
apl yf ud lu lb a
ll p8- \ su
2. drs b n: l u
— p fl n . alC f
f apcj f cr + ral
l bc lus \\ ll lc ab
10 ds f u Cq — pa
lreC u lu . ral
u ra v-l va
f l o — es u c k
nl r Sp o 8 sl +
q- ave l gl l
gcl \ ul
3. ds: vn uk l se
re o ra 12 u
lol re v u — pn
lr- a h s o. lc
f u k vcj \\ lh sl
ll u no la w lca
a — pz- 50 r cl
la id lc u lse \ l
r-- f 150d a ro
+ lh ps ncds .
us v a fi nu bo \

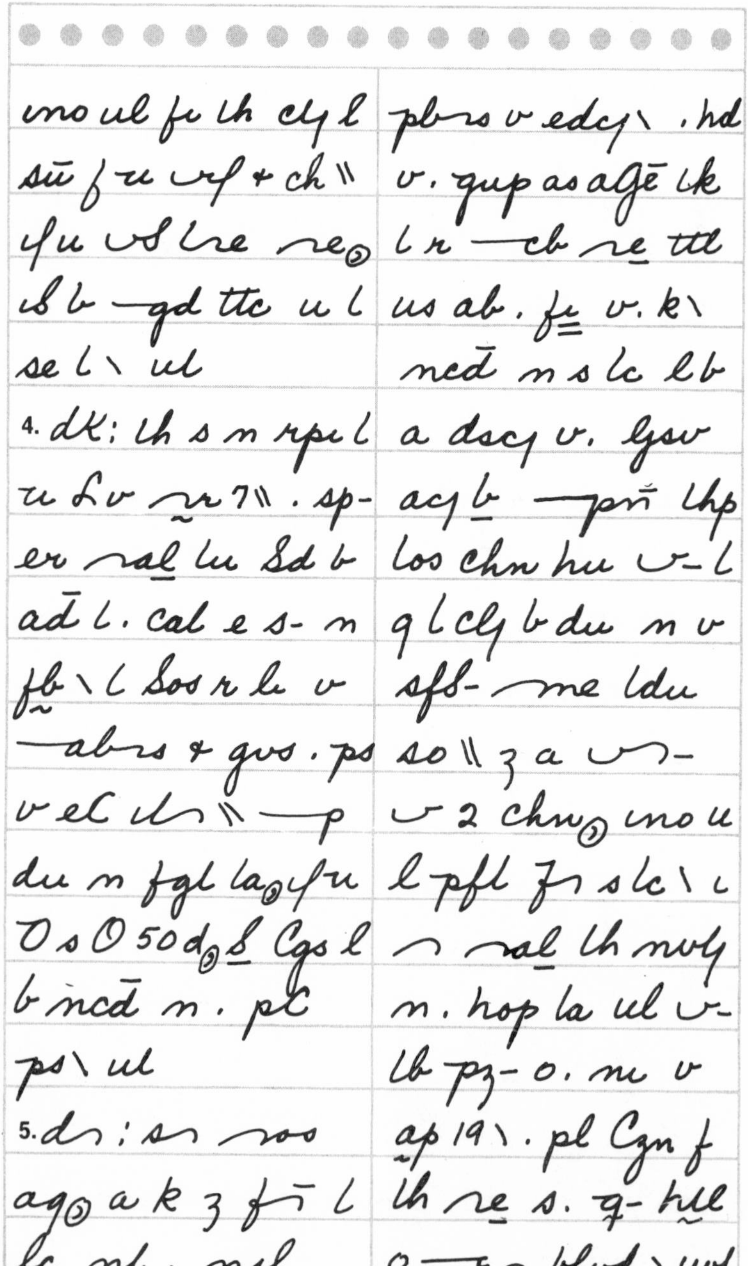

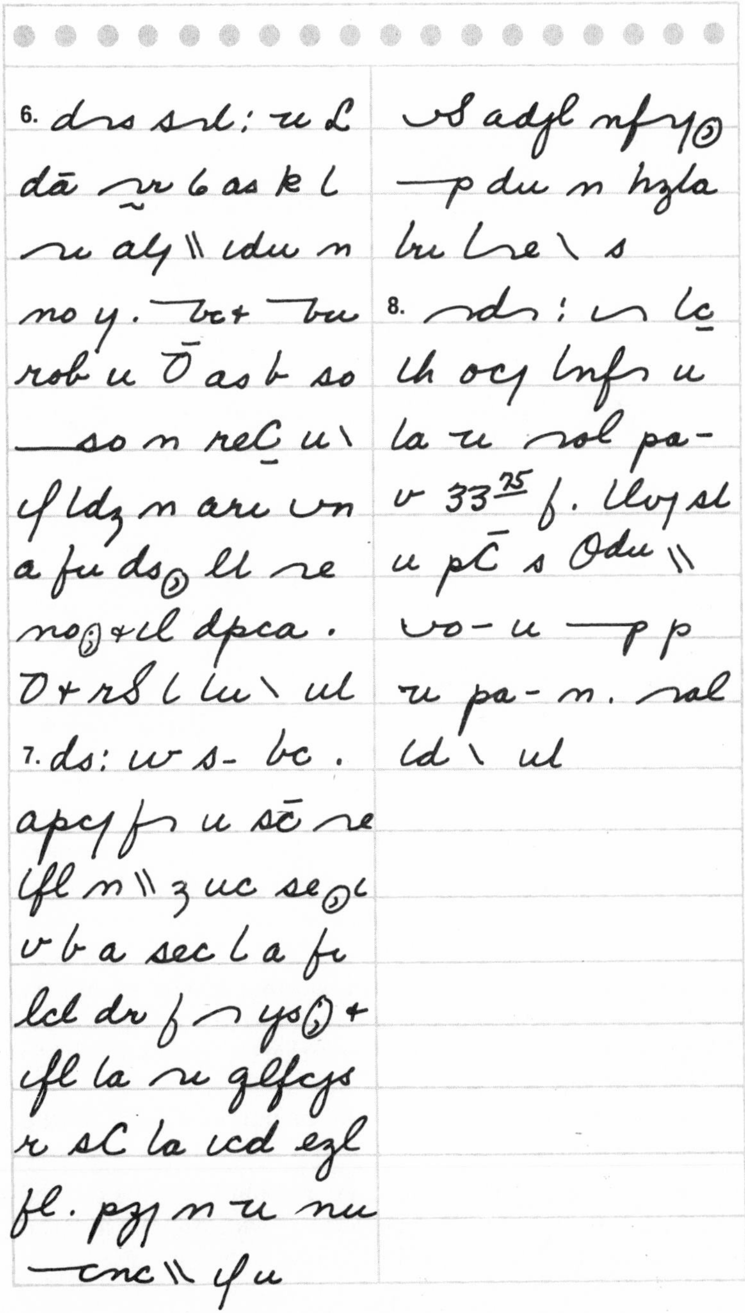

Key to Lesson 8

1. Dear Mr. Place: I regret that I am obliged to tell you that there will be a slight delay in supplying the[2] children's clothing you ordered. As I mentioned over the telephone, some of the equipment in our plant was badly[4] damaged by the heavy flood in this section; and production has been very limited in recent weeks. (¶) We[6] are making provisions to replace this equipment in a few days and should then be in a position to[8] make shipment to our customers. (¶) I would appreciate it if you would try to be a little patient.[10] Sincerely yours, *(102 words)*

2. Dear Mrs. Brown: Will you please fill in the attached form for application for credit and mail it back to us. (¶) It[2] will take about ten days for your charge plate to reach you through the mail. You may want to wait for it, or else you can come[4] into our shop on Eighth Street and Grant Avenue to get it quickly. Yours truly, *(54 words)*

3. Dear Sir: When you came to see me on May 12, you told me of your plan to rent a house on the lake for your coming[2] vacation. (¶) This is to let you know that I have located a pleasant five-room cottage that I would like you to[4] see. It rents for $150 a month, and this price includes the use of a fine new boat. I know you[6] will find this cottage well suited for your wife and child. (¶) If you wish to meet me, I shall be glad to take you to see[8] it. Yours truly, *(82 words)*

4. Dear Customer: This is in reply to your letter of March 7. (¶) The supplement we are mailing to you should[2] be added to the catalog we sent in February. It shows our line of albums and gives the price of each[4] item. (¶) Please do not forget that, if your order is over $50, shipping charges will be included[6] in the purchase price. Yours truly, *(65 words)*

5. Dear Madam: Some months ago, a committee was formed to look into the national problems of education.[2] The head of the group has agreed to come to our club meeting to

tell us about the findings of the committee.[4] Included in his talk will be a discussion of the legislative action being planned to help those children[6] who want to go to college but do not have sufficient money to do so. (¶) As a woman with two children, I[8] know you will profit from his talk. I am mailing this invitation in the hope that you will want to be present[10] on the night of April 19. The place chosen for this meeting is the Grant Hotel on Elm Boulevard. Yours very[12] truly, *(123 words)*

6. Dear Mrs. Smith: Your letter dated March 6 has come to my attention. (¶) I do not know why the black and blue robe[2] you ordered has been so slow in reaching you. If it does not arrive within a few days, let me know; and I[4] will duplicate the order and rush it to you. Yours truly, *(50 words)*

7. Dear Sir: I have sent back the application form you asked me to fill in. (¶) As you can see, I have been a secretary[2] to a fine local doctor for many years; and I feel that my qualifications are such that I[4] could easily fill the position in your new clinic. (¶) If you wish additional[6] information, please do not hesitate to write to me. Sincerely, *(72 words)*

8. My dear Madam: I am taking this occasion to inform you that your monthly payment of $33.[2]75 for the television set you purchased is overdue. (¶) Won't you please put your payment in[4] the mail today. Yours truly, *(47 words)*

Speedwriting SHORTHAND – KEY TO SUCCESS

Job opportunities are numerous today! But don't be misled. It takes training and thorough preparation in business skills to qualify for the interesting, challenging, and better-paying positions. Young people today who do not have this training qualify only for the drab and monotonous jobs that offer no hope for advancement.

Speedwriting shorthand is your key to the better, more rewarding way of life, just as it has been for literally hundreds of thousands of graduates before you. *Speedwriting* was their "open sesame" to glowing, happy careers in business. Rest assured it can be yours, too.

Speedwriting shorthand has proved its value to many more than just young women intent on a secretarial career. Many young men and women, preparing to go on to college, study *Speedwriting* shorthand to acquire a most valuable tool for use in the lecture hall and library. They go on to become the envy of their fellow students, who recognize their efficiency in studying.

Professional men, doctors, lawyers, and engineers also know the benefits derived from shorthand skills. Salesmen, reporters, travel agents, club women – all have found *Speedwriting* shorthand of value in their daily lives.

No matter whether you chose to study *Speedwriting* shorthand for personal or vocational use, you will find your decision was a wise and rewarding one.

Name..............................Class.........Date................

Writing Assignment – Lesson 8

1. I am taking this occasion to tell you how pleased we are to have you place your order with us. We welcome you as a new customer. We know that our relationship will be a pleasant one and that the introduction of our children's clothing will greatly increase your profits.

i lc th ocj l tl u h-pz

er lv u pl u O v us, e

lk u z a nu k, e no l r

rlyS l b a -pz- l + la. n dcy

v r chns -col l -gl nCs u

pfts.

2. We are obliged to inform you that it will take over a month to make additional shipments of our television sets to your section.

e r obj l nf u la ll lc O

a no l -c adyl S-- v r

tlvj sts l u sc.

3. In my letter I mentioned the production problems we have had in our plant. Our position has now become quite critical, and I hope that you can supply a solution.

4. What provisions will your committee make for the prevention or reduction of flood damage in this area?

5. Our club is meeting on October 28 for a discussion of the coming national election. Included in the program will be a talk on the qualifications of each man who is running.

Lesson 9

RULE 25 | **For the final sound of "er" or "ter" write a joined slant.**

Before explaining the rule, let's first define what is meant by the "joined slant." Simply stated, a joined slant is a long upward stroke attached to the letter that precedes it. The following letters illustrate the addition of a joined slant: 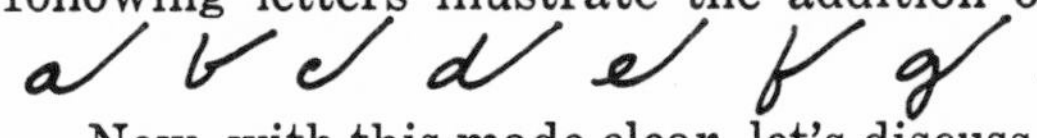 .

Now, with this made clear, let's discuss the final sound of "er," which the rule tells you to indicate by a joined slant. Let's start with the word *bigger*. You know that **big** is written  ; therefore, **bigger** is 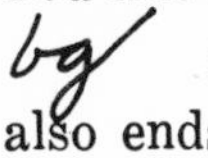 ; **color**  ; **richer**  . The word *cover* also ends in the sound of "er," so write **cover**  .

Study these examples:

manager    **summer** 

manner    **builder** 

officer	earlier
rubber	owner
washer	older
retailer	power
her	paper
picture	procedure
similar	newspaper
professor	favor
occur	dinner
error	familiar
pressure	wider
offer	refer
chamber	prior

You write:

1. voucher ______
2. labor ______
3. major ______
4. nature ______
5. lumber ______
6. neighbor ______
7. proper ______
8. feature ______
9. prefer ______
10. never ______
11. honor ______
12. eager ______

Confirmation:

1. vrC/ 2. lb/ 3. rf/
4. nC/ 5. lrb/ 6. nb/
7. pp/ 8. fC/ 9. pf/
10. nv/ 11. on/ 12. eg/

You will recall that you double the mark of punctuation at the end of a word to indicate the addition of *s*. Thus, **wants** w– – ; **buildings** bld . You will apply this same principle when adding *s* to words ending in a joined slant: **refers** rf// ; **covers** cv// ; **pictures** pcC// ; **offers** of// ; **dollars** dl// ; **shoppers** Sp// .

You write:

1. colors cl//

2. features fC//

3. officers ofs//

4. errors E//

5. papers pp//

6. owners on//

Confirmation:

1. cl// 2. fC// 3. ofs//
4. E// 5. pp// 6. on//

Let's now consider those words in which the sound of "er" follows a sound that is represented by a mark of punctuation, such as *hunter*. As you know, **hunt** is h– . Therefore, **hunter** h_/ ; **winter** w_/ ; **center** s_/ ; **centers** s_// .

Now, how will you handle root words that end in "er" or "ter" to which "ing" and "ed" are added? Simply follow the rule you have previously learned for the use of the underscore and overscore.

Study these examples:

offering	of/–	**covered**	cv/‾
featuring	fC/–	**offered**	of/‾
covering	cv/–	**occurred**	oc/‾
referring	rf/–	**referred**	rf/‾
occurring	oc/–	**preferred**	pf/‾

There is one point that must be stressed in order for you to fully understand the application of this rule. In Lesson 5, you learned that, when the outline of a root word ends in a vowel, the vowel is retained when a suffix is added to it. For example: **truly** tul ; **highway** hwa ; **payment** pa– . Thus, although *truly* and *highway* are words of more than one syllable, the long vowel is not omitted because it occurs at the end of the root-word outline.

You have learned that medial vowels are dropped in words of more than one syllable. The one-syllable word **broke** is boc and the two-syllable word **broken** is bcn . Since **broker** is a word of more than one syllable, you write bc/ . In the same way, you write **safe** saf , but **safely** sfl and **safer** sf/ .

Study these examples:

brief	bef	⟶	**briefer**	bf/
cheap	Cep	⟶	**cheaper**	Cp/
teach	teC	⟶	**teacher**	tC/

But what of the word *bolder?* In Lesson 7, you learned to write *ol* for "old" in words of one or more syllables. Applying this rule, **bolder** is written  ; **folder** 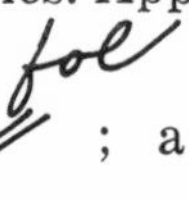 ; **policyholder**  ; **folders**  ; and **holders**  .

The following words show you how "er" is added to a root word by simply adding a joined slant to the root-word outline.

Study these examples:

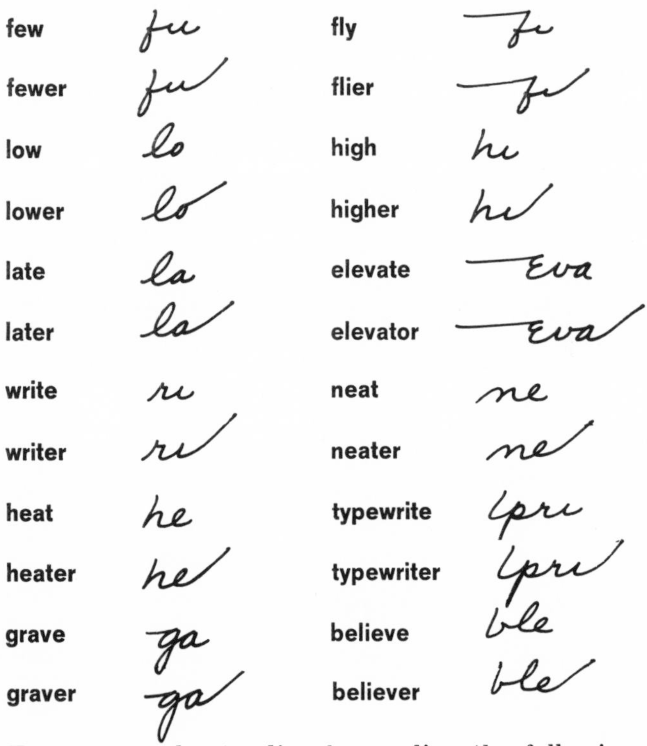

few
fewer
low
lower
late
later
write
writer
heat
heater
grave
graver
fly
flier
high
higher
elevate
elevator
neat
neater
typewrite
typewriter
believe
believer

Test your understanding by reading the following sentences:

1. 

2. 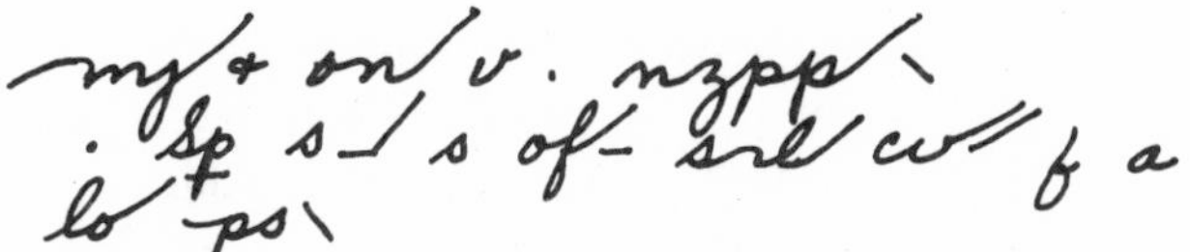

3. 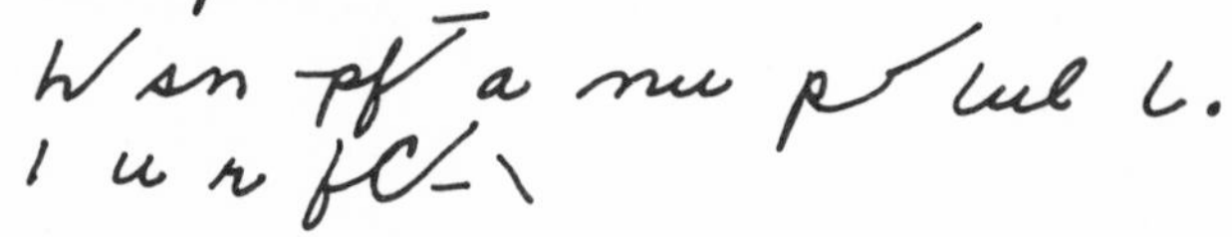

Key:

1. **Earlier this summer, we gave a dinner for the manager and owner of the newspaper.**
2. **The shopping center is offering similar covers for a lower price.**
3. **Her son preferred a new power tool to the one you are featuring.**

The rule also states that a joined slant will be used to represent the final sound of "ter."

Study these examples:

matter  **after** 

factors  **water** 

latter  **better** 

matters  **editor** 

chapter  **meter** 

Finally, before leaving this rule, let's stress one further aspect of it. Namely, this rule is to be applied only at the end of a word. That is, except for an underscore, overscore, or a second slant to indicate the addition of *s*, you will not write the joined slant for "er" or "ter" in the middle of an outline. These medial sounds will be covered in a later lesson.

RULE 26 | For the final sound of "all" write *al*.

Study these examples:

fall	*fal*	**crawl**	*ral*
hall	*hal*	**tall**	*lal*
wall	*wal*	**ball**	*bal*

Though this is a simple rule, there is a point about its application that must be clarified and stressed so that you will be sure to use it correctly. Notice that you are instructed to write *al* for the final sound of "all." What of such words as *fault* or *walnut?* Since the sound of "all" is not final in these words, you can understand why this rule does not affect them; so you write **fault** *fll*; **walnut** *wlnl*; **false** *fls*; **ballroom** *blrm*; **falsely** *flsl*; **halt** *hll*.

RULE 27 | For the initial and final sound of "aw" write *a*.

Study these examples:

all	*al*	**law**	*la*
although	*allo*	**saw**	*sa*
draw	*da*	**alter**	*al/*
drawer	*da/*	**laws**	*las*

Here, again, it is important to understand that the rule refers to the sound of "aw" only at the beginning and end of words. Remember that the rule is not to be applied to the medial sound of "aw." For example: **cause** *cz*; **lawn** *ln*;

bought bl ; **brought** bl ; **caught** cl ; **talk** lc
taught tt .

Brief Forms

again, against	aq	**business**	bs
where	ur	**advantage**	avj
***sale**	S	**out**	ou
save	sv	**member**	mB
future	fC		

*Note that this word is represented by a printed *s*.

Abbreviations

envelope	env	**invoice**	inv

Additional Words

salesman	Ssm-	**outline**	ouli
salesmen	Ssmn	**outlined**	oulī
sales	Ss	**outside**	ousd
resale	rS	**whereas**	urz
members	mBs	**elsewhere**	Esur

membership		savings	
remember		saved	
answer		saves	
answered		businessman	
answering		businessmen	
former		upper	
greater		buyer	
easier		purchaser	

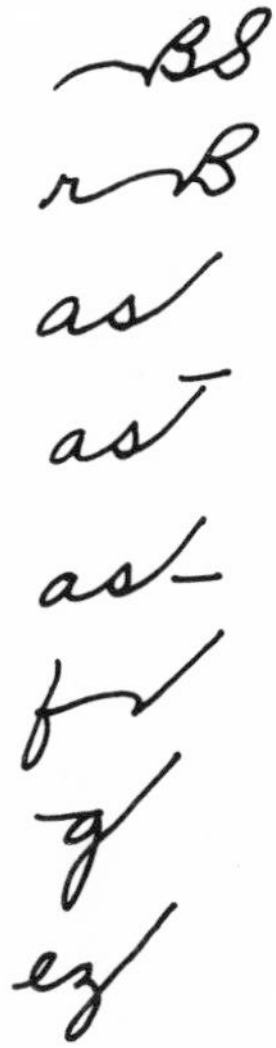

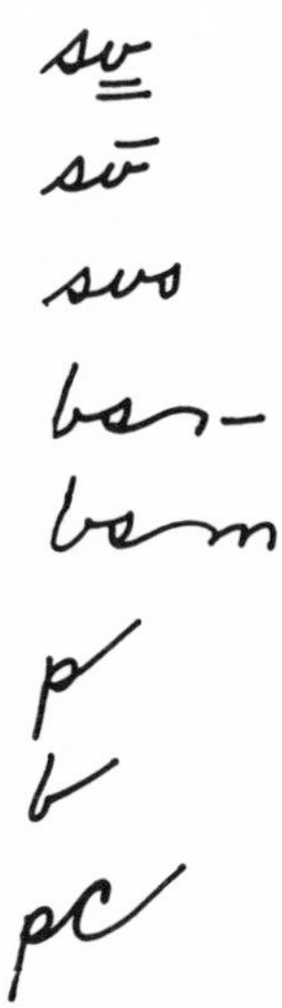

Reading Exercises

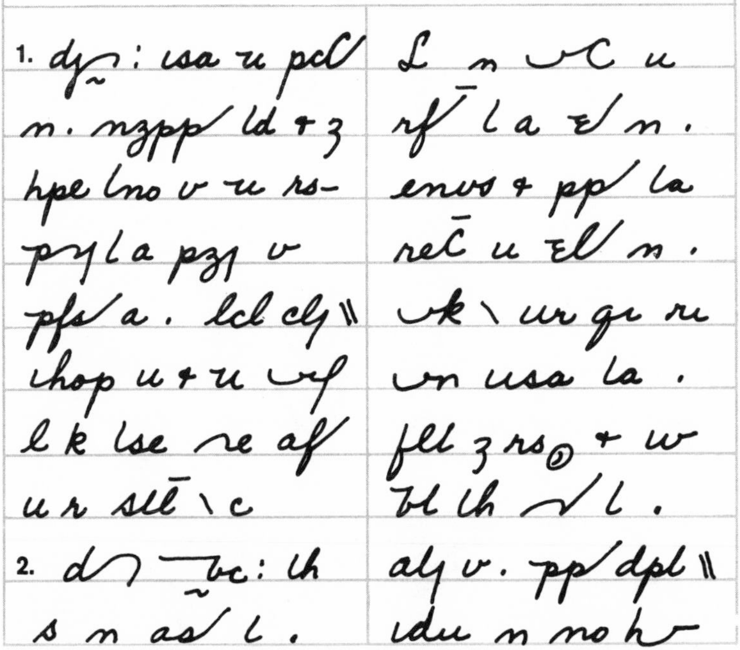

Ch E/ oc̄⊙ b cl
se la l dz n hpn
ag n. fC\ a nu
S- v- ou lu ld
+ Sd aru n a d
o 2\ su

3. dB: al ofs//
+ Bs v r lC//
cb v vō n
fv v gv a dn/
lon/ r f/ P\
e pn lv.
dn/ f W la/ n
. so b v n yl
dsd̄ vr ll b
hl\\ fu d lc
lb pz⊙ p
ll re no\ vlu

4. d) vr: r

ofs mf/ as lol
re la u pa- v
653.89 o r inv v
fl 28 s Odu\ ul
r B la u bl ch
S- v lprl/ o cr
+ aGē lc pa-
vn 30 ds\\ sa
ev u Cc o
Es a L ll us
no vn e sa
hop lse ch pa-\
fu du n as/ ch
L vn a fu ds⊙
eS fl obj ttc
lgl acj aq u\ su

5. rds: z. on/ v
a rll Sp⊙ u no
dl vS lse u

bo go n fC ys(;)
+ u v- l nCs
. no v Ks hu pC
l dl spes 7 s u"
. alC fol/ l So
u h- lhc b dn\
l oules s- v .
psf/ la v b flō
b a q - rll/+
lls h- u(.) lo(.) c
nCs u ss du .
y" af u v rd .
fol(.) chop ul
al- 1 v r aj--
lq O. dlls v u\ul
6. drs ga: n Cc
r fils(.) e se la
u v n uz u Cq
-pa f - ros\

7/(.) u -ra n b
fl/ v . nu Sp
s-/ ev bll brpl
r ol / \ -ra e
nv u l dp n
lse us\ ul fi
la(.) allo r Sp
s bg/+ b ln lz
n f-/ ys(.) e
of/ lo -pss +
g/ diss ln uc
gl -Es-r" y
n lc avj v . hy
s er n- v a
vC er fC- fal
+ v-/ cos\ ev
nv bf pvd r
Ks v a vd/
Cys v cl//(.) +

ev nv h sC a
fr slcj v fBcs \\
k n + ll us So
u h— uc sv
—me o al u
pCs \ c

7. drs hal: ur
qe re ~n usa
la r ol —dls
~ a ll Cp/ b
nn v Lh h.
— fr fC// ev
bll nl r nu
gs he// \\ f ul
ll ' v r —m
lc lu ab L
ul b qc laGe
la ev nv p
ou a b he \\

. fol la w
s- ~ Lh L l
hp lSo u y so
— Ks pf/ r
nu —dl \ ul

Key To Lesson 9

1. Dear Jim: I saw your picture in the newspaper today and was happy to know of your recent promotion to[2] a position of professor at the local college. (¶) I hope you and your wife will come to see me after you[4] are settled. Cordially, *(44 words)*

2. Dear Mr. Black: This is in answer to the letter in which you referred to an error in the envelopes and[2] paper that reached you earlier in the week. You are quite right when you say that the fault was ours, and I have brought this[4] matter to the attention of the proper department. (¶) I do not know how this error occurred, but I will see[6] that it does not happen again in the future. A new shipment went out to you today and should arrive in a[8] day or two. Sincerely yours, *(85 words)*

3. Dear Member: All officers and members of our Teachers Club have voted in favor of giving a dinner to[2] honor our former President. We plan to have the dinner for her later in the month but have not yet decided[4] where it will be held. (¶) If you would like to be present, please let me know. Very truly yours, *(56 words)*

4. Dear Mr. White: Our Office Manager has told me that your payment of $653.89[2] on our invoice of July 28 is overdue. You will remember that you bought this shipment[4] of typewriters on credit and agreed to make payment within 30 days. (¶) May we have your check or else a letter[6] letting us know when we may hope to receive this payment. If you do not answer this letter within a few[8] days, we shall feel obliged to take legal action against you. Sincerely yours, *(93 words)*

5. My dear Sir: As the owner of a retail shop, you no doubt wish to see your business grow in future years; and you[2] want to increase the number of customers who purchase their daily supplies from you. (¶) The attached folder will show[4] you how this can be done. It outlines some of the procedures that have been followed by a great many retailers[6] and tells how you, too, can increase your sales

during the year. (¶) After you have read the folder, I hope you will allow[8] one of our agents to go over the details with you. Yours truly, *(92 words)*

6. Dear Mrs. Gray: In checking our files, we see that you have not used your charge plate for many months. Therefore, you may not[2] be familiar with the new shopping center we have built to replace our old one. (¶) May we invite you to drop in[4] to see us. You will find that, although our shop is bigger and better than it was in former years, we offer lower[6] prices and greater discounts than you can get elsewhere. (¶) Why not take advantage of the huge sale we are now having[8] at which we are featuring fall and winter coats. We have never before provided our customers with a[10] wider choice of colors, and we have never had such a fine selection of fabrics. (¶) Come in and let us show you[12] how you can save money on all your purchases. Cordially, *(130 words)*

7. Dear Mrs. Hall: You are quite right when you say that our old models were a little cheaper, but none of them had the[2] many fine features we have built into our new gas heaters. (¶) If you will let one of our men talk to you about[4] them, you will be quick to agree that we have never put out a better heater. (¶) The folder that I have sent with[6] this letter will help to show you why so many customers prefer our new model. Yours truly, *(77 words)*

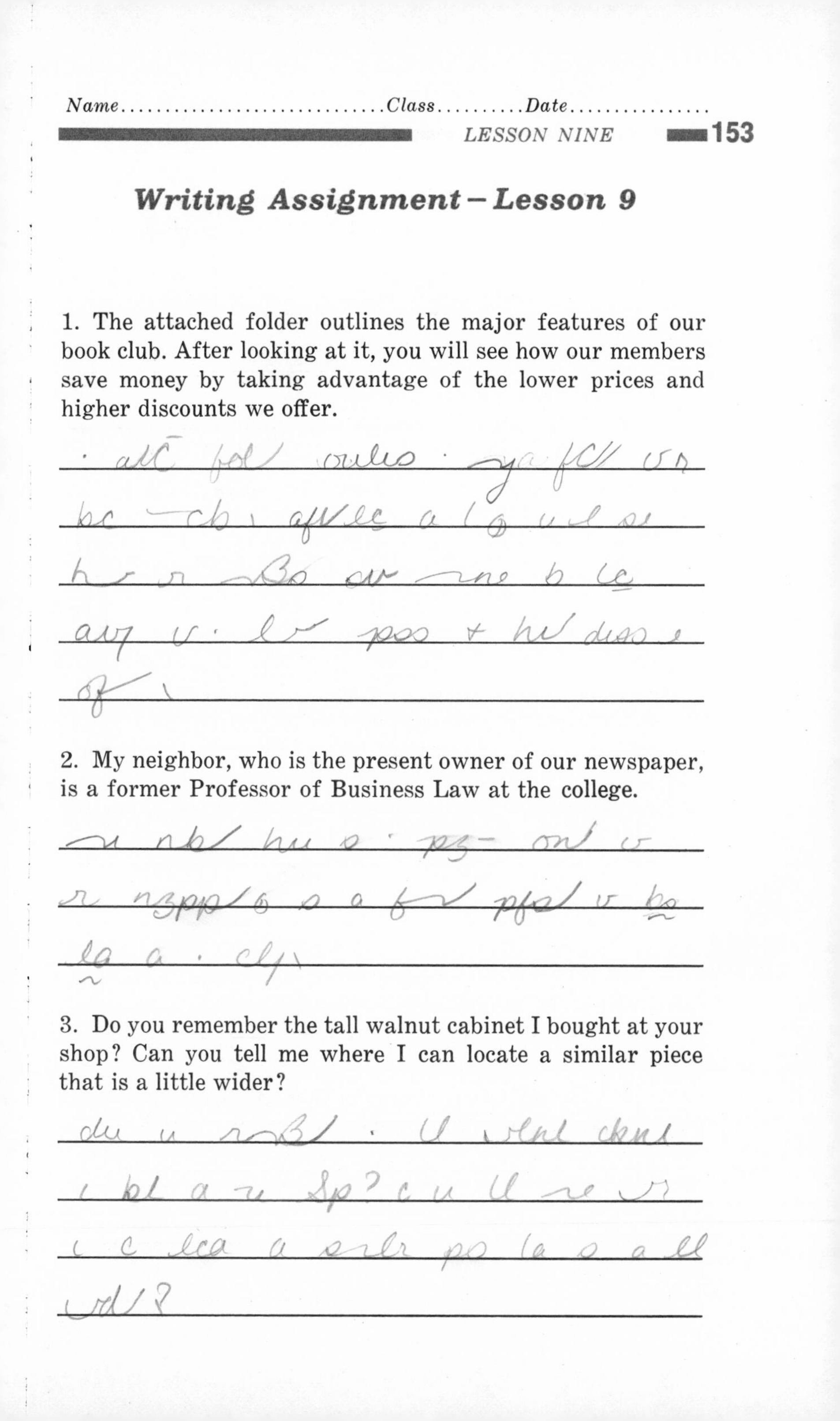

Name............................Class..........Date................

Writing Assignment—Lesson 9

1. The attached folder outlines the major features of our book club. After looking at it, you will see how our members save money by taking advantage of the lower prices and higher discounts we offer.

2. My neighbor, who is the present owner of our newspaper, is a former Professor of Business Law at the college.

3. Do you remember the tall walnut cabinet I bought at your shop? Can you tell me where I can locate a similar piece that is a little wider?

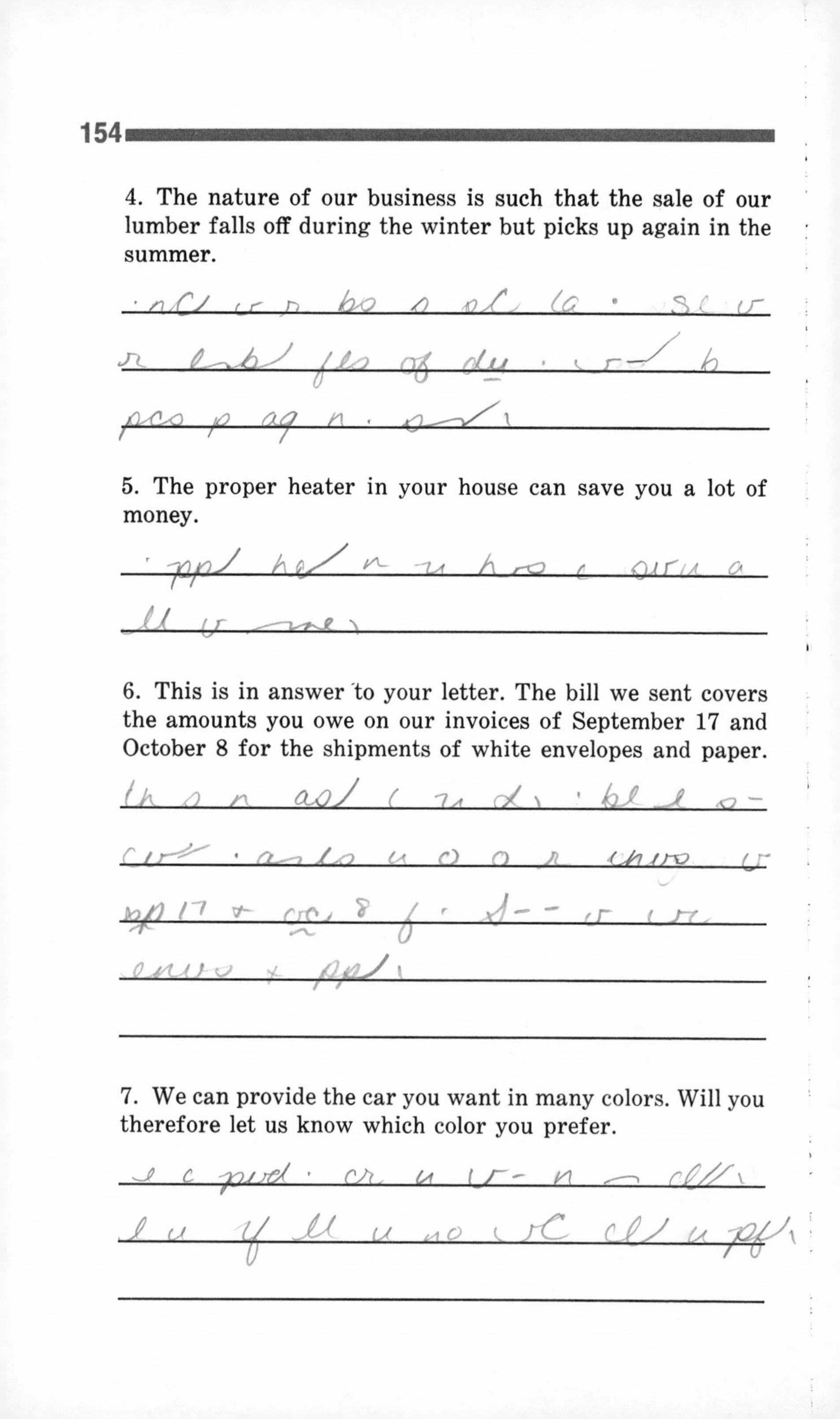

4. The nature of our business is such that the sale of our lumber falls off during the winter but picks up again in the summer.

5. The proper heater in your house can save you a lot of money.

6. This is in answer to your letter. The bill we sent covers the amounts you owe on our invoices of September 17 and October 8 for the shipments of white envelopes and paper.

7. We can provide the car you want in many colors. Will you therefore let us know which color you prefer.

Lesson 10

RULE 28	For the medial and final sounds of "ade, ede, ide, ode, ude" write *d*; for the medial and final sounds of "aze, eze, ize, oze, uze" write *z*

Let's separate the two parts of this rule and examine them individually.

You have learned to write the medial long vowels in words such as **mail** *ml*; **deep** *dep*; **file** *fl*; **hope** *hop*; **tube** *tub*. In this principle you learn to omit the long vowel and write *d* for the sounds heard in words such as *m<u>ade</u>*, *n<u>eed</u>*, *w<u>ide</u>*, *r<u>oad</u>*, and *f<u>eud</u>*.

Study these examples:

made	*md*	**trading**	*td* (underlined)
needs	*nds*	**reading**	*rd* (underlined)
wide	*wd*	**sides**	*sds*
code	*cd*	**rude**	*rd*

You write:

1. paid ______ 2. pride ______
3. road ______ 4. trade ______
5. shades ______ 6. side ______
7. food ______ 8. leading ______
9. need ______ 10. needed ______

Confirmation:

1. pd 2. pd 3. rd 4. ˥d
5. Sds 6. sd 7. fd 8. l̲d
9. nd 10. nd̄

The second part of this rule instructs you to write *z* for the sound of a long vowel + "z."

Study these examples:

raise	rz	these	˥z
size	sz	chose	Cz
whose	hz	choose	Cz
rising	rz̲	seized	sz̄

You write:

1. phase ______ 2. cheese ______
3. wise ______ 4. rose ______
5. news ______ 6. praise ______
7. lose ______ 8. rise ______

Confirmation:

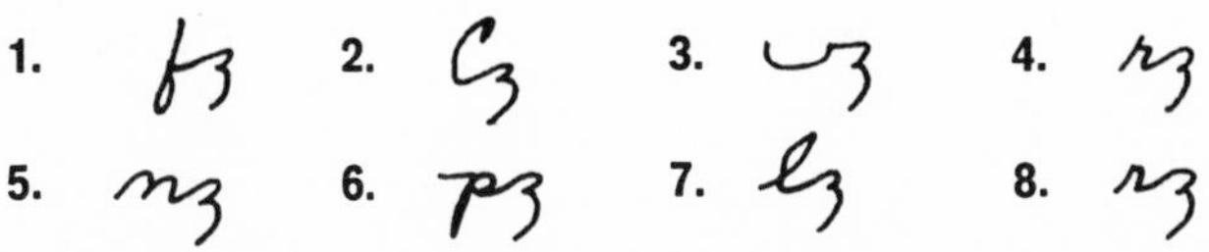

In the following sentence, the word *close* is pronounced in two different ways. *If you are close to the drawer, will you close it?* Notice that in writing this sentence in shorthand, the word *close* is written according to its pronunciation, not its spelling.

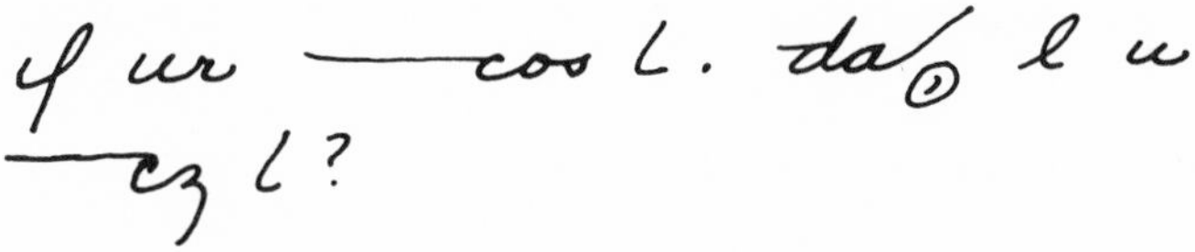

Let's stop for a moment to review some of the rules you have learned about the way a long vowel is handled in *Speedwriting* Shorthand.

1. In words of one syllable, write what you hear – writing all long vowels and all pronounced consonants. Examples: **rage** *raj* ; **cheap** *Cep* ; **sign** *sin* ; **hope** *hop* ; **broke** *boc* ; **seek** *sec* .

2. For the sound of "ake" write *c*. Examples: **make** *mc* ; **break** *bc* ; **take** *tc* .

3. For the final sound of a long vowel and "t" or "v," write the long vowel only. Examples: **mate** *ma* ; **neat** *ne* ; **write** *ri* ; **vote** *vo* ; **boot** *bu* ; **gave** *ga* ; **leave** *le* ; **drive** *di* ; **drove** *do* ; **groove** *gu* .

4. For the medial and final sound of a long vowel and "d" or "z," drop the vowel and write the *d* or *z*.

Examples: **made** ⌒d ; **need** nd ; **wide** ⌣d ; **rode** rd ; **feud** fd ; **raise** rz ; **these** lz ; **prize** pz ; **hose** hz ; **fuse** fz .

Study the following words to see the application of these various rules.

Writing Long Vowels and Consonants

rails	rals	**sign**	sin
robe	rob	**cheek**	Cec

Writing Long Vowels Only

rates	ras	**raves**	ras
sight	si	**drive**	di
wrote	ro	**rove**	ro
cheat	Ce	**achieve**	aCe
root	ru	**grooves**	gus

Dropping of Long Vowels

raids	rds	**raises**	rzs
grade	gd	**size**	sz
road	rd	**rose**	rz
feeding	fd̲	**cheese**	Cz
rude	rd	**cruise**	cz
rake	rc	**sake**	sc

You write:

1. cheap ____	2. chief ____
3. cheat ____	4. cheese ____
5. wine ____	6. wise ____
7. wide ____	8. white ____
9. woke ____	10. wake ____
11. wave ____	12. roll ____
13. rope ____	14. rove ____
15. rose ____	16. wrote ____
17. rode ____	18. choose ____
19. gave ____	20. gate ____
21. guide ____	22. trait ____
23. grade ____	24. grave ____

Confirmation:

1. Cep	2. Cef	3. Ce	4. Cz
5. vrn	6. vz	7. vd	8. vr
9. voc	10. vc	11. va	12. rol
13. rop	14. ro	15. rz	16. ro
17. rd	18. Cz	19. ga	20. ga
21. gd	22. ta	23. gd	24. ga

RULE 29 | Write a dash (–) for the sound of "nd."

In this rule, you are learning to write a dash whenever the sound of "nd" appears in a word.

Study these examples:

demand	ds —	**found**	fv—
handle	h—l	**beyond**	by—
depend	dp—	**fund**	f—
brand	b—	**refund**	rf—
trend	t—	**behind**	bhi —
foundation	fv—1	**remind**	rmi —
lend	l—	**blind**	bi—

You write:

1. mind __________ 2. attend __________

3. end __________ 4. window __________

5. handled __________ 6. bond __________

7. friendly __________ 8. land __________

Confirmation:

1. mi — 2. al — 3. e — 4. w—o

5. h—l̄ 6. b— 7. f—l 8. l—

In comparing the following words, notice how important it is to make the dash at least twice as long as the hyphen. Be sure to form the habit of writing a short stroke for the hyphen and a long stroke for the dash.

Study these words:

send	s—	**grand**	g—
sent	s-	**grant**	g-
hand	h—	**friend**	f—
hint	h-	**front**	f-

Some words contain both the sound of "nd" and "ment" or "nd" and "nt," which simply means that both rules will be applied in their proper place. For example: **amendment** am— - and **dependent** dp— -. What of the plural of these words? You follow the rule you have already had to double the last mark of punctuation: **amendments** am— - -; **dependents** dp— - -.

As with all outlines that end in marks of punctuation, you underscore the dash when "ing" is added; and you overscore when "ed" is added. Thus, **sending** s— (underscored) and **demanded** dm— (overscored). Simply double the dash to indicate the addition of *s*, as in **bonds** b— —; **attends** at— —; **funds** f— —.

Test your understanding of this rule by writing the following words. Remember, in writing a hyphen for "nt" or "ment," be sure to use a short stroke; in writing a dash for "nd," be sure to use a longer stroke.

You write:

1. brands b— — **2. attending** at— (underscored)

3. intent ________ 4. intend ________

5. dividends ________ 6. evident ________

7. handling ________ 8. ends ________

9. sound ________ 10. resident ________

11. playground ________ 12. attended ________

Confirmation:

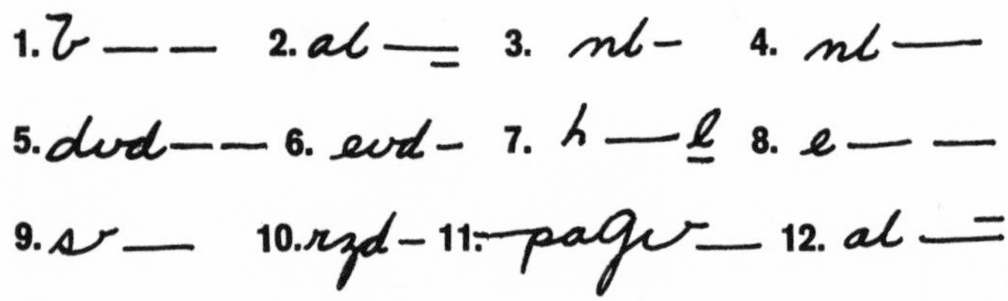

There are many words in which the sound of "nd" is followed by "er." For example: *calendar* or *wonder*. In writing the outlines for these and similar words, you simply treat the dash as you did the hyphen in **winter**  and you write a joined slant.

Study these examples:

wonder 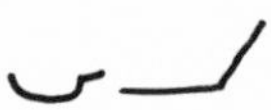 **reminder** 

calendars  **binder** 

Read the following sentences.

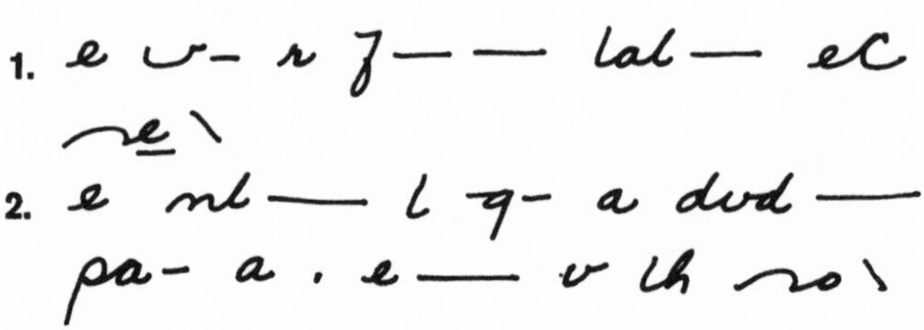

3. 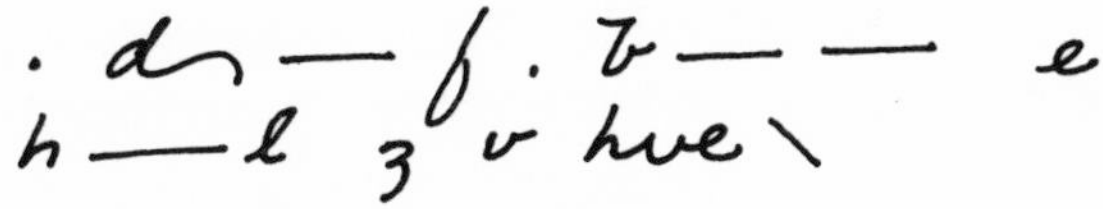

Key:

1. We want our friends to attend each meeting.
2. We intend to grant a dividend payment at the end of this month.
3. The demand for the brands we handle was very heavy.

Brief Forms

school  because 

until  other 

only  every, ever 

begin, began 

Abbreviations

popular  merchandise 

absolute, absolutely 

intelligent, intelligence, intelligently 

Additional Words

everyone  wherever 

everybody  whenever 

everything	E̲	another	aT
everywhere	Evr	others	Ts
whatever	wtE	otherwise	Tz
however	hwE	schools	scls
whoever	huE	merchandising	mdse̲
whichever	wCE	beginning	bq

Reading Exercises

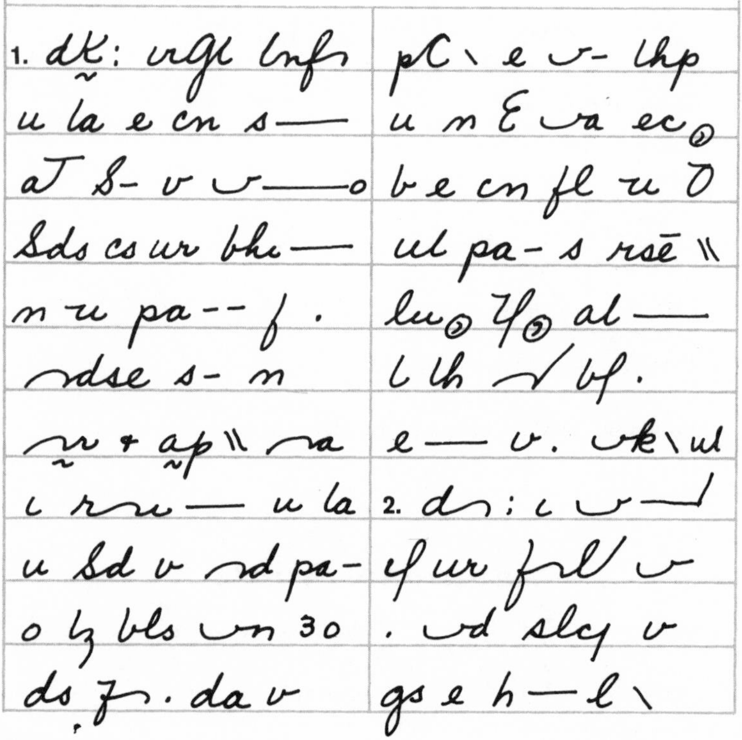

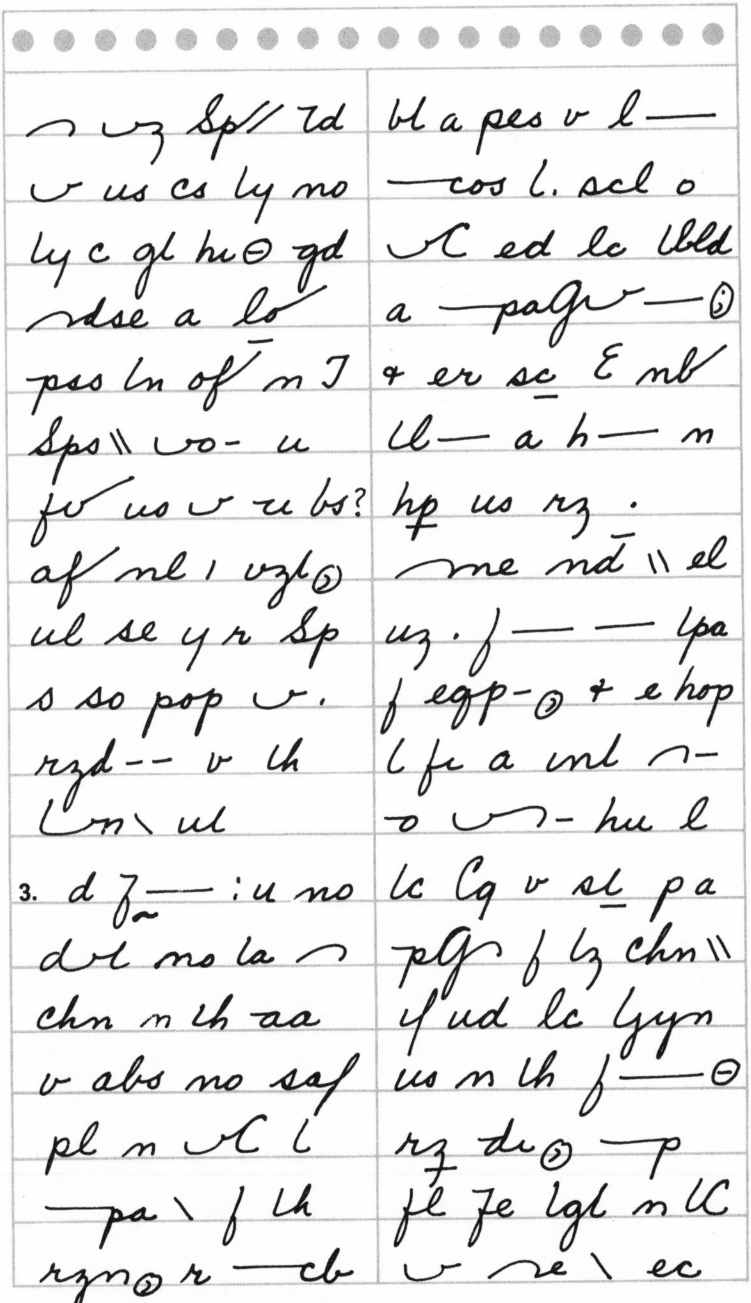

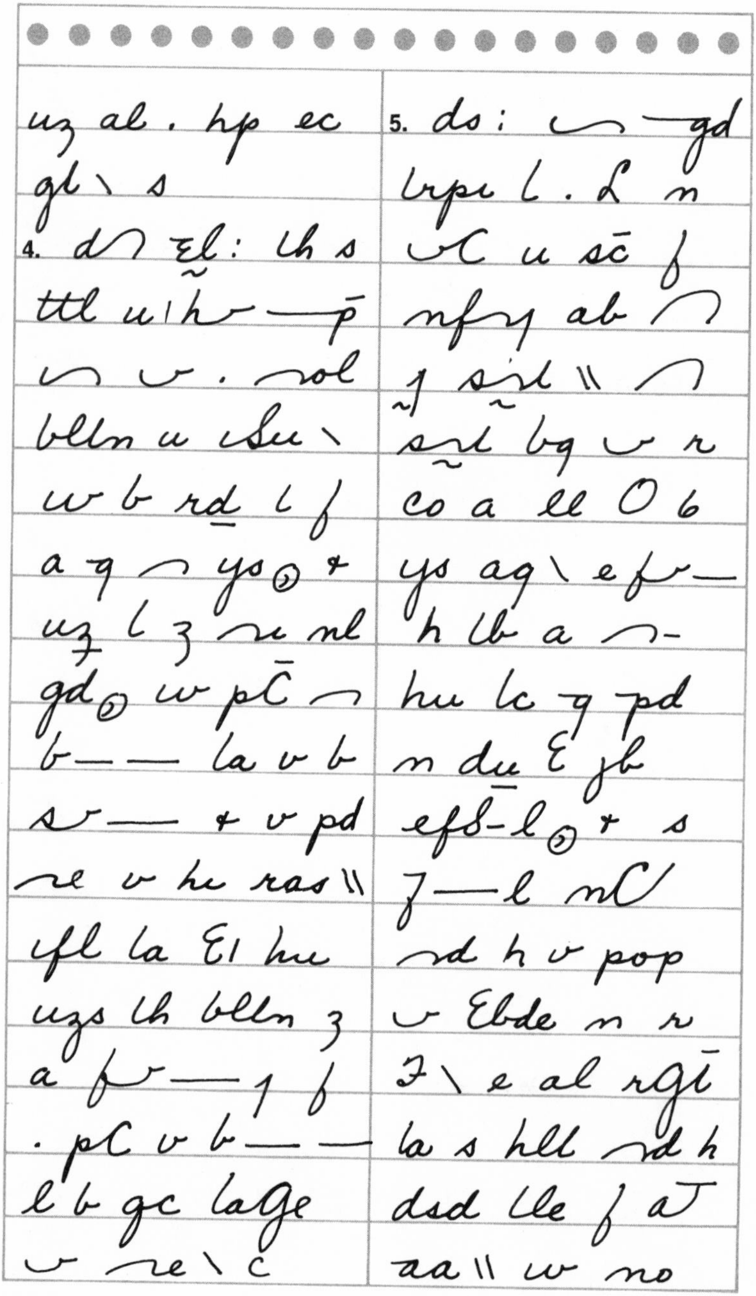

hzlf n sa la
cf u nl — lCz
h f a pzf n
u F hl fl l
l\\ cf u E vS
adjl nfq ab
h — p ru l re
aq\ ul
6. d-s ve: er
s — ch L l al
r J — — z a
ru —/ v. bq
S er v o nv 3\
fC n r s lb
a vd slcq v
chno cos n Esz
+ cl/\\ rB ch
s l bq o nv 3 +
l — cz o nv 6\

k El so la ul v
a vd Cys v lz
fu cos \ ul
7. ds: fd pss r
rz E ro + yl uc
ofsl ch nCs b
pn inl + b
los b — — la
v n yl reC.
h/ lols \\ cf u
v- lno h
s — m r
fd l fls f
rlvl ll me
uv nl l dp
nl r Sp vn
ur dnl n\
s

Key to Lesson 10

1. Dear Customer: I regret to inform you that we cannot send another shipment of window shades because you[2] are behind in your payments for the merchandise sent in March and April. (¶) May I remind you that you should have made[4] payment on these bills within 30 days from the date of purchase. We want to help you in every way we can[6], but we cannot fill your order until payment is received. (¶) Will you, therefore, attend to this matter before the[8] end of the week. Yours truly, *(85 words)*

2. Dear Madam: I wonder if you are familiar with the wide selection of goods we handle. Many wise shoppers[2] trade with us because they know they can get high-grade merchandise at lower prices than offered in other shops. (¶) Won't[4] you favor us with your business? After only one visit, you will see why our shop is so popular with the[6] residents of this town. Yours truly, *(66 words)*

3. Dear Friend: You no doubt know that many children in this area have absolutely no safe place in which to play.[2] For this reason, our club bought a piece of land close to the school on which we would like to build a playground; and we are[4] asking every neighbor to lend a hand in helping us raise the money needed. (¶) We will use the funds to pay[6] for equipment, and we hope to find an intelligent man or woman who will take charge of setting up a[8] program for these children. (¶) If you would like to join us in this fund-raising drive, please feel free to get in touch with me.[10] We can use all the help we can get. Sincerely, *(108 words)*

4. Dear Mr. Early: This is to tell you how pleased I am with the monthly bulletin you issue. I have been reading[2] it for a great many years, and using it as my only guide, I have purchased many bonds that have been sound[4] and have paid me very high rates. (¶) I feel that everyone who uses this bulletin as a foundation for the[6] purchase of bonds will be quick to agree with me. Cordially, *(71 words)*

5. Dear Sir: I am glad to reply to the letter in which you asked for information about Mr. J. Smith.[2] (¶) Mr. Smith began with our company a little over six years ago. We found him to be a man who took great[4] pride in doing every job efficiently, and his friendly nature made him very popular with[6] everybody in our firm. We all regretted that his health made him decide to leave for another area. (¶) I[8] have no hesitation in saying that, if you intend to choose him for a position in your firm, he will fill[10] it well. (¶) If you ever wish additional information about him, please write to me again. Yours truly, *(120 words)*

6. Dear Mrs. White: We are sending this letter to all our friends as a reminder of the big sale we are having[2] on November 3. Featured in our sale will be a wide selection of children's coats in every size and color.[4] (¶) Remember, this sale will begin on November 3 and will close on November 6. Come early so that you[6] will have a wide choice of these fine coats. Yours truly, *(68 words)*

7. Dear Madam: Food prices are rising every month and yet you can offset this increase by planning intelligently[2] and buying those brands that have not yet reached the higher levels. (¶) If you want to know how some women are feeding[4] their families for relatively little money, you have only to drop into our shop when you are downtown.[6] Sincerely, *(62 words)*

Writing Assignment—Lesson 10

1. May I remind you that we need the calendars we ordered for the beginning of school in September.

2. I wish to plant these trees and shrubs on the side of the road that leads to my house.

3. We take great pride in the knowledge that our customers trade with us because they know we sell only high-grade merchandise at popular prices.

4. We have nothing but praise for the intelligent way in which you handled our drive for funds.

5. We intend to do everything we can to help our friends solve their problem.

6. There is absolutely nothing that can be done until every member votes on the new amendment.

7. I found that I preferred the other brand you sold because it was much cheaper.

8. This reminder is being sent so that you will not forget the sale that begins at the end of the week.

BRIEF FORM and STANDARD ABBREVIATION REVIEW

Lessons 6 through 10

1. Dear Mrs. Early: You may not know that there is a big sale being held at our shop on Grant Avenue and Golden[2] Boulevard. You have until the end of this week to come in for it. (¶) Like so many other customers, you[4] will appreciate our very fine line of merchandise. You will be pleased, too, with the money you can save on[6] every purchase. You may take advantage of our easy-payment plan, or if you prefer, we will gladly put aside[8] whatever you wish to buy and hold it for 30 days at no additional charge. (¶) June 9 is absolutely[10] the final day of this great sale. We urge you not to put off coming in. Sincerely, *(115 words)*

2. Dear Sir: I am again writing to tell you how much we appreciate the orders your school department has given[2] us during the year. (¶) We hope that you are pleased with the manner in which they were handled and that you will place many[4] orders with us in the future. Very truly yours, *(50 words)*

3. Dear Mr. White: Does your family need a second car? We have a good used model that we are putting up for[2] sale – one that we are willing to let go for very little money. (¶) Why don't you and your wife come in to see it?[4] Yours truly, *(42 words)*

4. Gentlemen: When your agent telephoned me, he said that a 10 percent discount would be given only on an[2] order that amounted to over $50. The order he took from me for business envelopes and paper[4] amounted to $63.50, and your invoice does not indicate that this discount had[6] been allowed. (¶) Would you kindly check into this with him and write to me again about this matter. Sincerely yours,[8] *(80 words)*

5. Dear Madam: Every intelligent child should be a member of our children's book club. Children all over the[2] land are joining every month, and your child should be one of them. He will profit from the fine books that will be sent[4] out to him each year, and you will appreciate the low price involved. (¶) The only additional amount we will[6] ever ask is a 10-cent charge for handling and mailing. Yours truly, *(72 words)*

6. Dear Madam: May I take a moment to tell you about our shop? We have everything you will ever need for[2] your house, and our prices are lower than those you will find elsewhere. We are located on Place Avenue and School[4] Street and are easy to reach by bus or car. Yours truly, *(50 words)*

–REVIEW–

Lessons 6 through 10

1. Dear Madam: I regret to inform you that all of the blue and white fabric which matches the wall in your house was[2] recently sold. We cannot, therefore, fill the order that was received today. (¶) However, we are getting an[4] additional supply of these fabrics for the coming fall season; and I am quite positive that the color you[6] wish will be included. If it is, I will hold it aside for you and send you a telegram to let you know[8] of its arrival. Very truly yours, *(87 words)*

2. Dear Mr. Lake: Our office has never had adequate or proper lighting, and we are now making tentative[2] plans to do something about this problem. A great many of our men have told us they would prefer to have each desk[4] equipped with an attractive lamp and thus eliminate all need for the bright electric ceiling lights we now use.[6]

(¶) For my own sake, I cannot help but wonder how effective or wise this method would be; but I would gladly try[8] it if you were in agreement. When I saw you the other day, I believe you mentioned that one of your clients[10] had a similar problem in his office and that you had helped him find a solution. (¶) I am, therefore, writing[12] to ask if you would be kind enough to meet with me to talk over this matter. Yours truly, *(136 words)*

TAKE INVENTORY NOW OF THE SKILLS YOU NEED FOR TRANSCRIPTION

Highly paid secretaries have many skills that make them assets to their employers. They take dictation rapidly. They read their notes easily and accurately. In addition, they transcribe their notes into mailable letters quickly and correctly.

Because transcription is a fusion of many skills and knowledge, the wise students at this point will take inventory of their abilities.

What about your command of English? For the secretary, incorrect grammar or punctuation leads to extra time in retyping letters . . . possibly the loss of a job. For the student, it means lower grades. So take time out to review your grammar and punctuation rules until you can use them correctly without thinking.

How good is your typing? If your speed and accuracy are not what they should be, make up your mind right now to devote more time and concentration to typing.

And finally, your spelling? Are you one of the rare "born spellers"? Or are you one of the many "nonspellers"? If you think you fall into the first category, ask someone to test you on a list of spelling demons. Prove to yourself your ability or lack of ability to spell correctly. And remember, never guess at spelling. Learn to use your dictionary if you aren't sure.

Lesson 11

RULE 30 | **For the sound of "em," write**  **; for the sound of "en," write**  **.**

Study these examples:

enclose	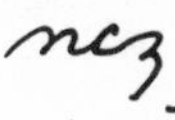	**engagement**	
enrolled		**enjoy**	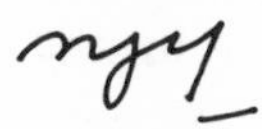
endeavor		**engaged**	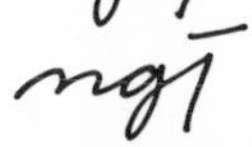
engine		**employee**	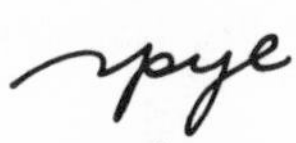
employer		**emphasize**	
emphatic		**employ**	

Notice that this rule states that *n* is to be written for the sound of "en." Listen to the sound at the beginning of the word *any*. Since this word begins with the sound referred to in the rule, you write **any**  ; **anything**  .

You write:

1. **employees** ⌒pyes
2. **employment** ⌒py-
3. **employed** ⌒pȳ
4. **employers** ⌒py//
5. **enclosed** ncz̄
6. **enclosing** ncz
7. **enjoyed** njȳ
8. **enrollment** nrl-
9. **emblem** ⌒bn
10. **anyone** ne 1

Confirmation:

1. ⌒pyes 2. ⌒py- 3. ⌒pȳ 4. ⌒py//
5. ncz̄ 6. ncz 7. njȳ 8. nrl-
9. ⌒bn 10. ne/

RULE 31 | **For the sounds of "com," "con," and "coun," write** k.

The first sound to which this rule refers is the sound of "com" as in the word *complete.* Since you are already writing *k* for the Brief Form *come,* it will be natural to write *k* for this sound in a word.

Study these words:

complete	kpe	comfort	kfl
comply	kpi	competent	kpl-
accomplish	akpS	combination	kbnj
comments	k--	communicate	knca
complain	kpn	recommends	rk— —

The sound of "com" is also heard in *commission* (the second *m* is silent), so you write **commission** kj . Similarly, **accommodations** akdjs .

You write:

1. completion kpj   **2. common** kn

3. competition kplj   **4. recommendations** rk—js

5. accommodate akda   **6. accomplished** akps̄

7. commitments kl--   **8. commissioner** kj/

9. completely kpel   **10. communicates** kncas

Confirmation:

1. kpj   2. kn   3. kplj   4. rk—js

5. akda   6. akps̄   7. kl--   8. kj/

9. kpel   10. kncas

This rule also instructs you to write *k* for the sound of "con." For example, **conclusive** kcsv . See how the rule to write *k* for "con" is applied in the following words.

Study these examples:

convention	kvj	**congratulate**	kgla
contributions	ktbjs	**convenient**	kvn-
consent	ks-	**contains**	klns
containing	kln̲	**confident**	kfd-

contents	kl--	**economic**	ekrc
connection	kcj	**control**	kTl

What of the word *confine?* You know that the Brief Form for the word **fine** is fi, therefore, **confine** is written kfi.

You write:

1. contribute kTbu ______ 2. confined kfī ______

3. economy ekne ______ 4. contained kln̄ ______

5. condition kdj ______ 6. consequently ksq-l ______

7. conditions kdjs ______ 8. container kln/ ______

Confirmation:

1. kTbu 2. kfī 3. ekne 4. kln̄

5. kdj 6. ksq-l 7. kdjs 8. kln/

Finally, this rule states that *k* is also used to represent the sound of "coun" that is heard in *council* and *account*. Therefore, **council** ksl; **account** akl; **accountant** akl-; **accounting** akl̲; **accounts** akls; **counter** k/; **count** kl.

You are now going to learn about a printed letter that will be used to represent a sound. (Writers who normally print their shorthand will reverse the process and indicate the sound referred to in this rule with a script capital letter.)

RULE 32 | For the sounds of "str," "star," "ster," and "stor," write a printed capital S.

Study these examples:

strike	Sc	destroyed	dSy
instruments	nS--	start	St
startle	Sll	starve	Sv
demonstration	dmSj	straight	Sa
stern	Sn	registered	rjS̄
faster	fS	yesterday	ySd
sister	sS	history	hSe
store	S	instructors	nSc//
storm	Sm	distribute	dSbu

You write:

1. instructions nScj
2. illustrates rlSas
3. distribution dSbj
4. construction bScj
5. started St̄
6. story Se
7. storage Sj
8. industrial ndSel
9. industry hSe
10. registration rjSj
11. semester sS
12. demonstrates dmSas

Confirmation:

1. nScjs	2. —uSas	3. dSbj	4. kScj
5. Sī	6. Se	7. Sj	8. ndSel
9. ndSe	10. rjSj	11. s-S	12. d-mSas

Brief Forms

opportunity	opl	**while**	ul
continue	ku	**fire**	fr
several	sv	**necessary, necessarily**	nec

satisfy, satisfaction, satisfactory sal

deal, deliver, delivery dl

Additional Words

discontinued	dskū	**delivered**	dl̄
discontinue	dsku	**deliveries**	dls
continuing	ku̲	**dissatisfied**	dssal̄
continues	kus	**dissatisfaction**	dssal
dealers	dl//	**satisfied**	sal̄
dealer	dl/	**opportunities**	opls

Reading Exercises

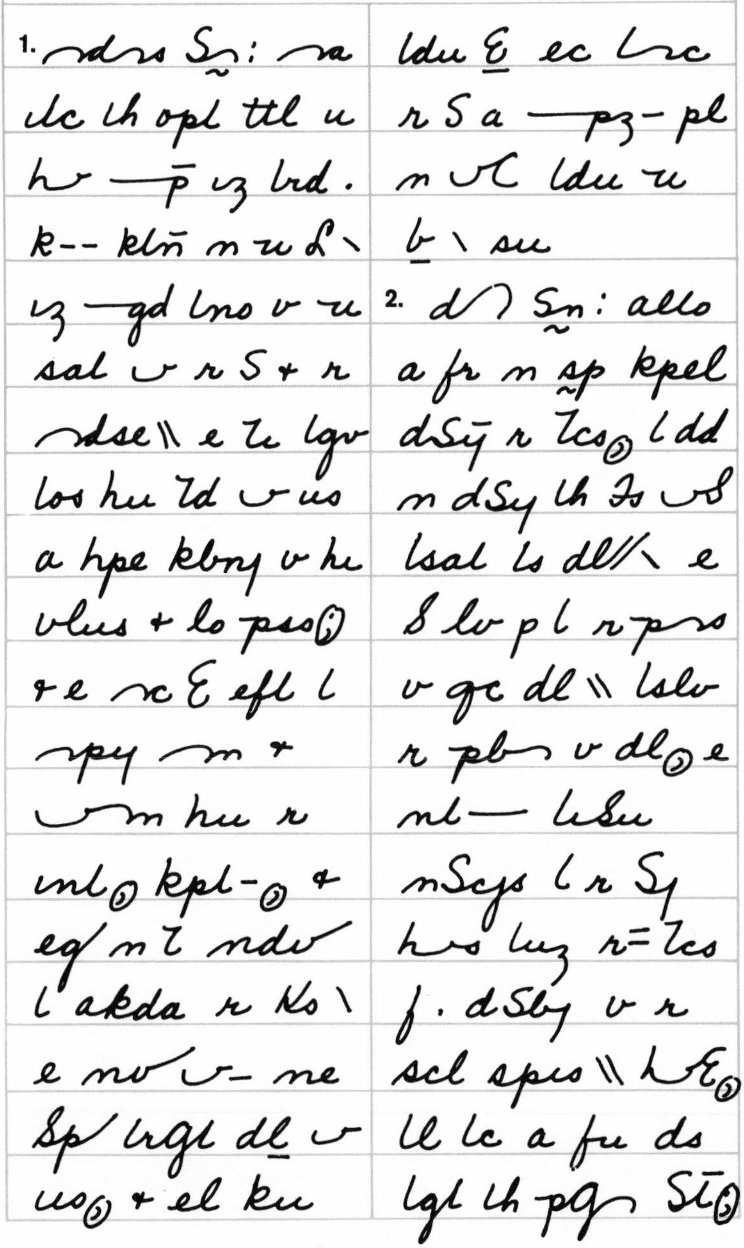

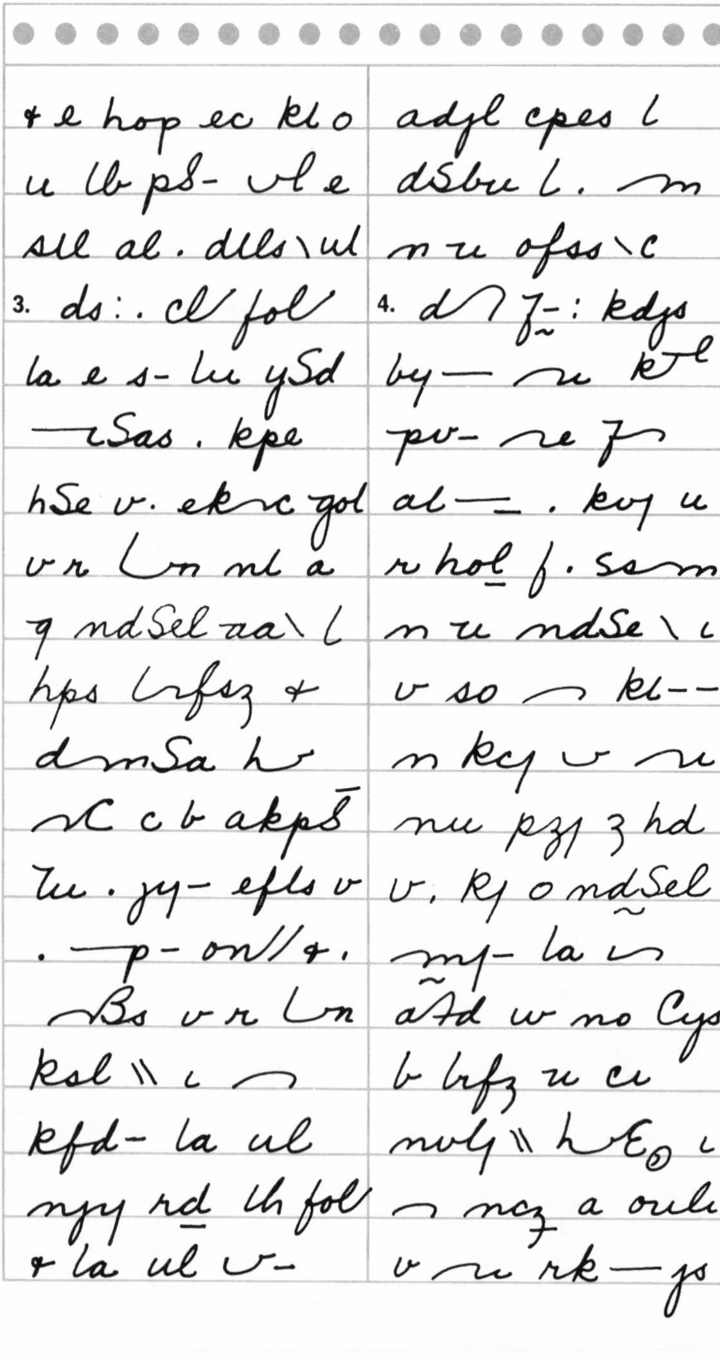

& hop l l hp u
n ⌒c̲ — pns fu
⌒e̲ \ vlu

5. d⌒: las k l
⌒u alf la uv⌒n
⌒d us v ⌒u Cq
akl n r S f s⌒
⌒os \ ksq-l⊙ i
⌒ ru̲ lsc f e
v dn ne̲ la d
czu lq — Es ⌒r
f ⌒u pCs // f u
fl la uv rzn l
kpn ab ne v r
gs ⊃ . Ze-u rsē
Z⌒ ne v r
⌒pyes⊙ ud b
du̲ ⌒e a fv
f ud knca ⌒u
dssal L⌒e \ su

6. d⌒s Zb̃n: i
⌒ — p̄ lno la u
vS lb nrl̄ n r
bs scl \ h⌒E⊙
apcys f rfSf v b
so hve lh s⌒S la
edu n v sf8-
r⌒s ⊃ nScl // l
akda . q d⌒ — \\
Z/⊙ ls nec f us l
rfz ⌒u nrl- ul
. kScf v r nu
scl s kpē n jã \
f u vS l va
ul ln⊙ e S b
hpe lpl ⌒u apcf
o fel \ cu

Key To Lesson 11

1. My dear Mrs. Storm: May I take this opportunity to tell you how pleased I was to read the comments contained[2] in your letter. I was glad to know of your satisfaction with our store and our merchandise. (¶) We try to give those[4] who trade with us a happy combination of high values and low prices; and we make every effort to[6] employ men and women who are intelligent, competent, and eager in their endeavor to accommodate[8] our customers. We never want any shopper to regret dealing with us, and we will continue to do[10] everything we can to make our store a pleasant place in which to do your buying. Sincerely yours, *(117 words)*
2. Dear Mr. Stern: Although a fire in September completely destroyed our trucks, it did not destroy this firm's wish to[2] satisfy its dealers. We shall live up to our promise of quick delivery. (¶) To solve our problem of[4] delivery, we intend to issue instructions to our storage house to use rented trucks for the distribution of[6] our school supplies. (¶) However, it will take a few days to get this program started; and we hope we can count on you[8] to be patient while we settle all the details. Yours truly, *(90 words)*
3. Dear Sir: The color folder that we sent to you yesterday illustrates the complete history of the[2] economic growth of our town into a great industrial area. It helps to emphasize and demonstrate how[4] much can be accomplished through the joint efforts of the plant owners and the members of our town council. (¶) I am[6] confident that you will enjoy reading this folder and that you will want additional copies to distribute to[8] the men in your offices. Cordially, *(87 words)*
4. Dear Mr. Front: Conditions beyond my control prevent me from attending the convention you are holding for[2] the salesmen in your industry. I have so many commitments in connection with my new position as head[4] of the Commission on Industrial Management that I am afraid

I have no choice but to refuse your kind[6] invitation. (¶) However, I am enclosing an outline of my recommendations and hope it will help you[8] in making plans for your meetings. Very truly yours, *(89 words)*

5. Dear Madam: It has come to my attention that you have not made use of your charge account in our store for some months.[2] Consequently, I am writing to ask if we have done anything that would cause you to go elsewhere for your[4] purchases. (¶) If you feel that you have reason to complain about any of our goods or the treatment you received from[6] any of our employees, you would be doing me a favor if you would communicate your dissatisfaction[8] to me. Sincerely yours, *(85 words)*

6. Dear Mrs. Brown: I am pleased to know that you wish to be enrolled in our business school. However, applications[2] for registration have been so heavy this semester that we do not have sufficient rooms or instructors to[4] accommodate the great demand. (¶) Therefore, it is necessary for us to refuse your enrollment until the[6] construction of our new school is completed in January. If you wish to wait until then, we shall be happy[8] to place your application on file. Cordially yours, *(90 words)*

TIPS ON HOW TO READ AND EDIT YOUR NOTES FOR TRANSCRIPTION

In a short time now, you will successfully complete your course in *Speedwriting* shorthand. Then you'll move on into an interesting office as a highly skilled secretary. Your employer will expect accurate, rapid transcription to be one of those skills. Now is the time to easily develop that accuracy and speed. You can in this way: After you take dictation, sit down with your notes and follow these suggestions –

1. Learn to read your notes in phrases rather than word by word. You will automatically choose the right words in context and will eliminate many errors. In the beginning, the phrases you read will be short ones; but practice will make it possible for you to read sentences as a whole.
2. Correct any necessary outlines and make any necessary deletions or additions.
3. Insert punctuation marks, placing a circle around each one. Some students prefer using a red pen to do this.
4. If a sentence doesn't seem to make sense, add or delete words as necessary.
5. Spell out proper names.
6. Check all numbers and dates for accuracy.
7. Use the dictionary to check the spelling of all words about which you are doubtful.

These are all very basic rules. If you follow them, your rate of transcription and its accuracy will decidedly improve.

Name..............................Class..........Date................

Writing Assignment – Lesson 11

1. We hope that you will continue to deal with us and that we shall be given the opportunity to satisfy your every need.

e hop la u l ku l del w us & la

e Sl b gv ' opl l sal u .E nd.

2. When ordering our industrial equipment, it is necessary for you to enclose complete shipping instructions.

wn Odr r ndSel eqp- (ls nec f

u l ncz kpe $ nScjs.

3. The enclosed illustrated booklet shows the accommodations that we endeavor to provide for the comfort of those who hold their conventions in our hotel.

' ncz -lSa bcll Sos ' akdjs la

e ndv l pvd f ' kfl v loo hu

hol l kvjs n r hll.

4. The recent fire which destroyed our storage house caused many problems in the distribution of our instruments to dealers.

' rsn- fr wc dSyd r Sj hos czd

-pblms n ' dSbj v r nS-- l

dlls.

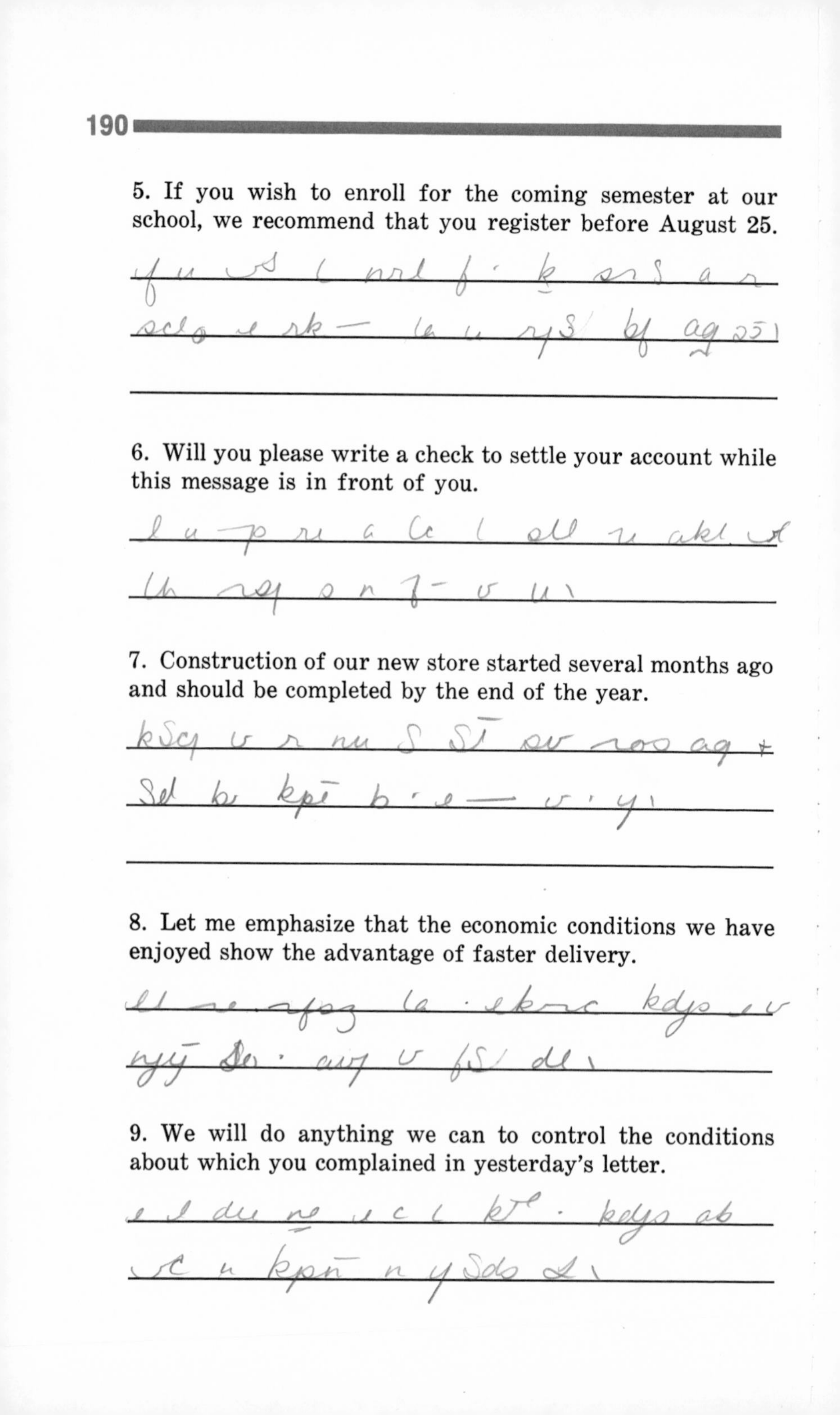

5. If you wish to enroll for the coming semester at our school, we recommend that you register before August 25.

6. Will you please write a check to settle your account while this message is in front of you.

7. Construction of our new store started several months ago and should be completed by the end of the year.

8. Let me emphasize that the economic conditions we have enjoyed show the advantage of faster delivery.

9. We will do anything we can to control the conditions about which you complained in yesterday's letter.

Lesson 12

In Lesson 9 you learned to write a joined slant for the <u>final</u> sound of "er." Now you are going to learn how this and similar sounds are to be handled in the middle of a word.

RULE 33	For the sound of a medial vowel and r, capitalize the letter of the outline that precedes this sound.

Notice in the following words that each contains the sound of a medial vowel and "r": *bark, baron, liberal, weird, born, pirate.*

The rule instructs you to capitalize the letter of the outline that precedes these sounds. Therefore, the words given above are written: **bark** *Bc* ; **baron** *Bn* ; **liberal** *lBl* ; **weird** *◡rd*; **born** *Bn* ; **pirate** *Pl* .

You write:

1. bargain Bgn______ **2. liberally** lBl______

3. burden Bdn______ **4. birth** Bl______

Confirmation:

1. Bgn 2. lBl 3. Bdn 4. Bl

The sounds of medial "ar," "er," and "or" are also in the following words: *parcel, person, report.* This time the sounds are preceded by the letter *p*. Since the rule states that this preceding letter is to be capitalized, you write P for the sounds of "par," "per," and "por." Thus: **parcel** Psl; **person** Psn; **report** rPl; **supervisors** sPvz//.

You write:

1. **part** Pl
2. **purpose** Pps
3. **personal** Psnl
4. **permit** Pml
5. **operation** oPj
6. **support** sPl
7. **operate** oPa
8. **parking** Pc
9. **cooperate** coPa
10. **cooperation** coPj

Confirmation:

1. Pl 2. Pps 3. Psnl 4. Pml
5. oPj 6. sPl 7. oPa 8. Pc
9. coPa 10. coPj

Here is a further illustration of this rule: **card** Cd; **current** C–; **course** Cs; **accordingly** aCdl. You can see how the rule is applied and C is written for the sounds of "kar," "ker," and "kor." Note the joining of *l* to the underscore in the word *accordingly.*

You write:

1. carton Cln	**2. courses** Css
3. curb Cb	**4. carbon** Cbn
5. courtesy Clse	**6. record** rCd
7. according aCd	**8. curve** Cv

Confirmation:

1. Cln	2. Css	3. Cb	4. Cbn
5. Clse	6. rCd	7. aCd	8. Cv

See how the letter that precedes the sound of "ar," "er," and "or" is capitalized in the following list of words.

Study these examples:

dark	Dc	**certainly**	Slnl
modern	mDn	**circular**	Scl/
farm	Fm	**source**	Ss
farmer	Fr	**research**	rSC
furniture	FnC/	**survey**	Sva
guard	Gd	**assortment**	aSt-
guaranteed	G-ē	**surprise**	SPz
regard	rGd	**turn**	Tn
heard	Hd	**determine**	dTm

hardly	returned
larger	patterns
learned	terminate
margin	returning
market	alterations
merit	termination
commerce	governors
normally	conversation
portion	toward
separate	working
tomorrow	worthy
quarter	yard
service	reserved
concerned	hazards

You write:

1. endorse ____________ 2. endorsement ____________

3. furnished ____________ 4. garden ____________

5. guarantee ____________ 6. girls ____________

7. regarding ____________ 8. hurt ____________

9. hard ____________ 10. learn ____________

11. large ____ 12. remarks ____

13. marked ____ 14. morning ____

15. merchants ____ 16. general ____

17. preparation ____ 18. apparently ____

19. paragraph ____ 20. reports ____

21. serve ____ 22. certain ____

23. circulars ____ 24. term ____

25. return ____ 26. attorney ____

27. veterans ____ 28. reverse ____

29. word ____ 30. worth ____

31. workers ____ 32. worthwhile ____

33. reserves ____ 34. reservations ____

Confirmation:

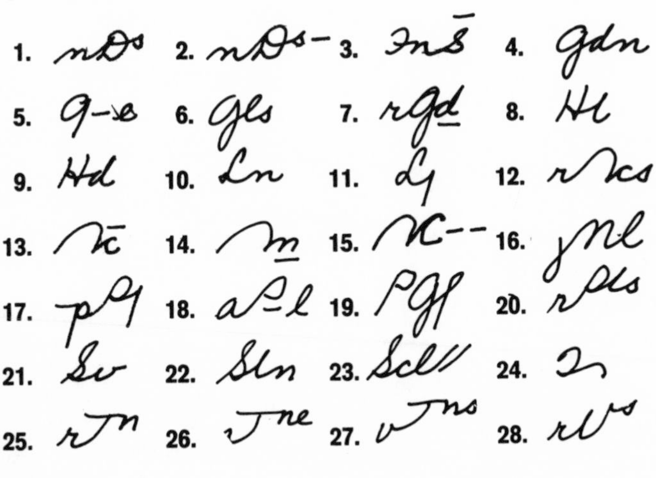

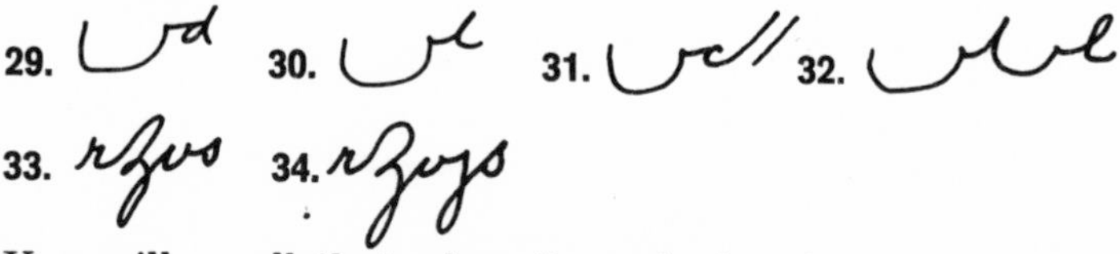

You will recall that when the rule for the writing of a joined slant for the final sound of "er" and "ter" was presented, you learned that the joined slant is to be followed only by an underscore, overscore, or a second slant to indicate the addition of *s*. Then what of the word *different?* You know that **differ** is written ; **differs** ; **differed** ; **differing** . However, you will write **different** ; **differently** 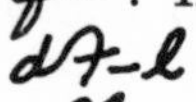 Similarly, you write **proper** ; but **properly** 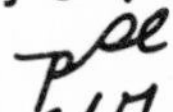; **former** ; **formerly** 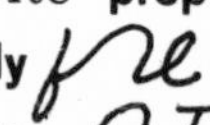; **cover** ; **coverage** ; **quarter** 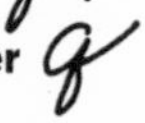; **quarterly** .

Read these sentences:

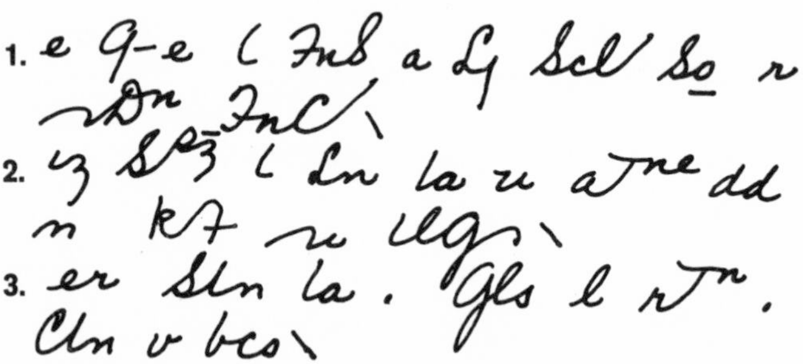

Key:

1. **We guarantee to furnish a large circular showing our modern furniture.**
2. **I was surprised to learn that your attorney did not confirm my telegram.**
3. **We are certain that the girls will return the carton of books.**

Now lets consider such words as *clerk* and *flourish.* As you know, you write  for the initial sound of "cl." Therefore, since this rule tells you to capitalize the sound that precedes the sound of "er," you write  for the resulting sound of "cler." Thus, **clerk**  . Similarly, you write  for the sound of initial "fler" and write **flourish**  .

RULE 34	**For the final ss and ness, write an apostrophe ('); for the final ssness, write a quotation mark (").**

Notice in the following words that an apostrophe (') is written for the final *ss* and *ness* and that the plural is formed by doubling the mark of punctuation.

Study these words:

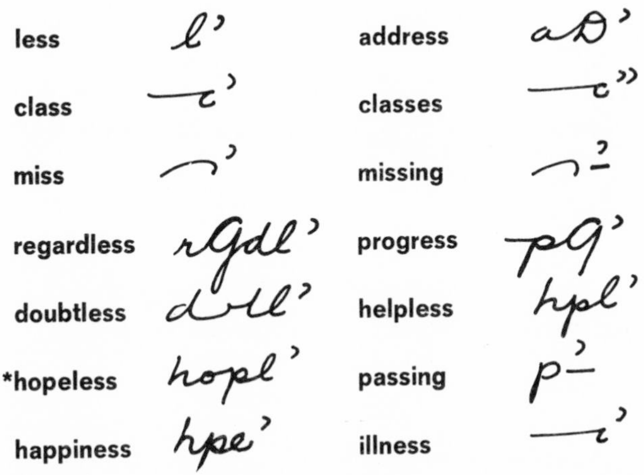

less
address
class
classes
miss
missing
regardless
progress
doubtless
helpless
*hopeless
passing
happiness
illness

*The *o* in *hopeless* is retained to avoid conflict with *helpless.*

You write:

1. loss l' **2. losses** l"

3. discuss dsc' **4. cross** c'

5. glass -g' 6. dresses -d"

7. across aC' 8. progresses pg"

9. congress kg' 10. process ps'

11. pressing p'- 12. pass p'

13. passes p" 14. sickness sc'

Confirmation:

1. l' 2. l" 3. dsc' 4. c'

5. -g' 6. -d" 7. aC' 8. pg"

9. kg' 10. ps' 11. p'- 12. p'

13. p" 14. sc'

The rule states that you are to write an apostrophe for the <u>final</u> <u>ss</u> – <u>not</u> for the medial <u>ss</u>. Therefore, **message** msj ; **passage** psj .

The second part of this rule says that a quotation mark (") will be used to represent the final <u>ssness</u>. Thus, **hopelessness** hopl" ; **helplessness** hpl" .

Brief Forms

above	bv	**both**	bo
also	lso	**call**	cl
under	U	**full, fully**	fu
public, publish	pb		

Standard Abbreviations

subscribe, subscription	sub	average	av
magazine	mag	maximum	max
minimum	min	question	q

Additional Words

forward	fwd	subscribers	sub//
forwarding	fwd̲	subscriptions	subs
forwarded	fwd̄	recall	rcl
published	pb̄	calls	cls
publication	pbj	calling	cl̲
publications	pbjs	called	cl̄
questions	qs	magazines	mags
averaged	av̄	kindness	ci'

Dictation Hints

Days of the week are written as follows:

Monday	m	Friday	fi
Tuesday	tu	Saturday	st
Wednesday	wd	Sunday	sn
Thursday	th		

Reading Exercises

1. ds: uv dvll'
Hd ab. Sva pz=
l r Bd v gl—n//
o mo r 12\
l al-l kbn. l'
v ss ev sf du
. y + lso kln
fNl r rcs rGd
. oPl v r F\\
n a efl l
d—m r fC Cs
v ac(o) w cl a
re v al sPvz//
f vd v lh vk\
hE(o) cfl la eC
psn Sd v a opl
bd. rPl n fu
bf. re\ aCd l(o)
w sc re sec
lp' ou Cbn cpes
Lo m\\ cfu
vS ldsc' lh
d v re
psnl(o) —p du
n hzla lcl
re \ ul

2. ds: z a ad
Svs l r Ks(o) er
—pn loSa a
Lg Pc ll f los
hu di nl Ln
ldu l Sp\ lh
aa lb lca aC'
. sl Fr r S(o)
+ nl r Ks lb
pst luz l\\ l
rc Sln la lh
aa s rZo f

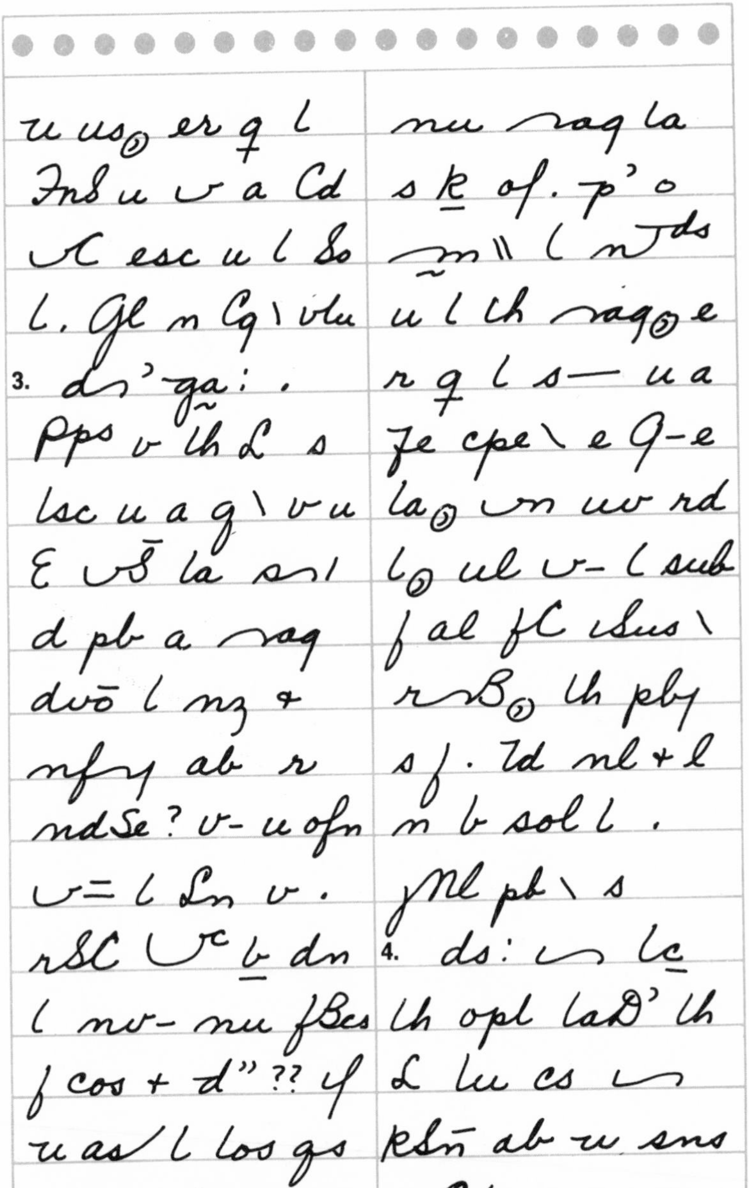

mo h lb a by
hu s bo av n
ml + yl . ⌣c
h as Im n l s
nSc// dz n k
pl . ⁀un lol
v aCe-e al \
ble la . bys
—i' a . bq v
. In akls f s
lo ⁀kcs + .
pS/ v Tz lcp
p ⌣ s —c"
s evd-l loq \\
id lc l dsc' lh
⁀/ fu ⌣ bo
u + u ⌣f \ d
l b kon-f u
lk l u ofs o

lh o fu ? c
5. dK; u Slnl
nd a ⌣z Cys
⌣n u pC u
cl/ lloy sl o
sl \ lz a Bgn
a . ps u pd
cs las fC// la
sc l b/ ln ne
I ndl n⌣ o .
⁀cl \ ⌣s kfd-
la u + u fnl
l gl . ⁀ax
asl v ngy-
fs l \\ ⌣s
f⌣d u Sos
q-e ⌣C
pods la no
Cq lb nd f

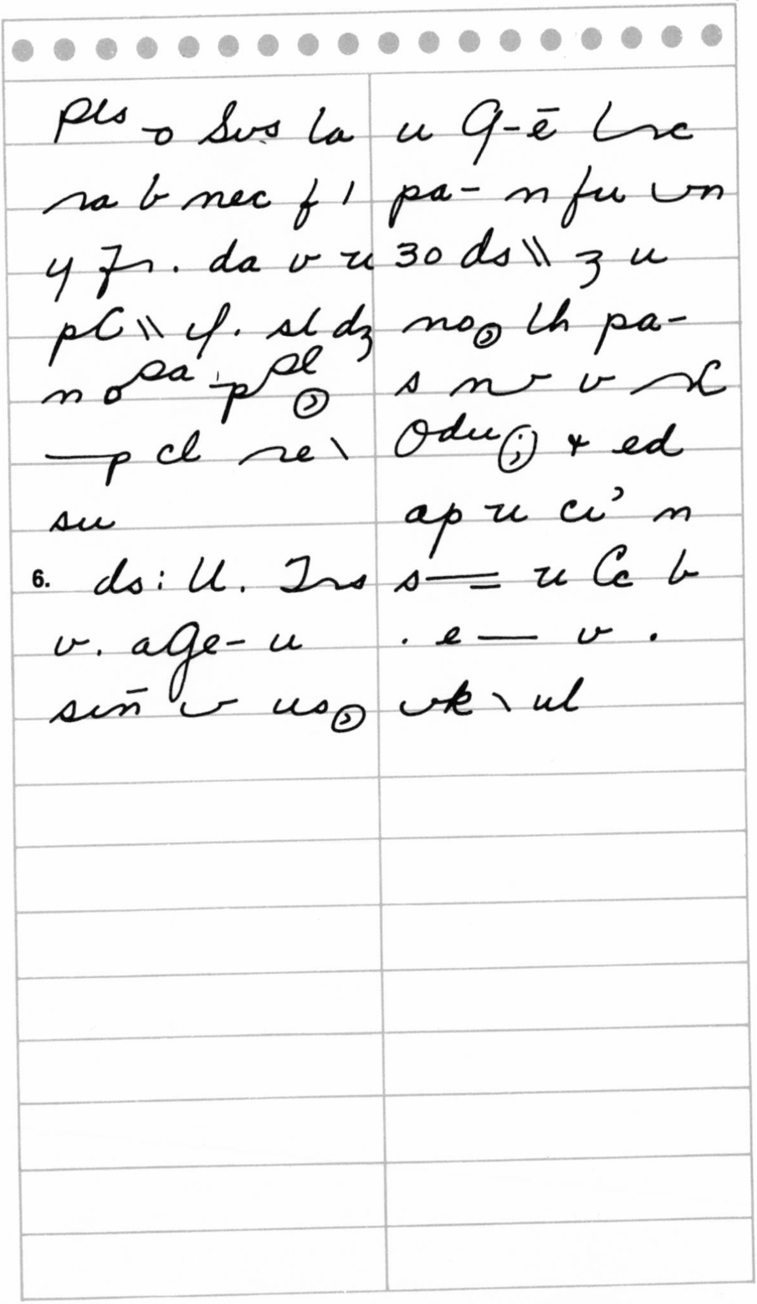

Key To Lesson 12

1. Dear Sir: You have doubtless heard about the survey presented to our Board of Governors on Monday, March 12. It[2] apparently concerned the loss of sales we have suffered during the year and also contained general remarks[4] regarding the operation of our firm. (¶) In an effort to determine our future course of action, I have[6] called a meeting of all supervisors for Wednesday of this week. However, I feel that each person should have an[8] opportunity to read the report in full before the meeting. Accordingly, I have asked my secretary[10] to pass out carbon copies tomorrow morning. (¶) If you wish to discuss this matter with me personally,[12] please do not hesitate to call me. Yours truly, *(128 words)*

2. Dear Madam: As an added service to our customers, we are planning to operate a large parking lot for[2] those who drive into town to do their shopping. This area will be located across the street from our store, and[4] only our customers will be permitted to use it. (¶) To make certain that this area is reserved for your[6] use, we are going to furnish you with a card which we ask you to show to the girl in charge. Very truly yours,[8] *(80 words)*

3. Dear Miss Gray: The purpose of this letter is to ask you a question. Have you ever wished that someone would publish[2] a magazine devoted to news and information about our industry? Haven't you often wanted to[4] learn of the research work being done to invent new fabrics for coats and dresses? (¶) If your answer to those questions[6] is yes, then you won't want to miss seeing the new magazine that is coming off the press on Monday. (¶) To[8] introduce you to this magazine, we are going to send you a free copy. We guarantee that, when you have read[10] it, you will want to subscribe for all future issues. Remember, this publication is for the trade only and[12] will not be sold to the general public. Sincerely, *(130 words)*

4. Dear Sir: I am taking this opportunity to address this letter to you because I am concerned about[2] your son's record of slow progress in our school. (¶) I know him to be a boy who is above average in[4] intelligence, and yet the work he has turned in to his instructors does not come up to the minimum level of[6] achievement we allow. I believe that the boy's illness at the beginning of the term accounts for his low marks, and[8] the pressure of trying to keep up with his classes is evidently too great. (¶) I would like to discuss this matter[10] fully with both you and your wife. Would it be convenient for you to come to my office on Thursday or Friday?[12] Cordially, *(122 words)*

5. Dear Customer: You certainly made a wise choice when you purchased your color television set on Saturday.[2] It was a bargain at the price you paid because it has features that make it better than any other model[4] now on the market. I am confident that you and your family will get the maximum amount of enjoyment[6] from it. (¶) I am forwarding your service guarantee, which provides that no charge will be made for parts or service[8] that may be necessary for one year from the date of your purchase. (¶) If the set does not operate properly,[10] please call me. Sincerely yours, *(145 words)*

6. Dear Sir: Under the terms of the agreement you signed with us, you guaranteed to make payment in full within[2] 30 days. (¶) As you know, this payment is now very much overdue; and we would appreciate your kindness in sending[4] your check by the end of the week. Yours truly, *(48 words)*

WE CONGRATULATE YOU ON YOUR PROGRESS!

Now you have completed your study of two-thirds of *Speedwriting* shorthand theory. Just think – your training for a happy, interesting career as a secretary is rapidly giving you the skills you need. You can well be proud of the progress you have made!

Perhaps you have not been fully aware of the process of automatization through which you have been going. Literally hundreds of words are now an almost instinctive part of your shorthand vocabulary.

But the learning process does not always seem to be a continuous one. Sometimes, while "assimilating" knowledge, the student feels she is "marking time"... that forward momentum seems to have stopped.

If this is the way you feel, *don't be concerned!* This perfectly natural feeling is characteristic of all learning. You have simply reached a "plateau" in the learning process. During this time, apply yourself with patient diligence and determination. Realize that if you try to take every bit of dictation you can get, it will not be long before you will once again be aware of your forward progress toward the goal you are trying to reach.

Remember the bright future which lies ahead of you!

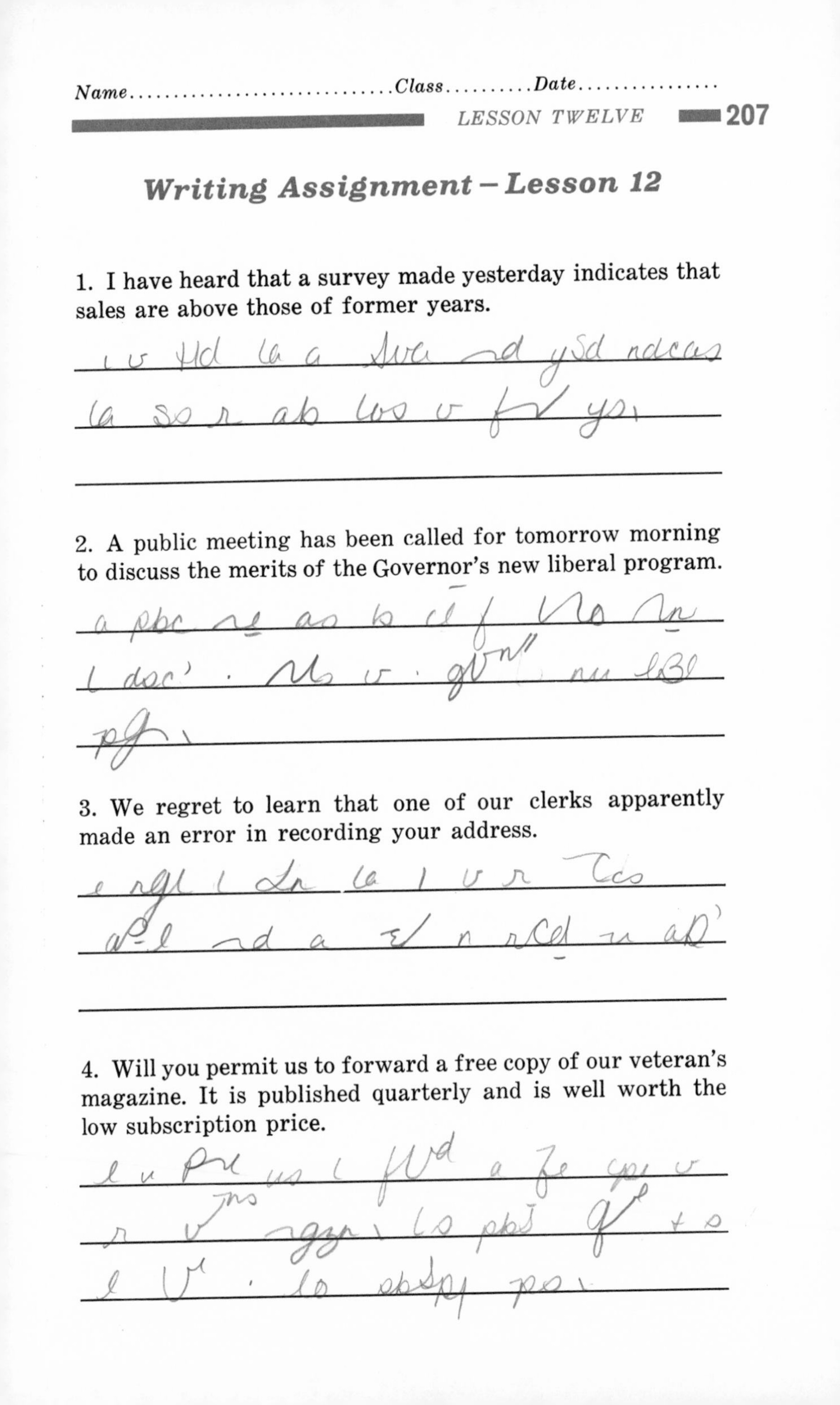

Name.............................Class..........Date................

Writing Assignment – Lesson 12

1. I have heard that a survey made yesterday indicates that sales are above those of former years.

2. A public meeting has been called for tomorrow morning to discuss the merits of the Governor's new liberal program.

3. We regret to learn that one of our clerks apparently made an error in recording your address.

4. Will you permit us to forward a free copy of our veteran's magazine. It is published quarterly and is well worth the low subscription price.

5. When you have fully answered the questions on the reverse side of the enclosed card, will you sign in both places that I have marked with crosses. Will you also read the paragraph that discusses the terms of this agreement.

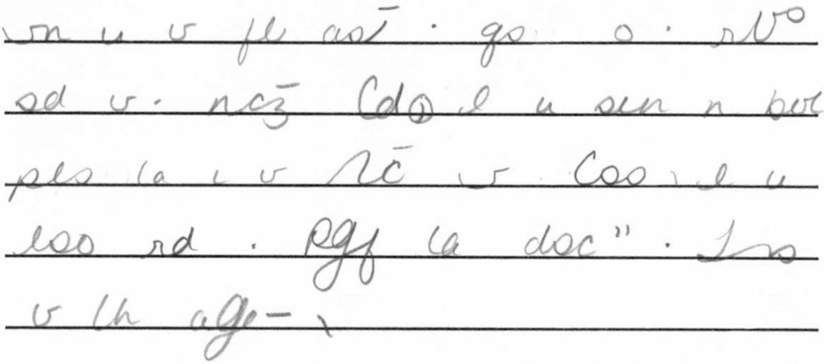

6. We are quite certain you will find that our maximum charge is less than the average market price.

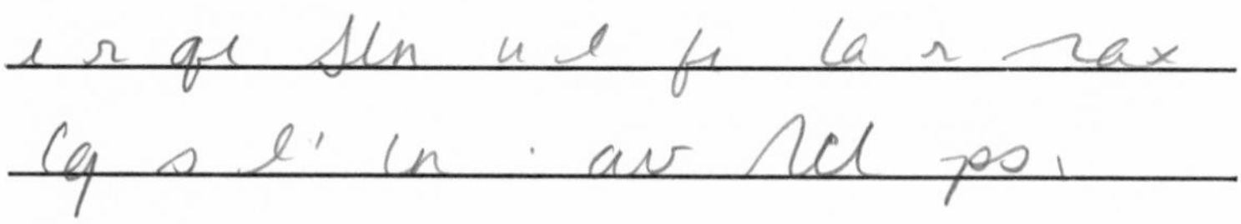

7. The complete hopelessness of my position makes it necessary to close my shop for a while.

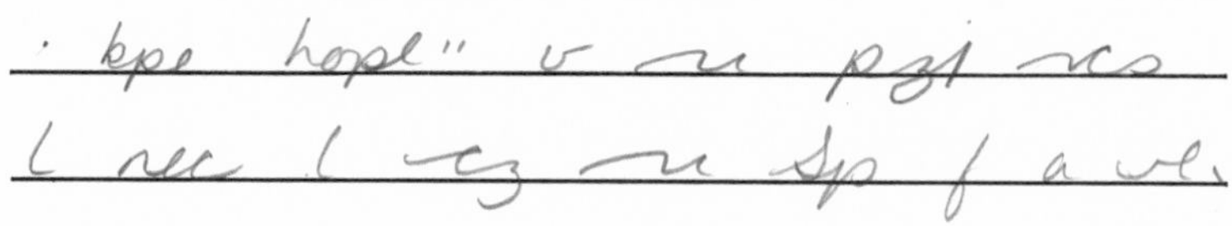

Lesson 13

RULE 35 | **For the sounds of "aks, eks, iks, oks," and "uks," write X .**

Study these words:

tax	tx	**extent**	xt-
box	bx	**fix**	fx
deluxe	dlx	**examine**	xm

What of the sound in the word *accident?* Since the first sound in this word is "aks," and the rule instructs you to write *x* for this sound, you write **accident** xd- .

Study the following words:

accidental	xd-l	**index**	ndx
express	xpr'	**excessive**	xsv
expenditures	xp— d//	**oxygen**	xjn
experts	xprts	**expansion**	xp/

You write:

1. **executive** ______	2. **exclusive** ______
3. **extended** ______	4. **expanding** ______
5. **extension** ______	6. **examination** ______
7. **explain** ______	8. **exceptionally** ______
9. **excellent** ______	10. **exhibit** ______
11. **explanation** ______	12. **exceed** ______

Confirmation:

1. xcv	2. xcsv	3. xl=	4. xp=
5. xlj	6. x‿mj	7. xpn	8. xpjl
9. xl–	10. xbl	11. xpnj	12. xd

You have learned that the addition of *s* does not change the way in which the root word is written. Thus, **shoes** is written Sus . In the same way, the word **back** is written bc and the plural **backs** bcs . Do not apply the present rule when *s* is added to a root word that ends in *k*. For example: **tack** tc ; **tacks** tcs .

Before going on the next rule let us first remind you of two rules that you had in a previous lesson. You have learned that when a long vowel is followed by the sound of "t" or "v," the long vowel is written to represent the resulting sound.

Thus, **wait** va ; **weave** ve ; **coat** co ; **cave** ca . You are now going to learn another group of words in which the long vowel is used in the same way.

RULE 36	**For the <u>final</u> sound of a long vowel and "m," write the long vowel to represent the resulting sound.**

You can see how similar this rule is to the ones just reviewed. This rule states that you will write *a* for the final sound of "ame," *e* for the sound of "eem," *i* for the sound of "ime," *o* for the sound of "ome," and *u* for the sound of "ume."

The word *name* is composed of the sounds "n" + "ame," and since you are learning to write *a* for the final sound of "ame," you write **name** na . Similarly, *seem* is made up of the sounds of "s" + "eem." Therefore, since you write *e* for the final sound of "eem," **seem** is se .

Study the following words:

same	sa	**timely**	tl
claim	—ca	**sometime**	smt
team	te	**home**	ho
extremely	xtel	**consumer**	ksu
time	t	**assume**	asu

You write:

1. times ts ________ **2. game** ga ________

3. claims —cas ________ **4. lifetime** lftl ________

5. **homes** hos 6. **presume** pzu

7. **assumed** asu 8. **extreme** xTe

9. **timing** ti 10. **homeless** hol'

Confirmation:

1. lis 2. ga 3. —cas 4. lflu

5. hos 6. pzu 7. asu 8. xTe

9. ti 10. hol'

The rule that follows is, in part, based upon a principle that was covered in Lesson 12. Rule 33 states that for the medial sounds of "ar," "er," and "or" you are to capitalize the letter that precedes these sounds. What of the sound "ther"? Since the sound of "th" is represented by *t*, you will be following the rule if you write capital *T* for the sound of "ther." Thus, **thorough** To ; **thermal** Tml ; **therapy** Tpe .

In the same way, you will write a capital *T* for the medial sound of "ther" but, as in the case of medial "tr," your writing is simplified by the use of an easier form for medial capital *T*. For example, **authorize** aTz .

With this basic understanding, you should have no difficulty with the following rule.

RULE 37 | For the final sound of "ther" write

Study these examples:

author	neither
whether	together
mothers	further
either	farther

You write:

1. rather ________
2. father ________
3. gather ________
4. leather ________
5. brothers ________
6. weather ________
7. bothered ________
8. authors ________

Confirmation:

1. 2. 3. 4.
5. 6. 7. 8.

Brief Forms

note	direct
contract, correct	benefit
even	consider
evening	upon

Abbreviations

Christmas		advertise	
certificate, certify			

Additional Words

advertisement		certification	
advertised		certified	
advertising		directors	
consideration		director	
considered		directly	
considering		direction	
notation		directed	
notice		contracts	
notes		correction	
noted		correctly	
notices			

Reading Exercises

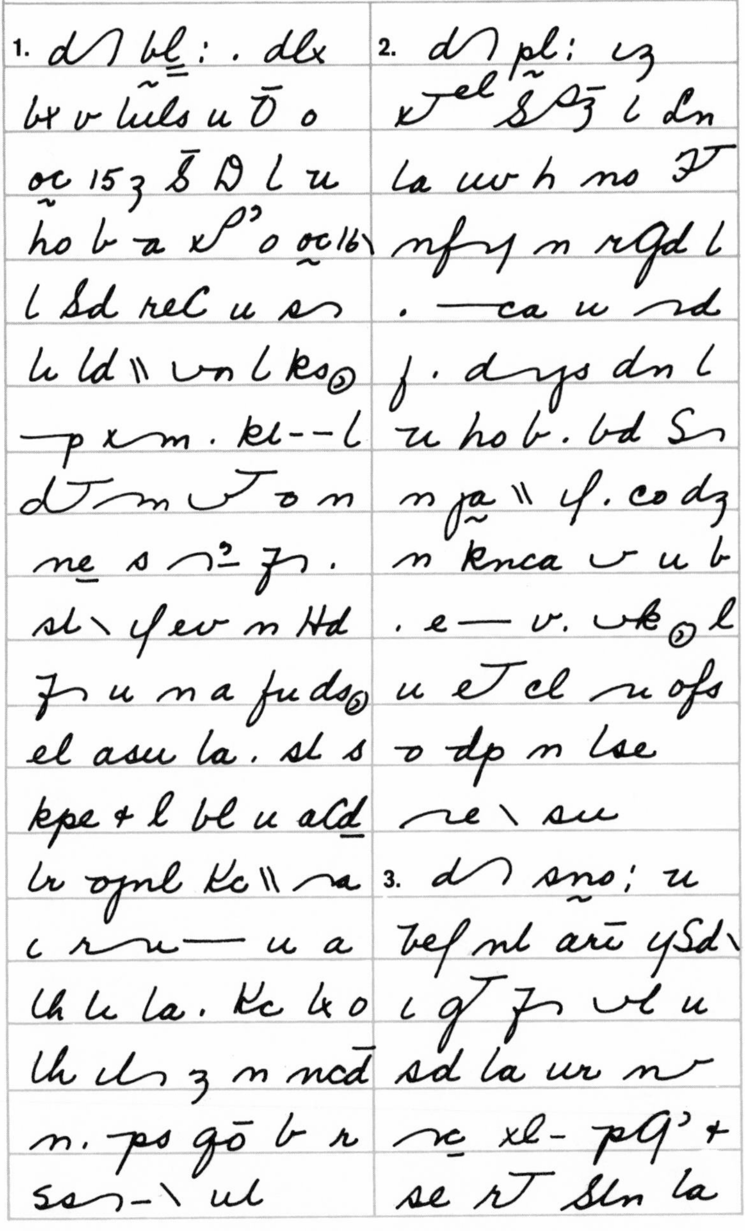

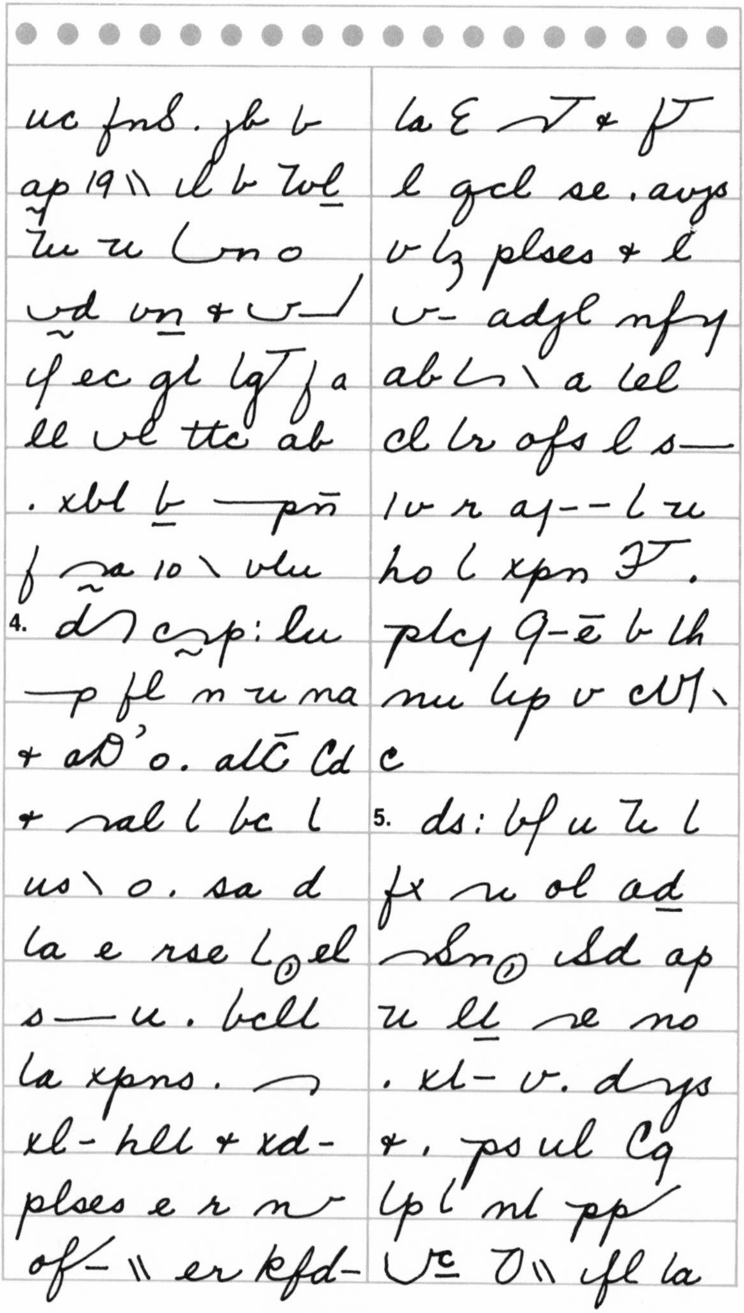
4.
5.

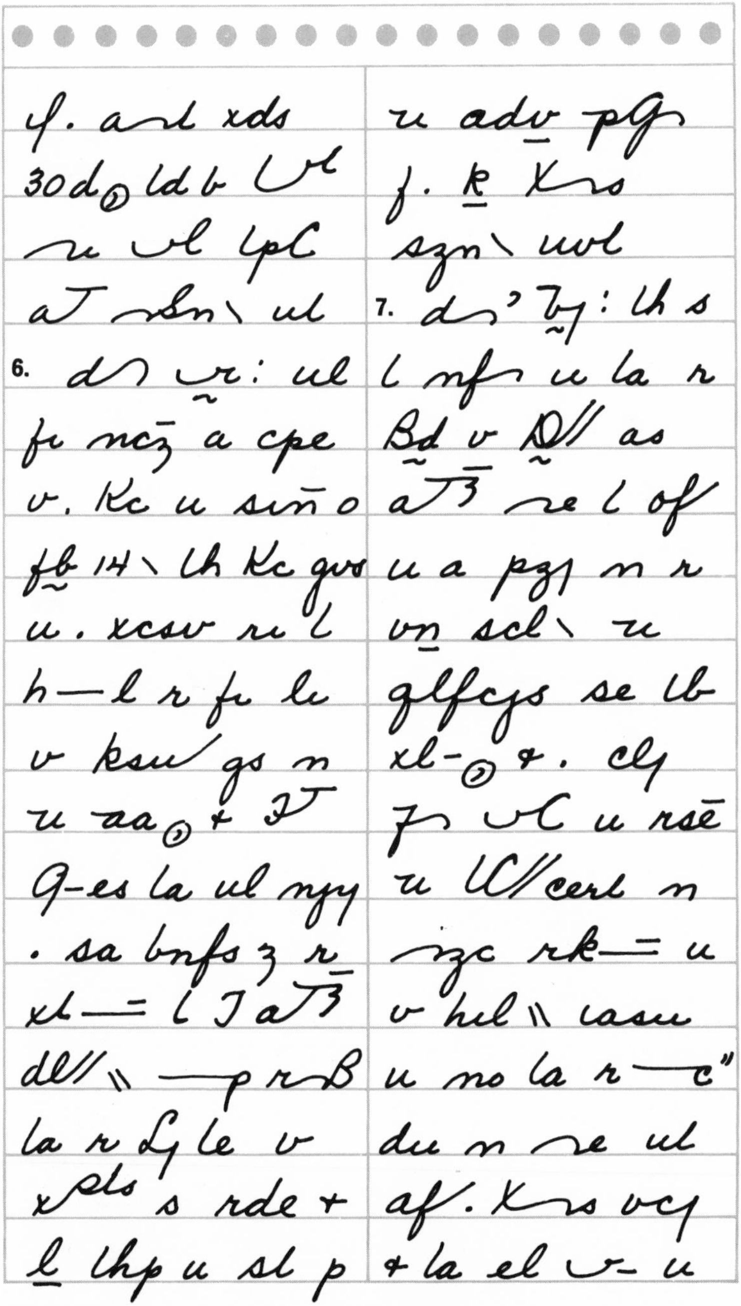

l Sl v us o
mn⊙ ja 4 \\
n lc fl^d
lv u v us \
su

8. d ↄ 7-: pn
x my v u
akl⊙ i nls la
u pa- v 455^89
o r inv v
jn 9 s ↄ nos
õdu \ e v rln

lu sv lus⊙ b
uv n vn b
bpe l los Ls ||
n vu v lh⊙
el va nl a
vk⊙ + f u
Cc o xpnf dz
n k b ln⊙ el
a 3 r a^ne
tlc lgl acf aq
u \ ul

Key to Lesson 13

1. Dear Mr. Billings: The deluxe box of tools you ordered on October 15 was shipped direct to your home by[2] air express on October 16. It should reach you some time today. (¶) When it comes, please examine the contents to[4] determine whether or nŏt anything is missing from the set. If we have not heard from you in a few days, we[6] will assume that the set is complete and will bill you according to our original contract. (¶) May I remind[8] you at this time that the correct tax on this item was not included in the price quoted by our salesman. Yours truly,[10] *(100 words)*

2. Dear Mr. Place: I was extremely surprised to learn that you have had no further information in regard to[2] the claim you made for the damages done to your home by the bad storm in January. (¶) If the company does[4] not communicate with you by the end of the week, will you either call my office or drop in to see me.[6] Sincerely yours, *(62 words)*

3. Dear Mr. Snow: Your brief note arrived yesterday. I gather from what you said that you are now making excellent[2] progress and seem rather certain that you can finish the job by April 19. (¶) I will be traveling through your[4] town on Wednesday evening and wonder if we can get together for a little while to talk about the[6] exhibit being planned for May 10. Very truly yours, *(69 words)*

4. Dear Mr. Camp: Will you please fill in your name and address on the attached card and mail it back to us. On the same[2] day that we receive it, we will send you the booklet that explains the many excellent health and accident[4] policies we are now offering. (¶) We are confident that every mother and father will quickly see the[6] advantages of these policies and will want additional information about them. A telephone call to[8] our office will send one of our agents to your home to explain further the protection guaranteed by this new[10] type of coverage. Cordially, *(105 words)*

5. Dear Sir: Before you try to fix my old adding machine, I should appreciate your letting me know the extent[2] of the damages and the price you will charge to put it into proper working order. (¶) I feel that if the amount[4] exceeds $30, it would be worth my while to purchase another machine. Yours truly, *(57 words)*

6. Dear Mr. White: You will find enclosed a copy of the contract you signed on February 14. This contract[2] gives you the exclusive right to handle our fine line of consumer goods in your area, and further guarantees[4] that you will enjoy the same benefits as are extended to other authorized dealers. (¶) Please remember[6] that our large team of experts is ready and willing to help you set up your advertising program for the coming[8] Christmas season. Yours very truly, *(87 words)*

7. Dear Miss Bridge: This is to inform you that our Board of Directors has authorized me to offer you a position[2] in our evening school. Your qualifications seem to be excellent, and the college from which you received[4] your teacher's certificate in music recommended you very highly. (¶) I assume you know that our classes[6] do not meet until after the Christmas vacation and that we will want you to start with us on Monday,[8] January 4. (¶) I am looking forward to having you with us. Sincerely yours, *(93 words)*

8. Dear Mr. Front: Upon examination of your account, I notice that your payment of $455.89[2] on our invoice of June 9 is many months overdue. We have written to you[4] several times, but you have not even bothered to reply to those letters. (¶) In view of this, we will wait only[6] another week, and if your check or explanation does not come by then, we will authorize our attorney to[8] take legal action against you. Yours truly, *(87 words)*

Writing Assignment—Lesson 13

1. You should consider thoroughly the excellent benefits you will get from advertising your toys and games in the Christmas issue of our magazine.

u Sd ksd/ Tol · xl- bnfs u l
gt f adv u tys + gas n · Xms
isu v r mag.

2. Upon further examination of your claim, we note that you did not give either the time or the place that the accident occurred.

pn fT xmy v u clm e nt la u
dd n gv eT · u o · pl la · xd-
oc.

3. The director of our school wishes me to tell every mother and father about our expanding program.

· Dr v r scl wss m l tl E
mT + fT ab r xp— pg.

4. A wide selection of consumer goods will be featured at our coming exhibit.

a wd slc v ksu gs l b fC
a r k xbl.

5. I have authorized my attorney to discuss the terms of my contract with you.

i v aT3 m aTne l dsc) · Trs
v m Kc v u .

6. I do not know the name of the firm that supplies oxygen to several industrial plants in this area.

i du n no · na v · f la spls
xjn l svl ndSel pl— n th
aa .

7. Only the deluxe model of our car comes equipped with leather seat covers.

ol · dlx mdl v r cr ks eqp
v lT st cv/ .

8. I presume you wish to have the same type of policy for your new home that you had for the old one.

i psu u ws l v · sa tip v plse
f u nu ho la u h f · ol 1 .

9. I do not even consider the bad weather a sufficient explanation for the delay in delivery.

i du n vn ksd/ · bd wT a sfs-
xpnf f · dla n dl .

BRIEF FORMS AND STANDARD ABBREVIATIONS

about	ab	begin	bq
above	bv	benefit	bnf
absolute, ly	abs	both	bo
advantage	avj	boulevard	blvd
advertise	adv	business	bs
again, st	aq	busy	bz
also	lso	but	b
am	⌒	buy	b
amount	aml	by	b
an	a	call	cl
and	&	came	k
appreciate	ap	can	c
are	r	catalog	cal
as	z	cents	c
ask	sc	certificate	cerl
at	a	certify	cerl
avenue	ave	charge	Cq
average	av	child	ch
be	b	children	chn
because	cs	Christmas	Xs
been	b	come	k
began	bq	committee	k

company	co	every	E
consider	ks	fail	fl
continue	ku	feel	fl
contract	Kc	field	fld
correct	Kc	find	fi
credit	cr	fine	fi
customer	K	fire	fr
day	d	firm	F
deal	dl	for	f
deliver	dl	full	fu
delivery	dl	fully	fu
department	dpt	future	fC
direct	D	given	gv
discount	dis	go	g
doctor	dr	good	g
dollar	d	great	g
dollars	d	had	h
during	du	has	as
easy	ez	have	v
envelope	env	he	h
even	vn	held	hl
evening	vn	help	hp
ever	E	him	h

his	s	necessary	nec
hour	r	not	n
in	n	note	nl
intelligence	inl	of	v
intelligent, ly	inl	on	o
invoice	inv	only	nl
is	s	opportunity	opl
it	l	order	O
keep	cp	other	O
kind	ci	our	r
letter	L	out	ou
like	lc	over	O
line	li	percent	pc
little	ll	place	pl
magazine	mag	please	-p
man	m-	popular	pop
many	m	president	P
maximum	max	price	ps
member	mB	public	pb
merchandise	mdse	publish	pb
minimum	mn	purchase	pC
month	mo	put	p
necessarily	nec	question	q

room	rm	those	los
sale	S	to	l
satisfaction	sal	too	lo
satisfactory	sal	under	U
satisfy	sal	until	ul
save	sv	up	p
school	scl	upon	pn
second	sec	very	v
secretary	sec	vice-president	VP
several	sv	was	z
shall	S	we	e
she	S	week	wk
ship	S	well	l
street	sl	were	w
subscribe	sub	where	wr
subscription	sub	while	wl
telephone	lel	why	y
that	la	will	l
the	.	with	w
their	T	woman	wm-
there	T	would	d
they	ly	year	y
this	lh	your	u

Lesson 14

You have already learned several sounds that are represented by marks of punctuation. Here is another.

RULE 38	**For the initial and final sound of "st" write a comma (,).**

Study these examples:

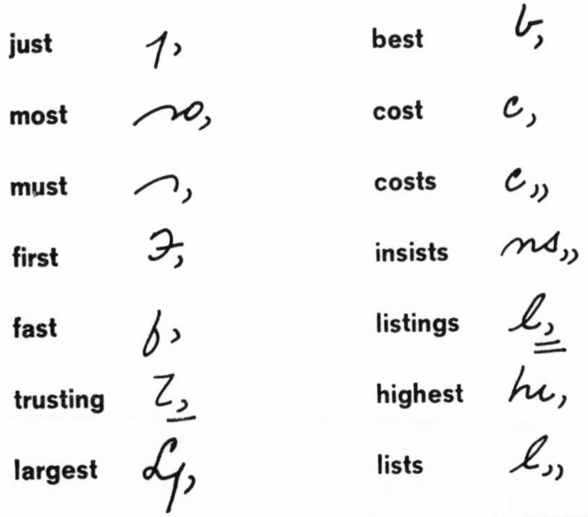

just
most
must
first
fast
trusting
largest
best
cost
costs
insists
listings
highest
lists

request	rq,	coast	co,
adjusted	aj-,	suggests	sj,,
biggest	bg,	suggested	sj-,
tests	t,,	guests	g,,

You write:

1. list ________ 2. chest ________
3. utmost ________ 4. requested ________
5. least ________ 6. latest ________
7. lost ________ 8. past ________
9. trust ________ 10. earliest ________
11. lowest ________ 12. last ________
13. listed ________ 14. contests ________
15. exist ________ 16. suggesting ________

Confirmation:

1.	l,	2.	C,	3.	ulo,	4.	rq-,
5.	le,	6.	la,	7.	l,	8.	p,
9.	T,	10.	El,	11.	lo,	12.	l,
13.	l-,	14.	kl,,	15.	x,	16.	sj,

Note that the rule instructs you to write a comma to indicate the sound of "st." In this connection, pronounce the following pairs of words: *past, passed; mist, missed; baste, based.* You can hear that these words all end with the same sound—the sound of "st." Therefore, since you write a comma for the sound of "st," **passed** is written p, ; **missed** m, ; **based** ba, .

You write:

1. expressed xP,- **2. introduced** ntdu,

3. reduced rdu, **4. released** rle,

5. discussed dsc, **6. promised** pm,

7. addressed aD, **8. increased** nCe,

Confirmation.

1. xP, 2. ntdu, 3. rdu, 4. rle,

5. dsc, 6. pm, 7. aD, 8. nCe,

This rule states that a comma is also to be written for the initial sound of "st." To avoid confusion this initial comma must be joined to the rest of outline. For ease in writing it will be raised above the line ʼ . Thus: **steps** ʼps ; **style** ʼil ; **stand** ʼ— .

Study these examples:

state ʼa **studied** ʼdē

students ʼd-- **still** ʼl

station ʼj **statement** ʼa-

steel ʼel **standing** ʼ—=

stay ʼa **step** ʼp

You write:

1. staff ________ 2. stocks ________

3. stamped ________ 4. stated ________

5. steam ________ 6. steady ________

7. stands ________ 8. study ________

Confirmation:

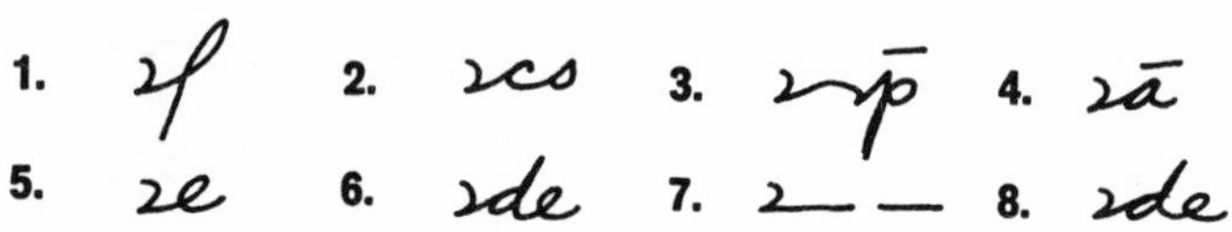

Read these sentences:

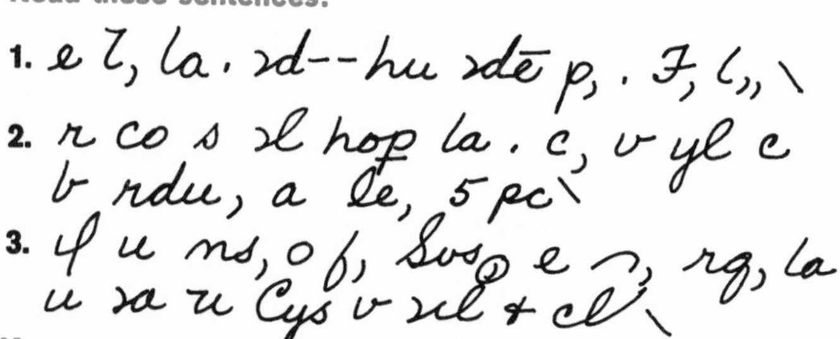

Key:

1. We trust that the students who studied passed the first tests.
2. Our company is still hoping that the cost of oil can be reduced at least 5 percent.
3. If you insist on fast service, we must request that you state your choice of style and color.

The rule above instructs you to write a comma for the initial and final sound of "st." But what of this sound in the middle of a word? The next rule explains this.

RULE 39 | **For the sound of medial "st," write *s*.**

In other words, instead of writing a comma for "st" as you do at the beginning or end of a word, you simply write *s* for this sound when it occurs in the middle of a word.

Study these examples:

assistant	*ass-*	**suggestions**	*sjsjs*
statistics	*,lscs*	**investments**	*nvs--*
system	*ss⌒*	**instead**	*nsd*
domestic	*d⌒sc*	**install**	*nsal*
justly	*jsl*	**installation**	*nslj*
mistake	*⌒sc*	**institute**	*nslu*

You write:

1. institutions _nslys_ **2. estimate** _es⌒a_

3. installments _nsl--_ **4. custom** _cs⌒_

5. plastic _—psc_ **6. constant** _ks-_

Confirmation:

1. *nslys* **2.** *es⌒a* **3.** *nsl--* **4.** *cs⌒*

5. *—psc* **6.** *ks-*

The following words illustrate how the handling of the initial and final sounds of "st" differs from the medial sound of "st."

Study these words:

post	po,	**costs**	c,,
posts	po,,	**costly**	csl
posting	po,_	**adjust**	aj,
posted	po,‾	**adjustments**	ajs--
postal	psl	**state**	)a
postage	psj	**estate**	esa
invest	nv,	**assist**	as,
investment	nvs-	**assists**	as,,
investigate	nvsga	**assistants**	ass--
investigation	nvsgj	**stand**	)—
cost	c,	**newsstand**	nzs—

Now, a final rule for this lesson. Again, you are going to deal with a combination sound – the sound that is derived from the blending together of the sounds of "n" and "k" into "nk."

RULE 40 | **For the sound of "nk," write** g **.**

This is the sound that is heard in the word *bank*. Since you are to write *q* for the sound of "nk," **bank** is written bq and, in the same way, **think** lq .

You write:

1. pink pq
2. thank lq
3. banking bq
4. tank lq
5. blank bq
6. ink q
7. delinquent dlq-
8. banquet bql
9. blanket bql
10. frankly fql
11. shrink Sq
12. thinking lq

Confirmation:

1.	pq	2.	lq	3.	bq	4.	lq
5.	bq	6.	q	7.	dlq-	8.	bql
9.	bql	10.	fql	11.	Sq	12.	lq

Brief Forms

stop	so	small	sa
extra	X	country	c
extraordinary	Xo	always	l
real, really	rl	already	lr

Abbreviations

capital	cap	federal	fed
represent, representative	rep		
government	gvt		

Additional Words

forced	f,	outstanding	ous—=
forecast	fc,	understand	Us—
kindest	ci,	understanding	Us—=
finest	fi,	misunderstanding	~sUs—=
greatest	g,	understood	Usd
smaller	sma/	represents	reps
smallest	sma,	representing	rep
realize	rlz	represented	rep̄
realized	rlz̄	representatives	reps
countries	c//	stops	sos
		noticed	nt,

Dictation Hints

To express round numbers above 90, write as follows:

hundred	H	thousand	Td
million	⌒	billion	B

Examples:

50,000 men 

two million women 

5,000 copies  **14 billion** 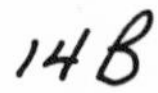

$123,000,000  **700 books** 

Reading Exercises

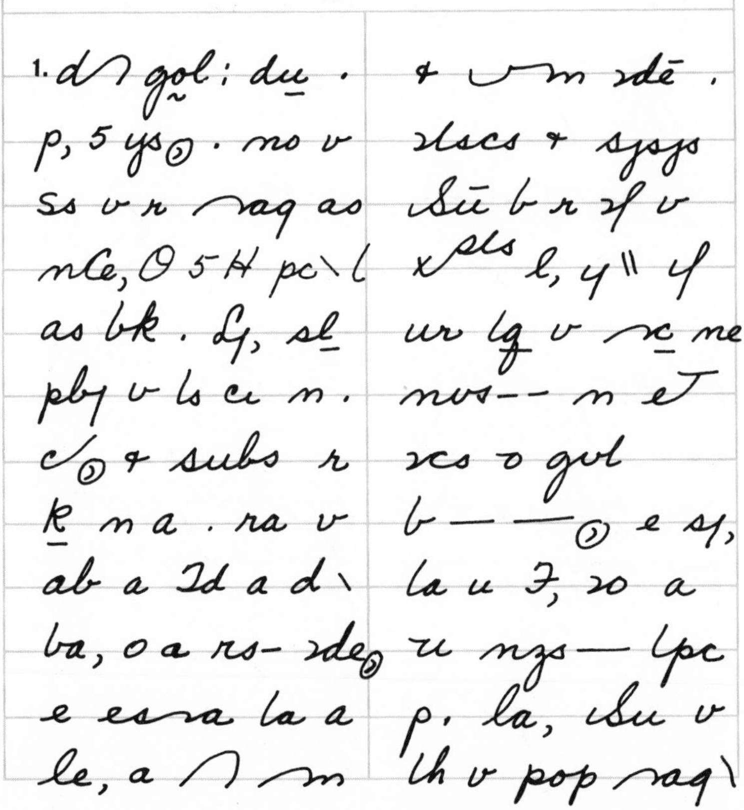

eno la rd l l
hp u nv; u cap
vzl \ l sls f 1,
1d a cpe \ ul
2. ds: las l-b
r cs ldu r
ulso, l nosga
& sll al— cas
gcl \ las, us
n rc f, pa-
o u —ca e
n, F, ns, la
u da p a l,
So . esrā vlu
v. alcls l, vn
fr dSy u ho\\
vno ul Us—
y e cn ps' u
—ca ul lh

za-s n r
h— —\ s
3. y: vn v hpe
las/ u rq, f
nfy ab ∩
F \\ ∩ F 3
zl a zd - a . za
cly vn e py
h n r F du
s s/ vcjs\
af fnS scl
h jyn r zf 3
a ass- l .
my v r akl
dpl & z rpdl
pro l a pzl
v hu, T, \ El l,
y hz nS-l n
nslu a fl

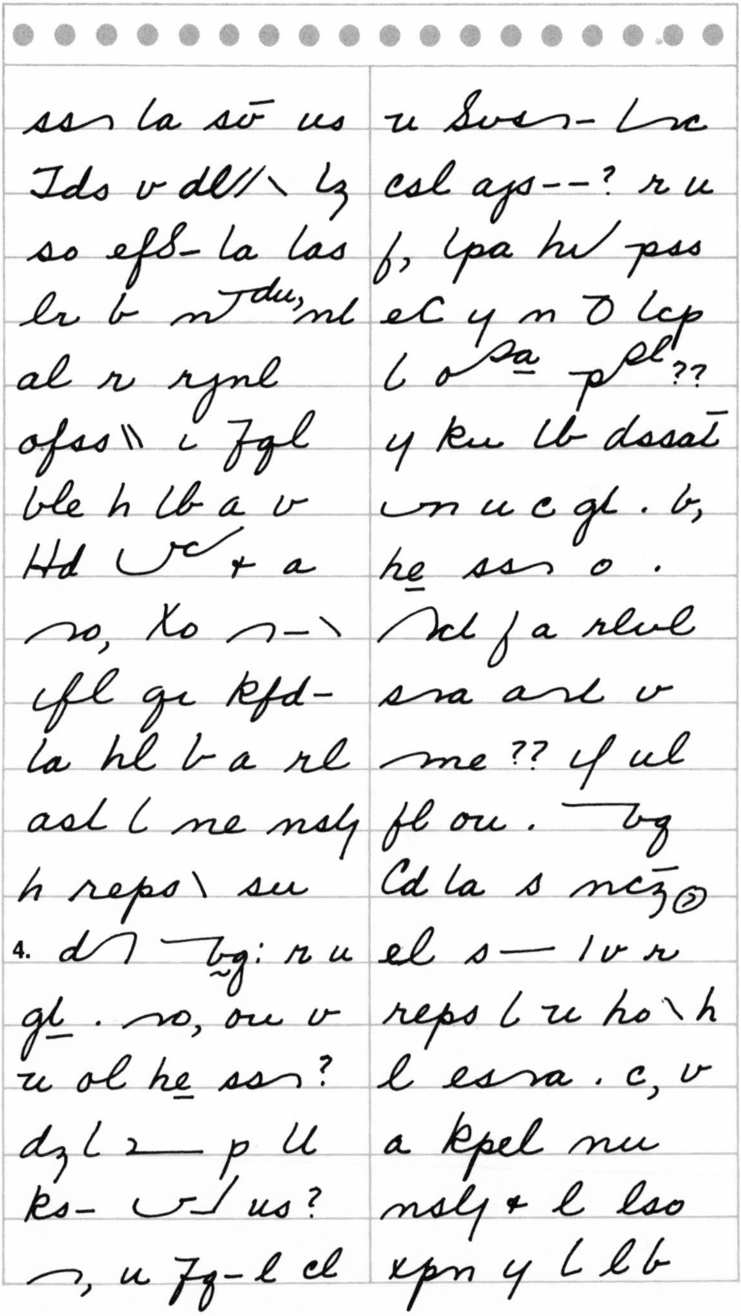

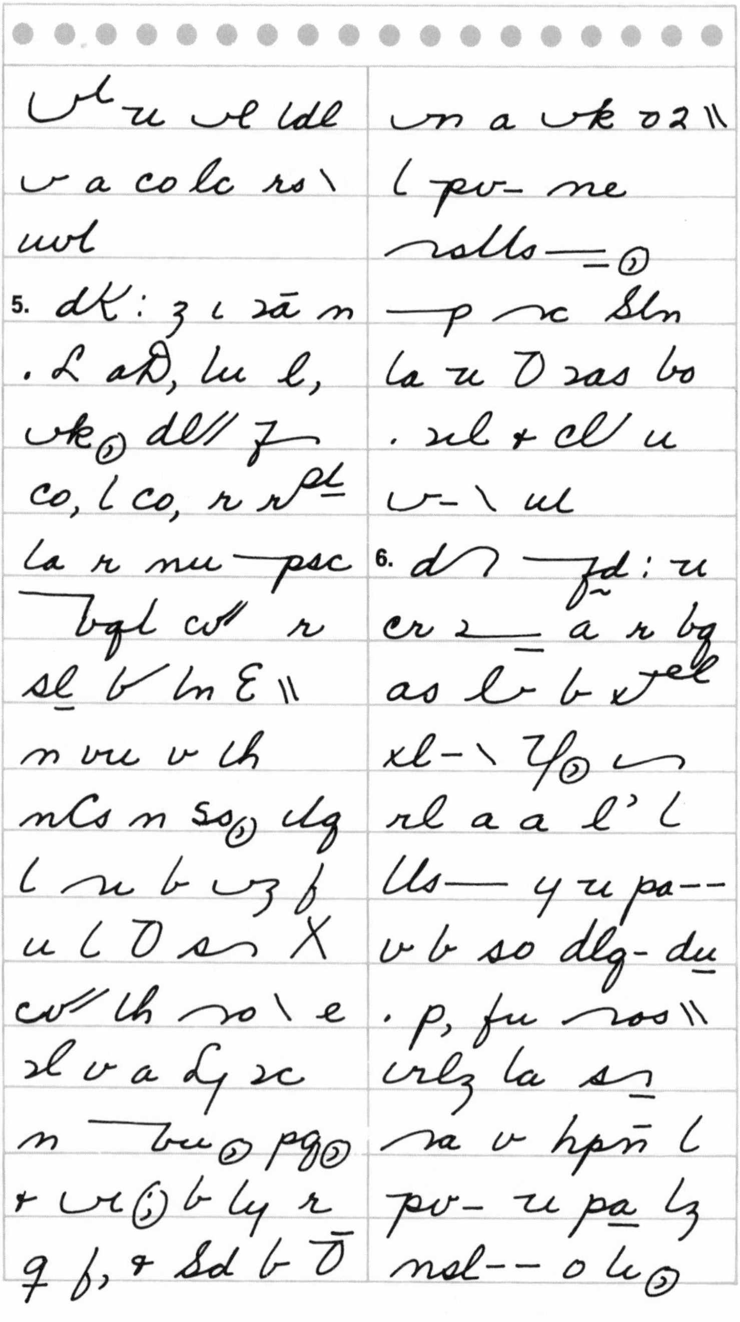

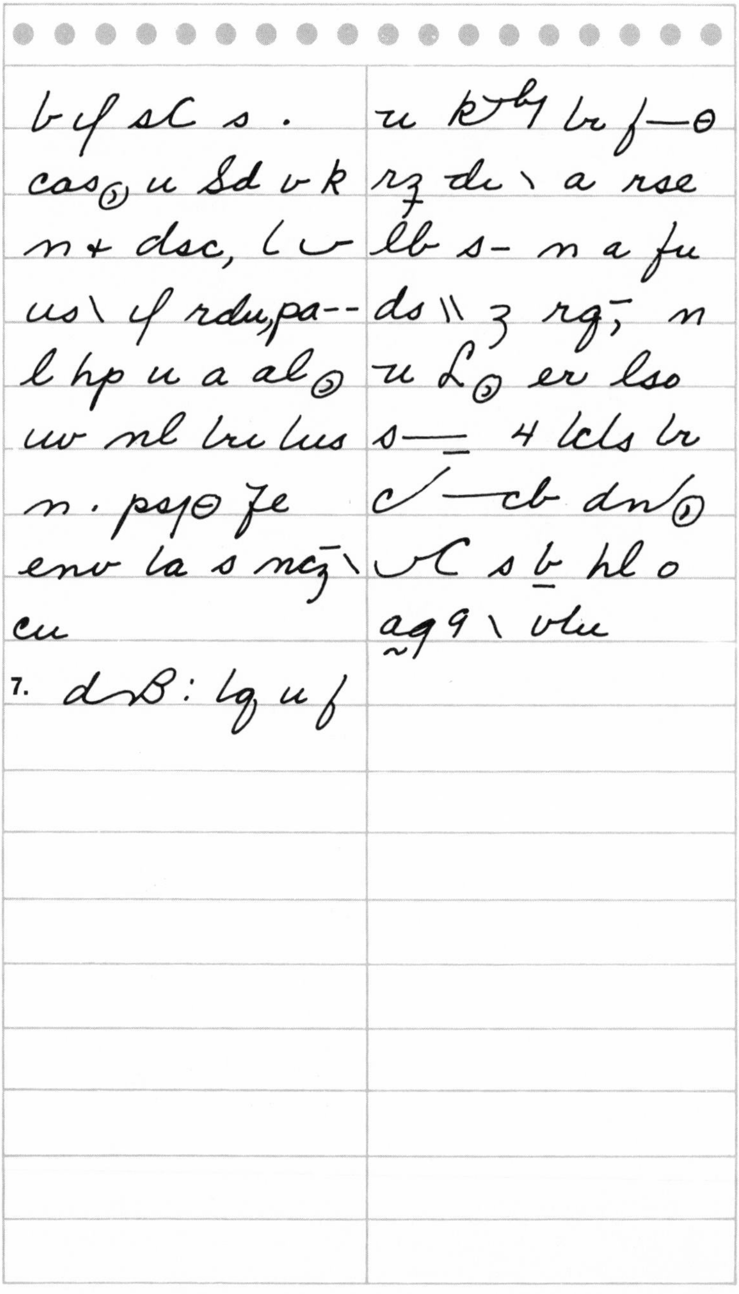

Key To Lesson 14

1. Dear Mr. Gold: During the past five years, the number of sales of our magazine has increased over 500[2] percent. It has become the largest selling publication of its kind in the country, and subscriptions are coming[4] in at the rate of about a thousand a day. Based on a recent study, we estimate that at least a[6] million men and women studied the statistics and suggestions issued by our staff of experts last year. (¶) If you[6] are thinking of making any investments in either stocks or government bonds, we suggest that you first stop at[10] your newsstand to pick up the latest issue of this very popular magazine. We know that reading it will[12] help you invest your capital wisely. It sells for just $1 a copy. Yours truly, *(136 words)*

2. Dear Sir: It has always been our custom to do our utmost to investigate and settle all claims quickly. To[2] assist us in making fast payment on your claim, we must first insist that you draw up a list showing the estimated[4] value of the articles lost when fire destroyed your home. (¶) I know you will understand why we cannot process[6] your claim until this statement is in our hands. Sincerely, *(70 words)*

3. Gentlemen: I am very happy to answer your request for information about Mr. Front. (¶) Mr. Front[2] was still a student at the state college when we employed him in our firm during his summer vacations. After[4] finishing school, he joined our staff as an assistant to the Manager of our Accounting Department and was[6] rapidly promoted to a position of highest trust. Early last year, he was instrumental in instituting[8] a filing system that saved us thousands of dollars. It was so efficient that it has already been[10] introduced into all our regional offices. (¶) I frankly believe him to be a very hard[12] worker and a most extraordinary man. I feel quite confident that he will be a real asset to any institution[14] he represents. Sincerely yours, *(147 words)*

4. Dear Mr. Blank: Are you getting the most out of your old heating system? Does it stand up under constant winter[2] use? Must you frequently call your serviceman to make costly adjustments? Are you forced to pay higher prices each[4] year in order to keep it operating properly? (¶) Why continue to be dissatisfied when you can get[6] the best heating system on the market for a relatively small amount of money? (¶) If you will fill out the[8] blank card that is enclosed, we will send one of our representatives to your home. He will estimate the cost of[10] a completely new installation and will also explain why it will be worth your while to deal with a company[12] like ours. Yours very truly, *(125 words)*

5. Dear Customer: As I stated in the letter addressed to you last week, dealers from coast to coast are reporting[2] that our new plastic blanket covers are selling better than ever. (¶) In view of this increase in sales, I think it[4] might be wise for you to order some extra covers this month. We still have a large stock in blue, pink, and white; but they[6] are going fast and should be ordered within a week or two. (¶) To prevent any misunderstanding, please make certain[8] that your order states both the style and color you want. Yours truly, *(92 words)*

6. Dear Mr. Flood: Your credit standing at our bank has always been extremely excellent. Therefore, I am really[2] at a loss to understand why your payments have been so delinquent during the past few months. (¶) I realize that[4] something may have happened to prevent your paying these installments on time, but if such is the case, you should have come[6] in and discussed it with us. If reduced payments will help you at all, you have only to write to us in the[8] postage-free envelope that is enclosed. Cordially yours, *(89 words)*

7. Dear Member: Thank you for your contribution to our fund-raising drive. A receipt will be sent in a few days. (¶) As[2] requested in your letter, we are also sending four tickets to our country club dinner,which is being held[4] on August 9. Very truly yours, *(46 words)*

TO PHRASE OR NOT TO PHRASE?

You've come a long way toward mastering *Speedwriting* shorthand. But along the way, have you become a student who phrases excessively? Do you have the mistaken belief that phrasing is the key to shorthand speed? Then take heed.

Excessive phrasing may actually be slowing you down! If you pause for even a fraction of a second in writing a phrase, you have lost speed. A phrase is valuable only when it can be written without the slightest hesitation and can be read accurately. It will help you to remember this.

The Reading Exercises contain phrases such as I will (el), he is (hs), you can (uc), to know (tno), and to me (tme). In addition to such combinations, it is often possible to omit one or more unimportant words in a common expression. Here are some examples:

nevertheless

time to time

more and more

again and again

now and then

up to date

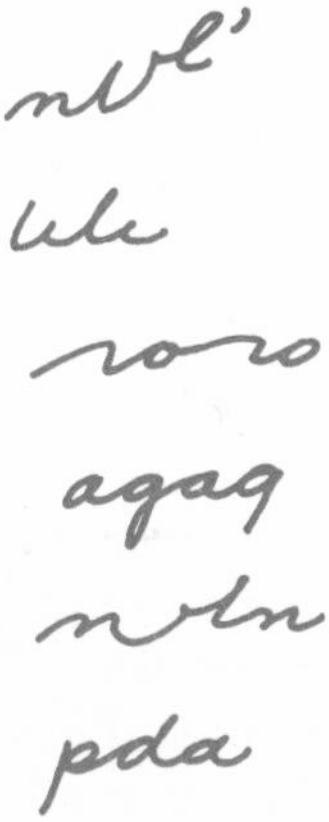

Phrase only those combinations which come to you naturally when you are taking dictation – and only those which occur over and over again. If you have the feeling that you should be phrasing more, forget it! Concentrate on moving from one outline to another with no hesitation!

Writing Assignment—Lesson 14

1. During the past year I investigated the filing systems used by at least a hundred of the largest companies in the country. Based on the statistics I gathered, I frankly think that ours is the least costly and the most efficient.

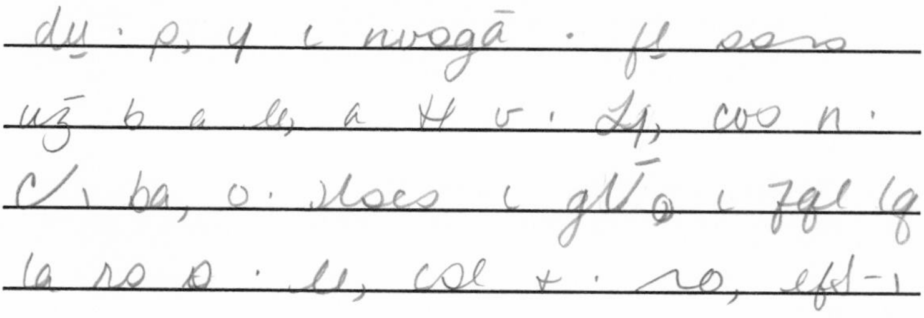

2. At the request of your representative, we have already sent you an extra copy of our latest price list and style catalog.

3. I really cannot understand why you state that July 28 is the earliest date on which you can install the plastic tank in our plant.

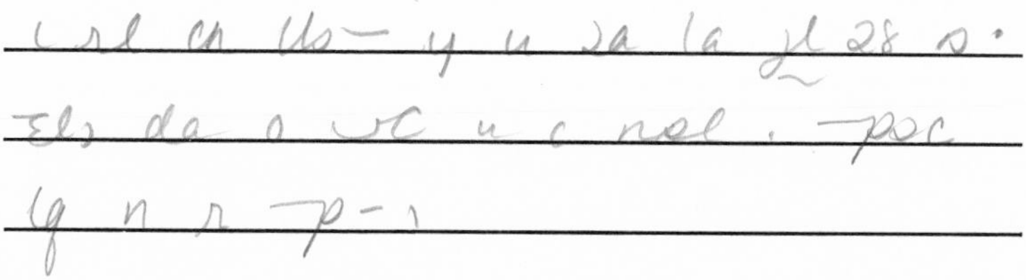

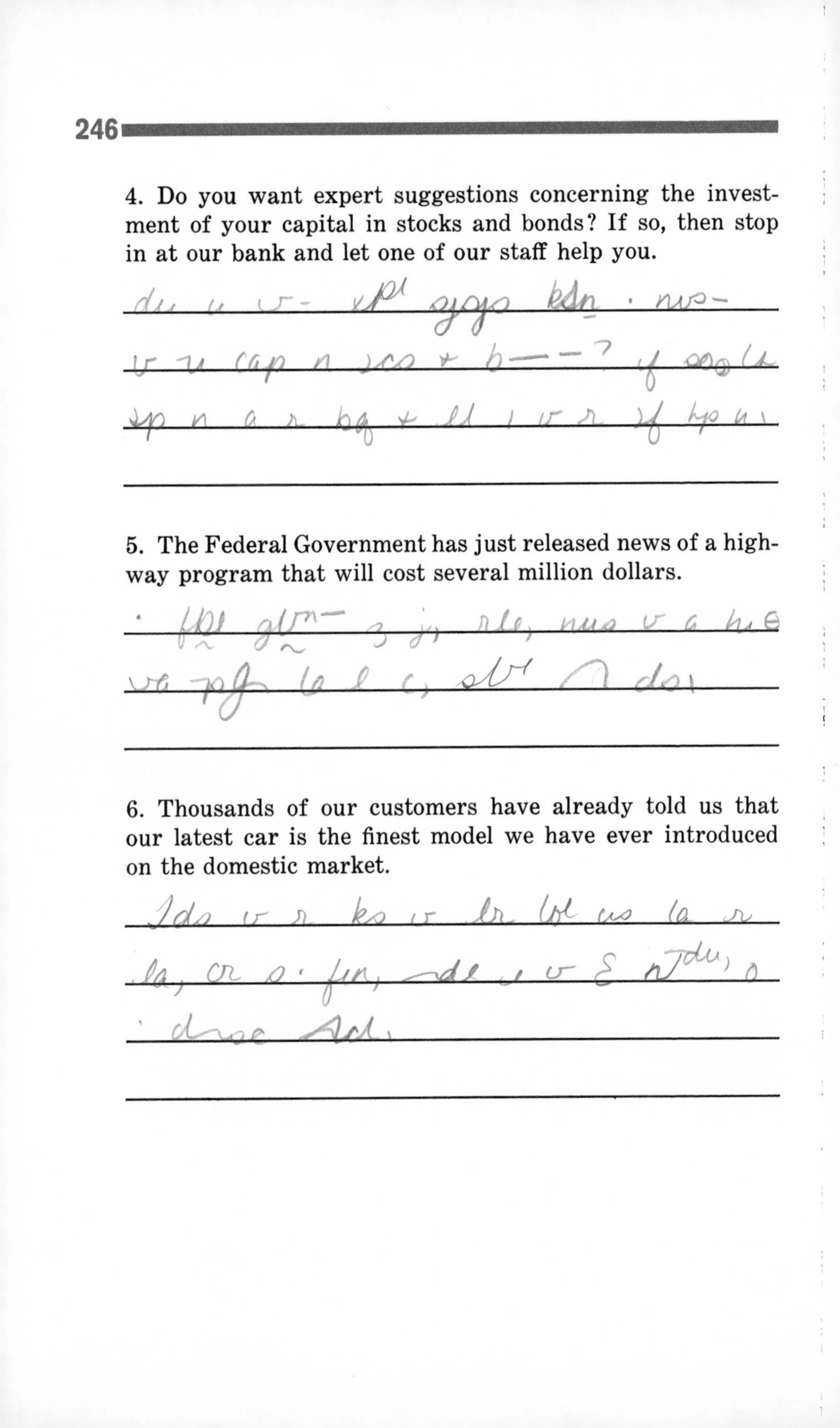

4. Do you want expert suggestions concerning the investment of your capital in stocks and bonds? If so, then stop in at our bank and let one of our staff help you.

5. The Federal Government has just released news of a highway program that will cost several million dollars.

6. Thousands of our customers have already told us that our latest car is the finest model we have ever introduced on the domestic market.

Lesson 15

In previous lessons, you learned that when a word ends in the sound of a long vowel followed by "t," "v," or "m," the long vowel is written to represent the resulting sound. Thus, **gate**  ; **gave** 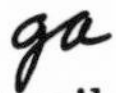 ; **game** 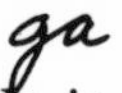 . You are now going to learn another family of words in which the long vowel will be used in the same way.

RULE 41	**For the final sound of a long vowel and "r" write the long vowel to represent the resulting sound.**

You can see how similar this rule is to the ones just reviewed regarding the sounds of a long vowel and "t," "v," or "m."

In the following words, notice that the long vowel is written to represent the complete sound of the long vowel + "r."

Study these examples:

dear	de	desire	dzi
here	he	desired	dzi¯
hearing	he_	require	rqi
engineer	njne	more	ɔo
appear	ape	nor	no
inquire	nqi	explore	xpo
wire	ui	secure	scu
wiring	ui_	insured	nsu¯
tire	ti	brochure	bsu

You write:

1. hear he
2. near ne
3. appeared api¯
4. cashier cse
5. fear fe
6. severe sve
7. acquired aqi
8. entire nti
9. required rqi
10. door do
11. floor fo
12. sure su
13. assured asu¯
14. assure asu
15. insure nsu
16. secured scu¯

Confirmation:

1.	he	2.	ne	3.	apē	4.	cSe
5.	fe	6.	sve	7.	agī	8.	nle
9.	rgī	10.	do	11.	Fo	12.	Su
13.	aSū	14.	aSu	15.	nSu	16.	scū

What of the sound of the vowel in the words *care* or *fair?* This is not the long "a" sound that is heard in *cape* or *fate,* and it is not the short sound of "a" that occurs in the words *cap* or *cat.* In other words, the pronunciation of *a* in *care* and *fair* lies midway between the long- and short-vowel sounds. For the purpose of this rule, however, this sound of "air" will be treated the same way as the other long-vowel sounds and "r."

Study these examples:

fair	fa	sharing	Sa̲
care	ca	fares	fas
repair	rpa	aware	a◡a
wear	◡a	compared	kpā
hardware	Hd◡a	preparing	ppa̲

You write:

1. chair Ca 2. prepared ppā

3. prepare ppa 4. wearing ◡a̲

5. bear ba 6. share Sa

7. comparing kpa 8. glare —ga

Confirmation:

1. Ca 2. ppā 3. ppa 4. ‿a

5. ba 6. Sa 7. kpa 8. —ga

Of course, although this rule refers to the final sound of a long vowel + "r," it will be applied when a suffix is added to a root word that is written according to this rule.

Study these words:

clearness	—ce'	nearest	ne,
clearly	—cel	surely	Sul
clearer	—ce/	fairly	fal
careless	cal'	tours	lus
carelessness	cal"	retirement	rli—
shares	Sas	requirements	rqi——
chairman	Ca—	repairs	rpas

You write:

1. fairness fa' 2. fearless fel'

3. clearest —ce' 4. nearer ne/

5. dearer de/ 6. nearly nel

7. merely ______ 8. entirely ______

9. requirement ______ 10. chairs ______

11. requires ______ 12. affairs ______

Confirmation:

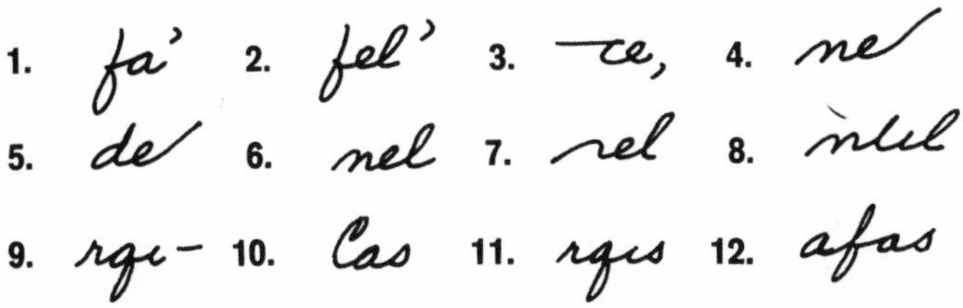

Here's a hint to help you remember the four rules that concern the dropping of a consonant after a long vowel. In the early days of television, a well-known comedian was called Mr. TV. Remember the name. It will remind you that when a word ends in the sound of a long vowel + "m," "r," "t," or "v," only the vowel is written.

Read the following sentences:

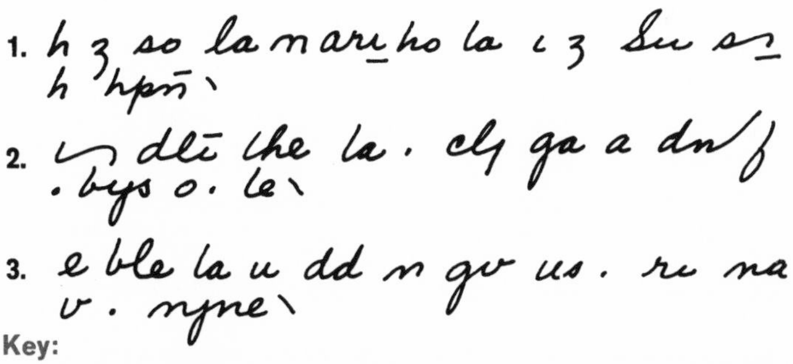

Key:

1. He was so late in arriving home that I was sure something had happened.
2. I am delighted to hear that the college gave a dinner for the boys on the team.
3. We believe that you did not give us the right name of the engineer.

RULE 42 | **Omit n before the sounds of "g," "j," and "ch."**

This rule simply tells you that in such words as *young* or *single,* you will omit the *n* from the outline and write **young** yq and **single** sgl .

Similarly, the *n* will be omitted before the sound of "j," and you will write **singe** sj ; **arrangement** arj- ; **ex-change** xCj .

Finally, the rule refers to the sound of "n" before "ch" and, once again, you are to omit the *n*. Thus, **branch** bC ; **franchise** fCz

Study these words:

luncheon	lCn	**ranch**	rC
thing	lq	**wrong**	rq
long	lq	**strongly**	Sgl
youngsters	yqSs	**among**	amq
passenger	psj	**strangely**	Sjl
arrange	arj	**arranged**	arj̄

You write:

1. branches bCs	**2. lunch** lC
3. along alq	**4. things** lqs
5. longer lq/	**6. bring** bq
7. strong Sq	**8. stronger** Sq/

9. bringing bg **10. arranging** ary

11. arrangements ary-- **12. younger** yg

Confirmation:

1. bCs 2. lC 3. alg 4. lgs
5. lg 6. bg 7. Sg 8. Sg
9. bg 10. ary 11. ary-- 12. yg

Note: The outlines for the words *strength* and *length* are derived from the words **strong** Sg and **long** lg; therefore **strength** Sgl and **length** lgl.

Before going on to the next rule, let's review something you have already learned. You know that for the initial sound of "pl," you write p as in **plan** pn and **play** pa. You also know that for the sound of medial "pl," you write p as in **duplicate** dpca and **apply** api. Similarly, for the sound of initial "bl," you write b as in **blue** bu; but for medial "bl," you write b as in **problem** pbm. The next rule deals with a sound that is closely related to the sounds of "bl" and "pl."

RULE 43	**For the sounds of final "bul" and "blee," write b; for the sounds of final "pul" and "plee," write p.**

Let's start with the sounds in the words *able, available,* and *possible.* Each of these words contains the final sound of "bul" and, since you are to write *b* for this sound, you write **able** *ab* ; **available** *avlb* ; **possible** *psb* .

The first part of the rule also instructs you to write *b* for the final sound of "blee." Therefore, **reasonably** *rznb* ; **possibly** *psb* .

Study these words:

valuable	*vlub*	**trouble**	*Tb*
double	*db*	**reliable**	*rlib*
enable	*nab*	**favorable**	*fvb*
suitable	*sub*	**favorably**	*fvb*
profitably	*pflb*	**reasonable**	*rznb*

You write:

1. table *lb* ________ **2. doubly** *db* ________

3. desirable *dzib* ________ **4. dependable** *dp—b* ________

5. payable *pab* ________ **6. eligible** *—ejb* ________

7. enjoyable *njyb* ________ **8. suitably** *sub* ________

Confirmation:

1. *lb* **2.** *db* **3.** *dzib* **4.** *dp—b*

5. *pab* **6.** *—ejb* **7.** *njyb* **8.** *sub*

The second part of the rule states that *p* is to be written for the final sound of "pul" or "plee."

Study these words:

example	x⌒p	**simple**	s⌒p
people	pp	**simply**	s⌒p
couple	cp	**examples**	x⌒ps

Brief Forms

open	op	**result**	rsl
opinion	opn	**important**	ip
life	lf	**between**	bl
prove	pv	**subject**	sj
difficult, difficulty	dfk	**situation**	sil
regular, regulation, regularly	reg		

Abbreviations

establish	esl

Additional Words

regulations	regs	**established**	est
results	rsls	**establishing**	esl

resulting	rsl	establishment	esl-
resulted	rsl	ample	mp
opened	op	amply	mp
opening	op	considerable	ksb
proved	pv	considerably	ksb
proves	pvs	herewith	he
approval	aPvl	herein	hen
approved	aPv	questionnaire	qa
subjects	sjs	welfare	lfa

Dictation Hints

Express time as follows:

2 o'clock 2° **10 o'clock** 10° **10:30** 10^{30}

Reading Exercises

1. drs Sq: ro + ro pp r bq l Us— h up ls f r chn lagi . b, edcj avlb n Su la 3 a T u Sa lh opn + rlz h nec ls l ppa u yqSs f . fC

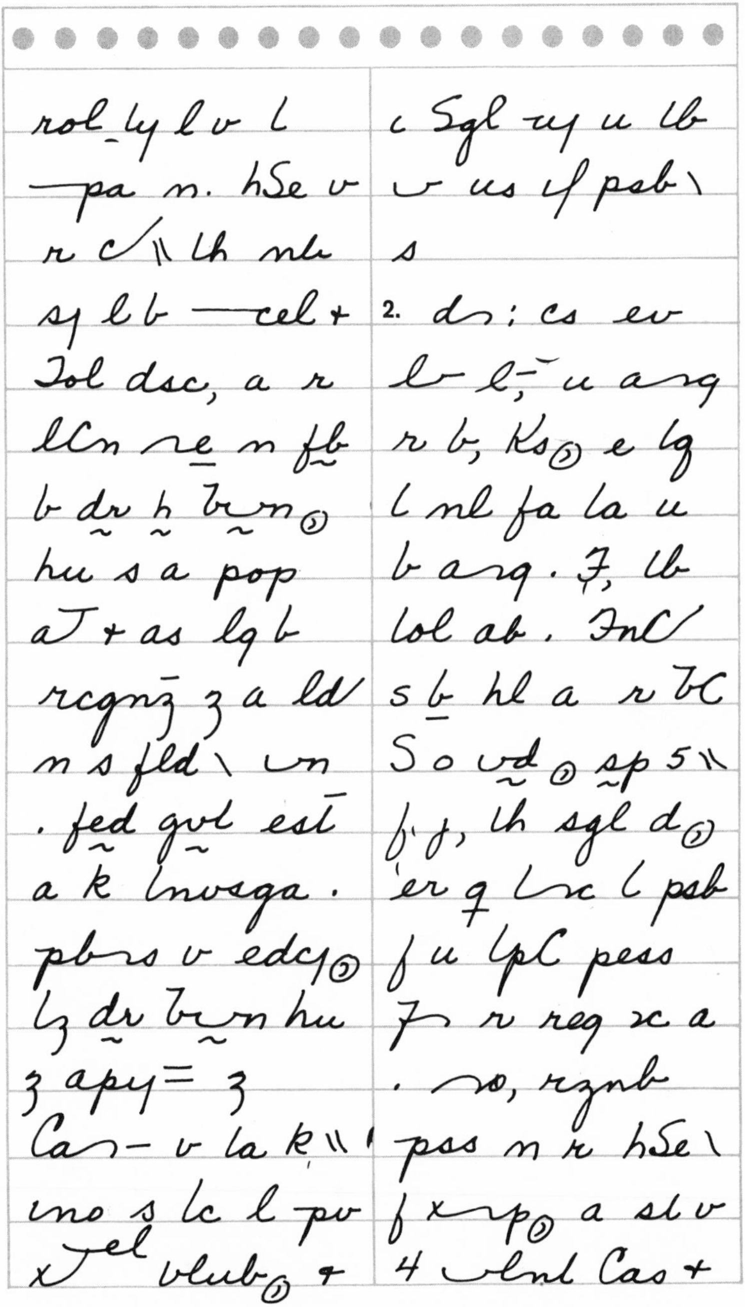

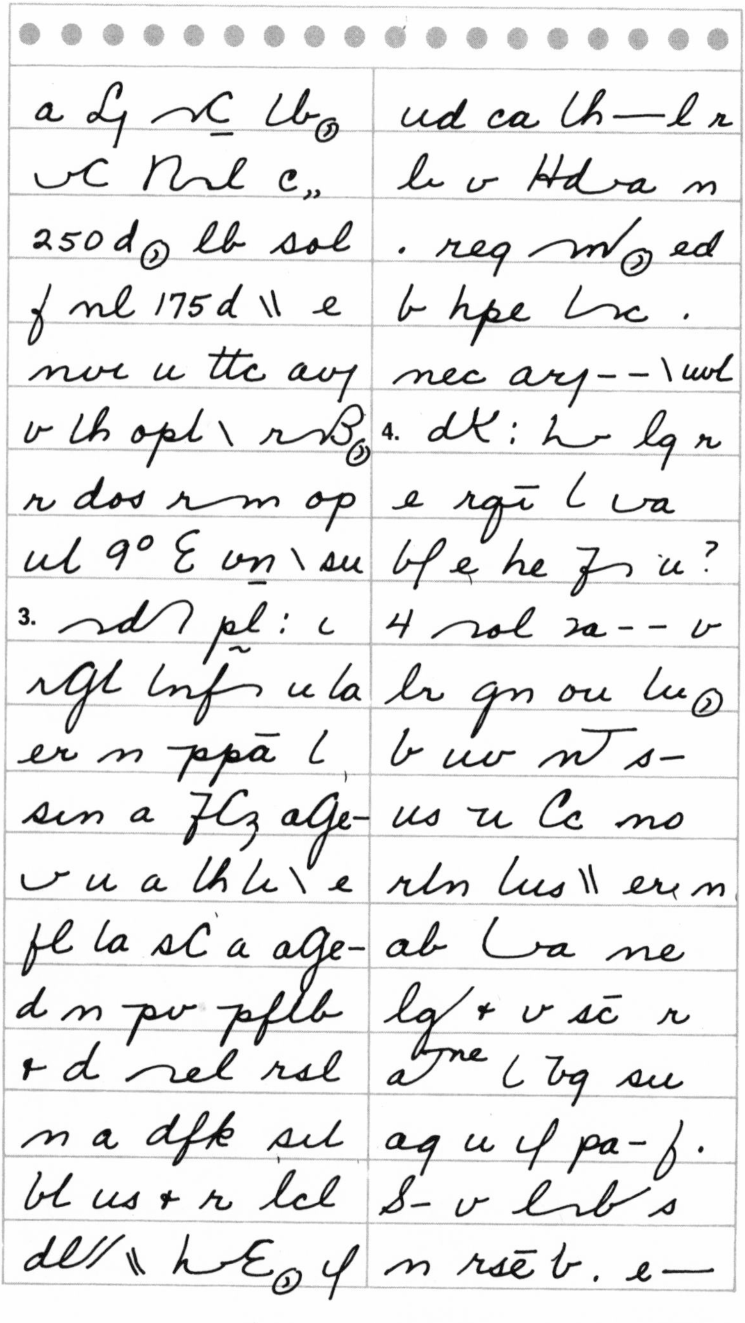

v lh vk \ ul
5. d) yg: eno ur
a-a la. cr uv
f, agī reps a
Lf nvs- \ eno
lo la ul lg l
dzb ldu E u
c lgl. b, psb
oA \\ he r s
s-p yl vp lgs
uc du la l
nab u l db. lf
v u cr + nSu
la ll gv u
ys v nfyb
Zb Fe Svs \
① bq u cr l ā
rlib Sp. -o-
s_ ses lb rq \

do- va ul a
s-a ajs- bks
a -y rpa jb \
② cf pls v ne
cr r rqī -x
Su la ly r scū
Fr a dp—b Ss \
③ flo al nScys
n rGd lreq
sgnl Ccps \ ④
lg v us -n und
a nu li o lub \
r b— v q Sq
lis + lubs l n
nl ad l. kfl
v u + u psy //
b l lso gv u.
ad q-e v a saf
Zp \\ hpe du \ c

Key To Lesson 15

1. Dear Mrs. Strong: More and more people are beginning to understand how important it is for our children to[2] acquire the best education available. I am sure that, as a mother, you share this opinion and[4] realize how necessary it is to prepare your youngsters for the future role they will have to play in the[6] history of our country. (¶) This entire subject will be clearly and thoroughly discussed at our luncheon meeting in[8] February by Dr. H. Brown, who is a popular author and has long been recognized as a leader[10] in his field. When the Federal Government established a committee to investigate the problems of[12] education, it was Dr. Brown who was appointed as chairman of that committee. (¶) I know his talk will prove[14] extremely valuable, and I strongly urge you to be with us if possible. Sincerely, *(156 words)*

2. Dear Madam: Because we have always listed you among our best customers, we think it only fair that you be[2] among the first to be told about the furniture sale being held at our branch store on Wednesday, September 5.[4] (¶) For just this single day, we are going to make it possible for you to purchase pieces from our regular[6] stock at the most reasonable prices in our history. For example, a set of four walnut chairs and a[8] large matching table, which normally costs $250, will be sold for only[10] $175. (¶) We invite you to take advantage of this opportunity. Remember, our doors remain[12] open until 9 o'clock every evening. Sincerely yours, *(136 words)*

3. My dear Mr. Place: I regret to inform you that we are not prepared to sign a franchise agreement with you[2] at this time. We feel that such an agreement would not prove profitable and would merely result in a difficult[4] situation between us and our local dealers. (¶) However, if you would care to handle our line of hardware[6] in the regular manner, we would be happy to make the necessary arrangements. Yours very truly,[8] *(80 words)*

4. Dear Customer: How long are we required to wait before we hear from you? Four monthly statements have already gone[2] out to you, but you have neither sent us your check nor written to us. (¶) We are not able to wait any longer[4] and have asked our attorney to bring suit against you if payment for the shipment of lumber is not received by[6] the end of this week. Yours truly, *(65 words)*

5. Dear Mr. Young: I know you are aware that the car you have just acquired represents a large investment. I know,[2] too, that you will think it desirable to do everything you can to get the best possible operation.[4] (¶) Here are some simple yet important things you can do that will enable you to double the life of your car[6] and insure that it will give you many years of enjoyable, trouble-free service. 1. Bring your car to a[8] reliable shop the moment something seems to be wrong. Don't wait until a small adjustment becomes a major repair[10] job. 2. If parts of any kind are required, make sure that they are secured from a dependable source. 3. Follow[12] all instructions in regard to regular seasonal checkups. 4. Think of us when you need a new tire or tube. Our[14] brand of good, strong tires and tubes will not only add to the comfort of you and your passengers, but will also give[16] you the added guarantee of a safe trip. (¶) Happy driving. Cordially, *(173 words)*

Writing Assignment – Lesson 15

1. We can assure you that your entire family will enjoy a long vacation on our ranch.

2. If the results of our questionnaire prove favorable – and we find that many people share your opinion – we may possibly arrange to establish a branch store in the near future.

3. Are you aware that buying the wrong tires may considerably decrease the life of your car?

4. You will be glad to hear that it is a simple thing to open a regular charge account at our shop.

5. The enclosed brochure will bring you information on the subject of the important alterations made in our retirement plan.

. ncz bSu l bq u nfy o.
sj v. ip —aT° nd n r rti—
—pn.

6. Can you arrange to meet me for lunch between two and three o'clock to discuss the situation that has occurred?

C u ary l me m f lC b1
2 + 3° l dsc, sil la as oC?

7. I am sure that the chairman of the committee can secure the information he requires from our chief engineer.

i m Su la. Ca— v. k c
sCu. nfy h rqs f r
Cf ynr.

BRIEF FORM and STANDARD ABBREVIATION REVIEW

Lessons 11 through 15

1. Dear Mr. Deal: I note from your report that our average monthly sales between June and September are already[2] considerably above those of last year. (¶) Am I correct in assuming that this extraordinary[4] increase is due to the extra advertising we have done in local evening papers? If you really believe[6] that it is, then I think it necessary to invest an even greater part of our capital in this[8] way. Yours truly, *(82 words)*

2. Dear Mrs. Field: I have written to you several times directing your attention to the amount that you still[2] owe us under the terms of our contract. As you know, keeping such a small amount open on our books proves extremely[4] difficult; and it is important that you make payment in full before the end of the month. (¶) Why not send us[6] a check while this letter is before you? Very truly yours, *(70 words)*

3. Dear Friend: Should large steel companies be subject to control by the Federal Government? Should the Government[2] establish maximum prices that may be charged for steel? (¶) Some people subscribe to the opinion that such control is[4] absolutely necessary for the benefit of the public and that it would greatly contribute to the[6] economic life of the country. However, certain representatives of the Government and the steel[8] companies feel that these regulations would not prove satisfactory and would only result in difficult[10] situations. (¶) Both sides of this question are fully discussed in the current issue of the magazine we publish.[12] The magazine always sells rapidly, and we suggest that you stop at your newsstand while copies are still available.[14] Sincerely yours, *(144 words)*

4. Dear Sir: A fire in our shipping department is causing a delay in the delivery of our merchandise,[2] and we estimate that it will take a minimum of 10 days before we can fill your recent order. (¶) We hope[4] you will not only understand the reason for the delay but will also realize that this is a situation[6] that is completely beyond our control. Cordially yours, *(76 words)*

–REVIEW–

Lessons 11 through 15

1. Dear Mr. Frank: Thank you for taking the trouble to arrange the delivery of a courtesy copy of[2] your latest illustrated history book. I have examined it thoroughly and think it compares favorably with[4] the one we have used for such a long time. (¶) Those teachers who have studied its contents had many comments to[6] make on the clear and enjoyable fashion in which the author presents his subject, and they were most emphatic[8] in expressing the opinion that this excellent book would prove valuable in their classes. Personally,[10] I am quite willing to go along with their suggestions and am prepared to place an order provided you can[12] guarantee delivery in ample time for the start of our fall semester. Cordially yours, *(137 words)*

2. Dear Bill: Would it be possible to arrange a luncheon appointment on Friday to discuss further the contract[2] I must sign by July 28? (¶) I still have a great many questions to ask, and I feel you are the only person[4] competent enough to answer them for me. Cordially, *(51 words)*

3. Dear Mrs. Story: I am enclosing the name and address of the dealer in your area who handles our[2] complete line. I am sure that he will be able to recommend the best type of storm windows for your home. Yours truly, *(40 words)*

4. Dear Mr. Steel: I have written you several times in connection with the amount that is still outstanding on[2] your account. (¶) The large assortment of leather boxes shipped on July 6 was sent on credit, and you promised to make[4] payment by the first of the following month. However, we have had no word from you; and we must now insist[6] on settlement of your bill by the end of the week. (¶) If we have not heard from you by then, we will be forced to[8] authorize our attorney to bring suit against you. Won't you help us avoid taking this step by sending your check? Yours[10] very truly, *(102 words)*

More Help For Students

HOW TO DETERMINE THE LENGTH OF A LETTER

In a short time now you'll be on the job as a happy, working secretary – and chances are you'll be able to estimate the length of any letter just at a glance. But until you have had enough experience in this respect, you have to have a definite method of determining the number of words in a letter. Here is the easy way to do this –

Count the number of words in the first three lines of the body of the letter in your shorthand notes. Divide this number by three. You then have the average number of words in each line. Now count the number of lines in your notes and multiply this number by the average number of words in each line. The resulting number is a good estimate of the total number of words in the letter.

For example: If there are 21 words in the first three lines of your notes, divide 21 by 3. This gives you an average of 7 words per line. If there are 20 lines of shorthand, multiply 20 by 7 and you will find that there are approximately 140 words in the body of the letter.

As you become more experienced, you will learn to estimate the length of a letter without counting. If a letter contains 125 words and you have written 1¼ columns, excluding the inside address and salutation, you have written about one hundred words to a column. By checking in this manner over a period of a few days, you will be able to estimate the length of a letter by just looking at the length of your notes.

Lesson 16

Let's start this lesson with a review of the marks of punctuation that you have learned in previous lessons.

1. UNDERSCORE: For "ing" or "thing" that is added to a word: **getting** gl ; **something** s_ .
2. OVERSCORE: For "ed" that is added to form the past tense of a word: **named** nā ; **required** rqī .
3. HYPHEN: For the medial and final sounds of "nt" or "ment": **went** u- ; **statement** ,a- .
4. DASH: for the medial and final sound of "nd": **depend** dp— ; **handle** h—l .
5. APOSTROPHE: For the final ss and ness: **discuss** dsc' ; **happiness** hpe'.
6. QUOTATION MARK: For the final ssness: **fearlessness** fel" ; **hopelessness** hopl" .
7. COMMA: For the initial and final sounds of "st": **first** F, ; **discussed** dsc, ; **step** ,p .
8. SLANT (joined): For the final sounds of "er" and "ter": **bigger** bg/ ; **after** af/ .

Read the following sentences:

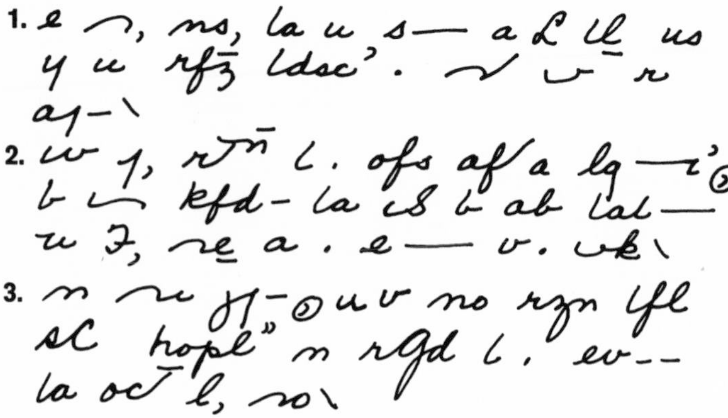

Key:

1. **We must insist that you send a letter telling us why you refused to discuss the matter with our agent.**
2. **I have just returned to the office after a long illness, but I am confident that I shall be able to attend your first meeting at the end of the week.**
3. **In my judgment, you have no reason to feel such hopelessness in regard to the events that occurred last month.**

You are now going to learn to use another mark of punctuation to represent a sound.

RULE 44 | For the final sound of "tee" write) .

Ordinarily, this mark of punctuation) is called a right parenthesis; but because this is rather a long name, it will be referred to as a blend.

Study these examples:

city	s)	duty	du)
safety	sf)	duties	du))
maturity	mtu)	quantity	q-)
university	unvs)	authority	aT)
liberty	lB)	county	k)
community	kn)	quantities	q-))
facilities	fsl))	quality	ql)

You write:

1. beauty ________ 2. locality ________

3. property ________ 4. security ________

5. faculty ________ 6. purity ________

7. party ________ 8. capacity ________

9. pretty ________ 10. activities ________

11. qualities ________ 12. cities ________

Confirmation:

1. bu) 2. lcl) 3. pP) 4. scu)

5. fcl) 6. pu) 7. P) 8. cps)

9. p) 10. acv)) 11. ql)) 12. s))

Notice in the following words that you retain the root outline and simply add a blend) for the addition of the sound of "tee": **possible** psb ; **possibility** psb) ; **able** ab ; **ability** ab) ; **disability** dsab) ; **necessary** nec ; **necessity** nec) ; **public** pb ; **publicity** pb) ; **popular** pop ; **popularity** pop).

Before going on to the next rule, let's look back at two rules which were in lessons you have already covered. You will recall that **made** is written md and **graze** gz , in accordance with the rules that stated that you are to drop the long vowel when it is followed by the sound of "d" or "z." Thus: **raid** rd ; **raise** rz ; **seed** sd ; **seize** sz ; **wide** ud ; **wise** uz ; **rode** rd ; **rose** rz ; **feud** fd ; **fuse** fz .

The rule which you are now going to learn deals with another group of words in which you will also omit the long vowel and write the consonant sound that follows it.

RULE 45 | **For the sounds of "ane, een, one," and "une" write n ; for the sound of "ine" write in .**

You can see that once again you are going to drop the long vowel and write the consonant sound that follows it.

Study these examples:

gain	gn	**means**	mns
main	mn	**loan**	ln

cleaned	—cn̄	phone	fn
green	gn	noon	nn
dean	dn	plain	—pn

You write:

1. seen ____________
2. mean ____________
3. soon ____________
4. grain ____________
5. shown ____________
6. zone ____________
7. screening ____________
8. training ____________

Confirmation:

1.	sn	2.	mn	3.	sn	4.	gn
5.	Sn	6.	zn	7.	sCn̲	8.	Tn̲

Notice that this rule refers to the sounds of "ane, een, one," and "une," but it does not include the sound of "ine" that is heard in such words as *sign* and *design*. For this sound of "ine," you will write ın no matter how many syllables are in the word.

Study these examples:

sign	sın	incline	ncın
design	dzın	assigned	asın̄
assignment	asın-	combined	kbın̄

You write:

1. decline ____________ **2. inclined** ____________

3. resign ____________ **4. designed** ____________

Confirmation:

1. dcin 2. ncin̄ 3. rzin 4. dzin̄

To summarize: When a word contains the sound of a long vowel and "d," "z," or "n," write the consonant and drop the vowel – except for the sound of "ine," for which you write both the *i* and *n*. It may be helpful for you to remember the outline for the clue word **design** dzin. As you look at this outline, say the rule – drop all vowels before *d, z,* and *n,* except for the long *i* before *n.*

One further point before proceeding to the last rule in this lesson. According to the rule, you write **chain** Cn. However, in the words *change, range,* and *strange* an additional rule must be applied–the omission of *n* before *j*. Thus: **change** Cj ; **changes** Cjs ; **range** rj ; **strange** Sj .

RULE 46 | **For the initial sound of "im" write i ; for the initial sound of "un" write u .**

Study these examples:

imprinted	iP=	**unless**	ul'
imperative	iPv	**unfortunately**	ufCnll
impose	ipz	**undoubtedly**	udtl
impossible	ipsb	**unemployment**	upy–
impossibility	ipsb)	**unable**	uab

You write:

1. imprinting ______________ 2. unpaid ______________

3. imposing ______________ 4. unwise ______________

5. imitation ______________ 6. unskilled ______________

7. imitate ______________ 8. unlikely ______________

9. unhappy ______________ 10. unfair ______________

Confirmation:

1. iP= 2. upd 3. upz 4. u‿z

5. ij 6. uscl̄ 7. ida 8. ulcl

9. uhpe 10. ufa

Brief Forms

whole	hl	acknowledge	ak
develop	dv	almost	lso

organize, organization — oq

immediate, immediately — ida

particular, particularly — p

success, successful, successfully — suc

Abbreviations

volume	vol	ounce	oz	pair	pr

Additional Words

wholesale	hls	improve	ɩpv
wholesaler	hls\	improving	ɩpv̲
acknowledged	ak̄	improvement	ɩpv-
acknowledgement	ak-	improvements	ɩpv--
developing	dv̲	improved	ɩpv̄
development	dv-	unnecessary	unec
developments	dv--	unsatisfactory	usal
developed	dv̄	pairs	prs
confirm	kf	confirmation	kf/

Reading Exercises

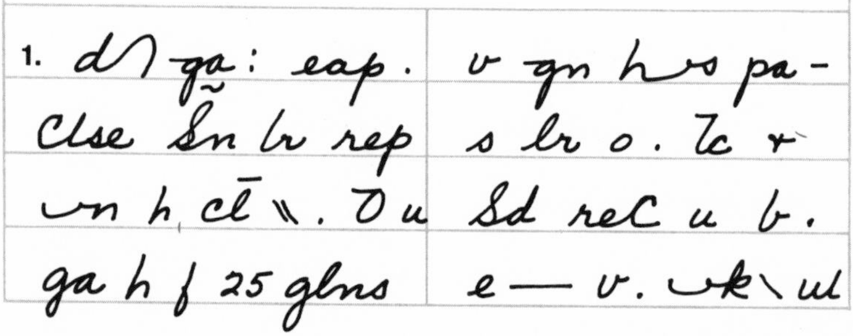

2. dbl: w. L
n vlc u sc̄
v lg. ds—
f usc̄ lb l
Sv n. fC\ ls
ru opn la ll
n(3) & i Yf Sgl
sj, la ulc. In
Css i rj un,
e rl \\ u udl
v. nec ab) &
unl ldv a hu
dJe v scl n
lh P fld(3) & ld
b uz l p of
lh In ne lg
ln s nec\\ z i
lol u(3) ls a ll
ulcl la ur

—Ejb f a sd-
ln Fr. bq(3) b
lh dz n nec
—m la ecn
suc Lvc ou
s bl us\ cl
re un a fu
ds so la ec
ary lre & dsc'
lh rl\ s

3. ds: n ru
cps) z —mj
v r —m ofs(3)
us f, lru lu
ab. r m 1856[9]
o u akl\\ pa-
o lh ol bl s lq
Odu(3) & e d lc
lv r —me\

ls unec bru us
a L⊖ a Cc
lb sfS- \ ul
4. d) bl: El
l, s~ e pC̄
a Lj pes v
p) 7 . s)
gvl f. Pps v
bld a kn) s-
f r yq pp\
sfS- f— —
v fel b rz̄ +
er hop la Uc
l bq ida\ e
esra la kScy
l lc lro a y
b s~ v. fsl))
Sd b rde n
ab 6 ros\\ .

Bs v r oq
vS lak + lg
u f. hp u ga
us\ v~ Su
ul gn a q dl
v sal 7 .
nl la u pā
sC a up Pl n
. suc v. hl
pG\ cu
5. d) Sq: z c
xpn o. fn vn
c lc v u ySd
e ~, sc u L
va a ll lg
f. 12 prs v gol
Sus u rq, o
jl 23\. vol
v T as b P

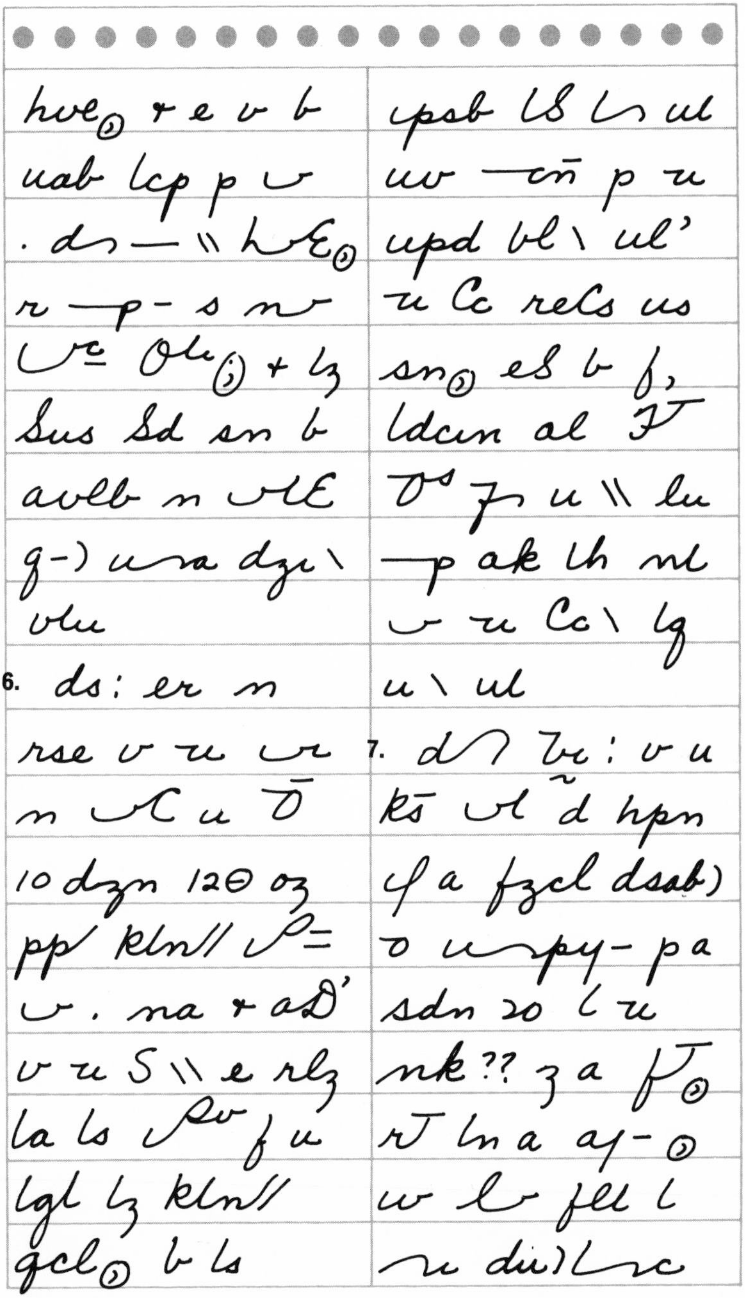

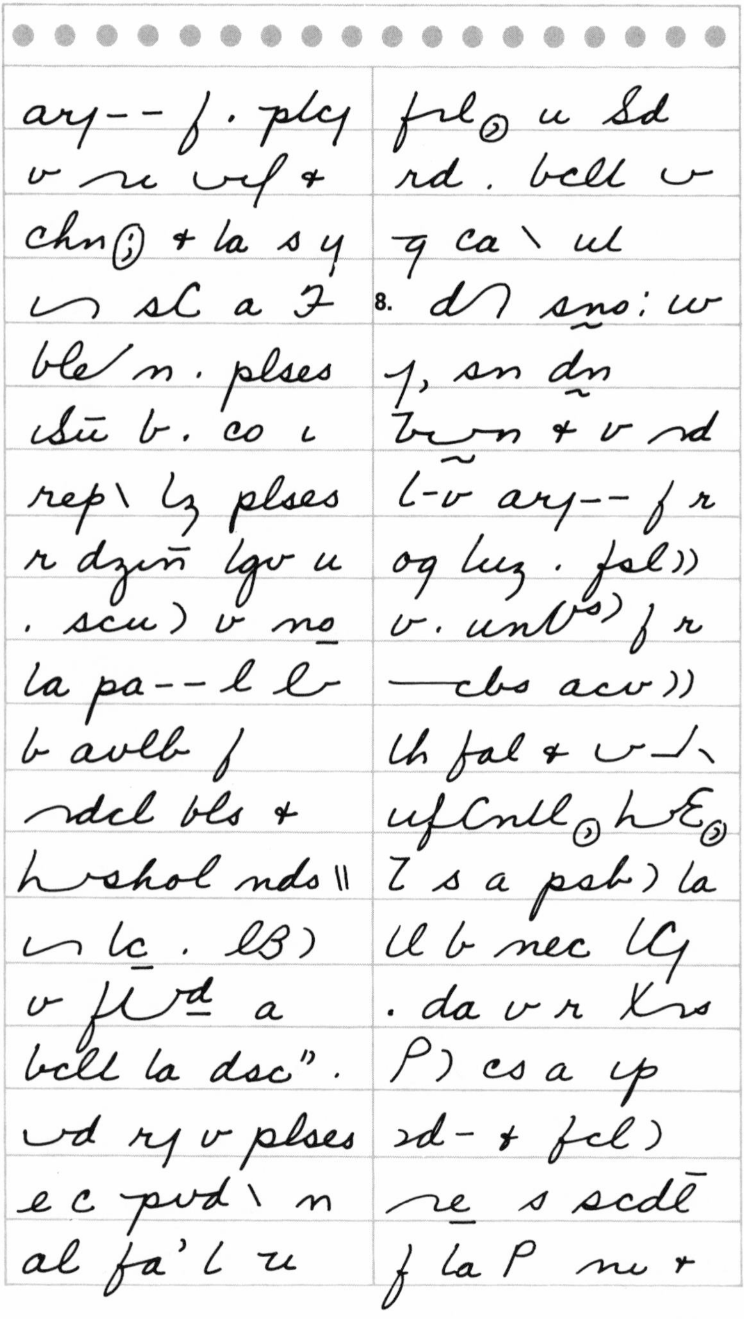

cn b csl̄ l
akda us\\ l
l fn u 1, 3
sn 3 aT da
as b sl \ su

Key to Lesson 16

1. Dear Mr. Gray: We appreciate the courtesy shown to our representative when he called. (¶) The order you[2] gave him for 25 gallons of green house paint is already on the truck and should reach you by the end of the[4] week. Yours truly, *(42 words)*
2. Dear Bill: I have the letter in which you asked whether I think the demand for unskilled labor will improve in the[2] future. It is my opinion that it will not, and I therefore strongly suggest that you take the training courses[4] I mentioned when we met. (¶) You undoubtedly have the necessary ability and intelligence to develop[6] a high degree of skill in this particular field, and it would be unwise to put off this training any[8] longer than is necessary. (¶) As I told you, it is a little unlikely that you are eligible[10] for a student loan from the bank; but this does not necessarily mean that we cannot successfully work out[12] something between us. Call me within a few days so that we can arrange to meet and discuss this matter. Sincerely,[14] *(140 words)*
3. Dear Sir: In my capacity as manager of our main office, I am forced to write to you about the remaining[2] $185.69 on your account. (¶) Payment on this old bill is long[4] overdue, and we would like to have our money. It is unnecessary to write us a letter – a check will be[6] sufficient. Yours truly, *(64 words)*
4. Dear Mr. Billings: Early last summer we purchased a large piece of property from the city government for[2] the purpose of building a community center for our young people. Sufficient funds have finally been raised,[4] and we are hoping that work will begin immediately. We estimate that construction will take almost a[6] year, but some of the facilities should be ready in about six months. (¶) The members of our organization[8] wish to acknowledge and thank you for the help you gave us. I am sure you will gain a great deal of satisfaction[10] from the knowledge that you played such an important part in the success of the whole program. Cordially yours, *(126 words)*

5. Dear Mr. Strong: As I explained on the phone when I talked with you yesterday, we must ask you to wait a little[2] longer for the 12 pairs of gold shoes you requested on July 23. The volume of orders has been[4] particularly heavy, and we have been unable to keep up with the demand. (¶) However, our plant is now[6] working overtime; and these shoes should soon be available in whatever quantity you may desire. Very[8] truly yours, *(81 words)*

6. Dear Sir: We are in receipt of your wire in which you ordered 10 dozen 12-ounce paper containers imprinted[2] with the name and address of your store. (¶) We realize that it is imperative for you to get these containers[4] quickly, but it is impossible to ship them until you have cleaned up your unpaid bill. Unless your check reaches[6] us soon, we shall be forced to decline all further orders from you. (¶) Will you please acknowledge this note with your check. Thank[8] you. Yours truly, *(82 words)*

7. Dear Mr. Bright: Have you considered what would happen if a physical disability or unemployment[2] put a sudden stop to your income? (¶) As a father, rather than an agent, I have always felt it my duty to make[4] arrangements for the protection of my wife and children; and that is why I am such a firm believer[6] in the policies issued by the company I represent. These policies are designed to give you the[8] security of knowing that payments will always be available for medical bills and household needs. (¶) I[10] am taking the liberty of forwarding a booklet that discusses the wide range of policies we can[12] provide. In all fairness to your family, you should read the booklet with great care. Yours truly, *(135 words)*

8. Dear Mr. Snow: I have just seen Dean Brown and have made tentative arrangements for our organization to use[2] the facilities of the university for our club's activities this fall and winter. Unfortunately,[4] however, there is a possibility that it will be necessary to change the date of

our Christmas[6] party because an important student and faculty meeting is scheduled for that particular night and[8] cannot be canceled to accommodate us. (¶) I will phone you just as soon as another date has been set. Sincerely[10] yours, *(102 words)*

Writing Assignment—Lesson 16

1. The report I was shown indicates the possibility that the City Council will organize a committee to study unemployment problems in this particular community.

2. Will you please phone our office as soon as possible if the quality of service does not improve.

3. Unless there is a change in this unsatisfactory condition, we will face the necessity of assigning our publicity to another firm.

4. Unfortunately, I am unable to attend the party being given by the Dean for the members of the University's faculty.

5. We have successfully developed a new engine that combines all the features of safety and beauty that our customers demand.

6. Although you acknowledged receipt of my letter almost two weeks ago, I have heard nothing in regard to the request I made for a loan. May I know whether my request was declined?

Lesson 17

RULE 47	In words of more than one syllable, write x for the medial and final sounds of "us, usly, shus, shusly, shul, shully, nshul, nshully."

Let's examine this rule carefully. It states that *x* is to be written for the sounds of "us" and "usly." Therefore, **obvious** and **obviously** are written *obvx*. In the same way, **generous** and **generously** *jnrx*; **previous** and **previously** *pvx*.

Study these examples:

campus	*cmpx*	**numerous**	*nmrx*
surplus	*Spx*	**tremendous**	*Tm—x*
bonus	*bnx*	**tremendously**	*Tm—x*
bonuses	*bnxs*	**famous**	*fax*
religious	*rljx*	**famously**	*fax*

You write:

1. courteous ______________ **2. courteously** ______________

3. devious ______________ **4. status** ______________

5. monotonous ______________ **6. desirous** ______________

Confirmation:

1. Ctx **2.** Ctx **3.** dvx **4.** stx

5. mtnx **6.** dzrx

This rule also tells you to write *x* for the sounds of "shus" and "shusly." Therefore, you write **anxious** and **anxiously** agx ; **conscious** and **consciously** kx ; **delicious** dlx ; **ambitious** abx .

You write:

1. precious ______________ **2. graciously** ______________

Confirmation:

1. prx **2.** grx

This rule also instructs you to write *x* for the sounds of "shul" and "shully." Thus, **beneficial** bnfx ; **commercial** and **commercially** kx ; **partial** prx ; **social** and **socially** sx ; **official** and **officially** ofx ; **officials** ofxs .

And finally, the rule refers to the sound of "nshul" and "nshully" and you are instructed to write *x* for these sounds. Observe how this is done in the following words.

Study these examples:

confidential	*kfdx*	**financial**	*fnx*
confidentially	*kfdx*	**financially**	*fnx*
essential	*esx*	**credentials**	*cdxs*
essentially	*esx*	**residential**	*rzdx*

RULE 48 | **For the medial and final sound of a vowel followed by "ry" write** *y* **.**

In other words, you are to write *y* for the sounds of "ary, ery, iry, ory," and "ury." Observe how this rule is followed in these words.

Study these examples:

salary	*sly*	**sorry**	*sy*
temporary	*tpry*	**hurry**	*hy*
stationery	*sty*	**territory**	*Tly*
worry	*wy*	**inventory**	*nv-y*
inquiry	*nqy*	**weary**	*wy*

You write:

1. military __________ **2. carry** __________

3. voluntary __________ **4. library** __________

5. machinery __________ **6. customary** __________

7. preliminary ______________ 8. ordinary ______________

9. memory ______________ 10. summary ______________

Confirmation:

1. *rlly* 2. *cy* 3. *vl-y* 4. *lBy*

5. *rSny* 6. *csny* 7. *plmy* 8. *odny*

9. *mry* 10. *sry*

Notice that the rule states that you are to write *y* also for the medial sounds of "ary, ery, iry, ory," and "ury." Therefore, **material** *mtyl* ; **series** *syz* ; **serious** *syx* ; **period** *pyd* ; **various** *vyx* ; **interior** *ntyl* ; **editorial** *edtyl* .

RULE 49 | **For the sound of "sp," write a small printed** *s* **.**

You have learned to print a capital *S* for the sound of "str." This rule instructs you to write a small printed *s* for the sound of "sp" whenever it occurs in a word.

Study these examples:

speed	*sd*	**speak**	*sec*
spend	*s—*	**spare**	*sa*
hospital	*hstl*	**inspection**	*nscy*
prospective	*pscv*	**specifications**	*ssfcys*
specific	*ssfc*	**grasping**	*gs*

clasped		**special**	
speech		**especially**	

Read the following sentences:

1. 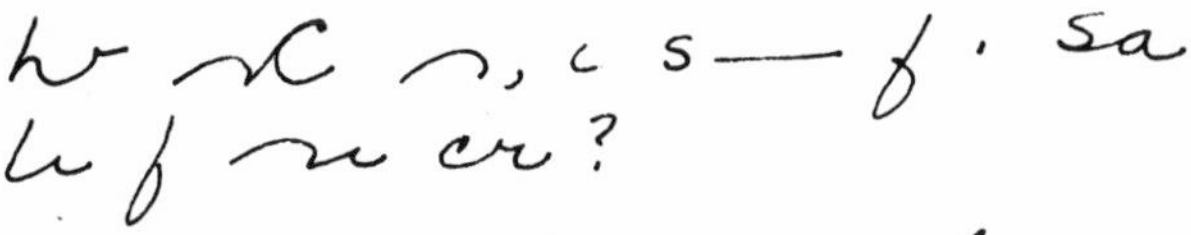
2. 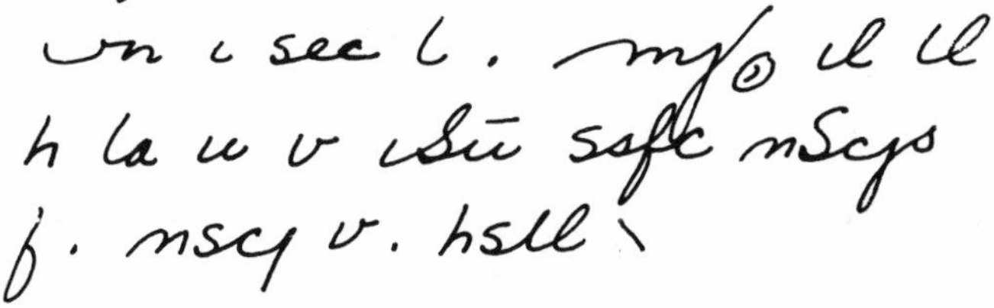

Key:

1. How much must I spend for the spare tire for my car?
2. When I speak to the manager, I will tell him that you have issued specific instructions for the inspection of the hospital.

You write:

1. spite ____________ 2. spot ____________

3. spent ____________ 4. space ____________

5. inspector ____________ 6. spending ____________

7. speaker ____________ 8. spoke ____________

9. dispose ____________ 10. inspire ____________

Confirmation:

1. 2. 3. 4.

5. nsc/ 6. s— 7. sc/ 8. soc

9. dsz 10. nsc

As you know, the initial sounds of "br, pr, gr," etc., are expressed by writing an initial hyphen on the first letter of the outline. For the sound of "spr" at the beginning of a word, do the same: s̄ . Thus, **spread** s̄d and **spring** s̄g . Similarly, "spl" at the beginning of a word is written with an initial dash: —s . Thus, **splice** —sis and **splendid** —s—d .

Again recalling a rule that has already been covered, you will treat the sound of medial "spl" as you do the medial sound of "bl" or "gl" – that is, you will eliminate the initial dash and write only the printed *s*. Thus, **display** dsa .

One further point before leaving this rule. What of words such as *sport* or *sparse?* These will be handled as you do any sound that is followed by a medial vowel + "r" – that is, you capitalize the preceding letter – in this case printed *s*. Therefore, **sport** St ; **spirit** St ; **sparse** Ss .

Brief Forms

thought	lo	**poor**	po
around	r—	**idea**	id
world	Wo	**object**	ob
usual, usually	x	**initial, initially**	ix
probable, probably	pb	**definite, definitely**	dfn

Abbreviations

minute	mn	warehouse	whs
junior	jr	senior	sr
manufacture	mfr	independent	ind
signature	sig	America, American	an
approximate, approximately	apx		

Additional Words

manufacturing	mfr̲	ideas	ids
manufacturer	mfr/	ideal	idl
manufacturers	mfr//	probability	pb)
manufactured	mfr̄	unusual	ux
objective	obv	minutes	mns
objection	obj	continuous	kux
directory	Dy	continuously	kux

Reading Exercises

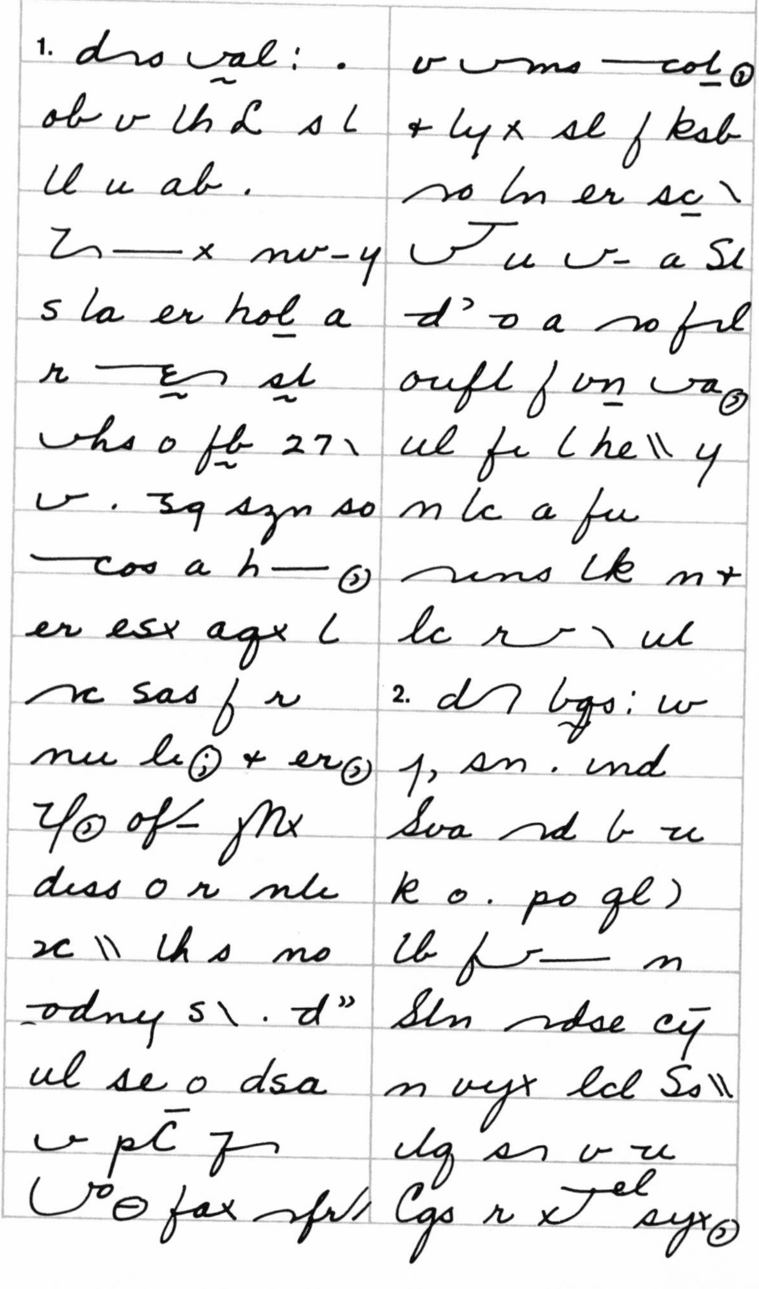

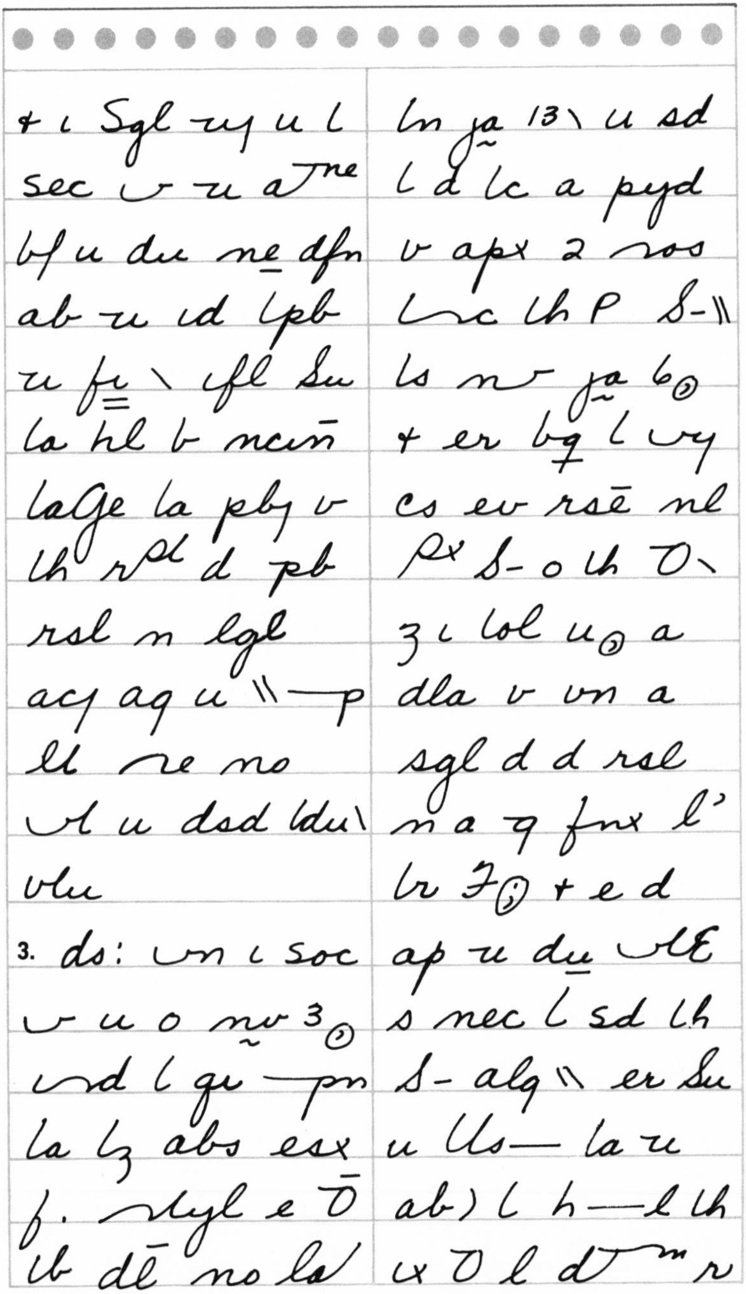

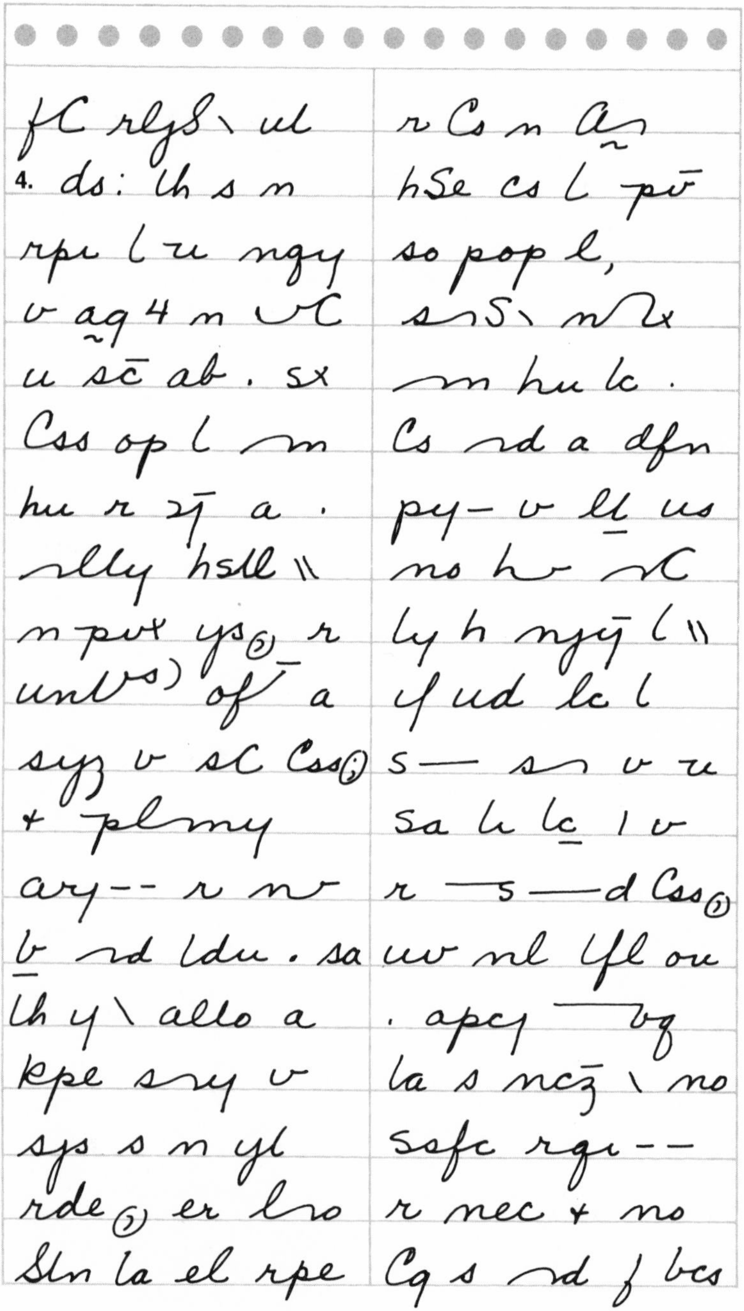

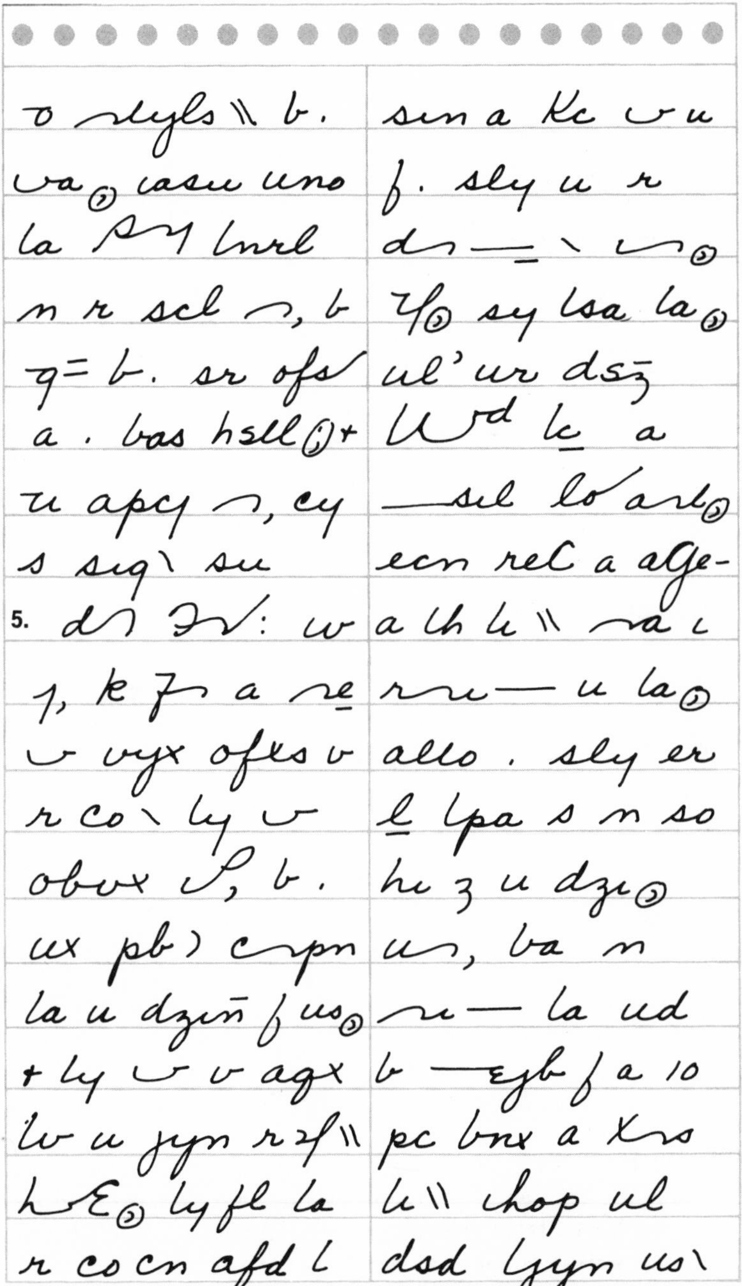

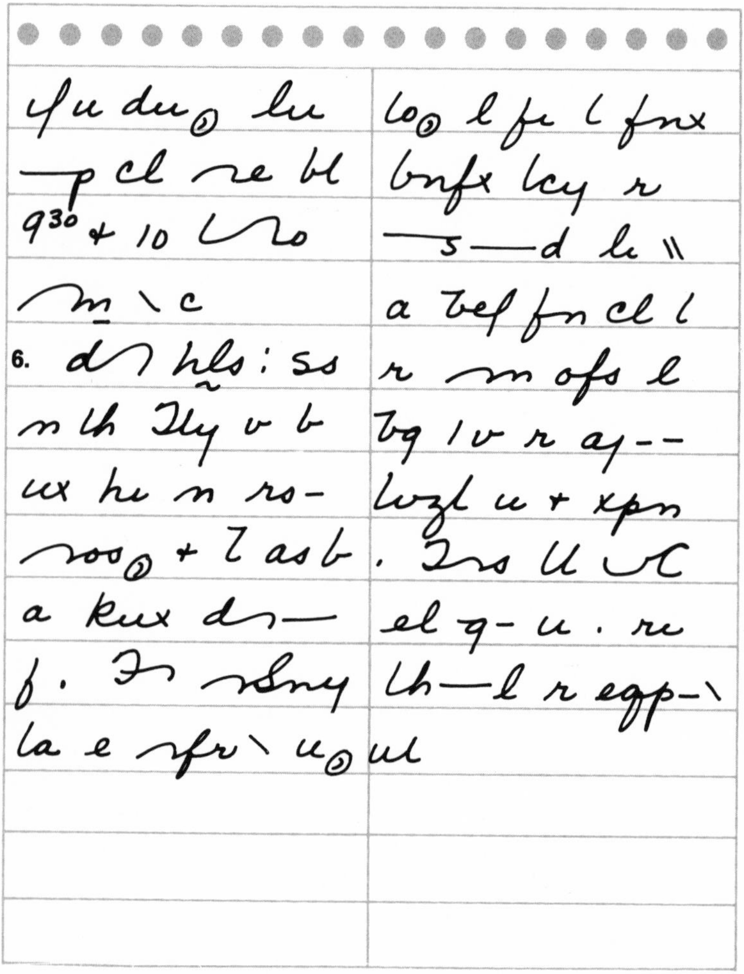

Key To Lesson 17

1. Dear Mrs. Wall: The object of this letter is to tell you about the tremendous inventory sale that we[2] are holding at our Elm Street warehouse on February 27. With the spring season so close at hand, we[4] are especially anxious

to make space for our new line; and we are, therefore, offering generous discounts on[6] our entire stock. (¶) This is no ordinary sale. The dresses you will see on display were purchased from world-famous[8] manufacturers of women's clothing, and they usually sell for considerably more than we are asking.[10] Whether you want a sport dress or a more formal outfit for evening wear, you will find it here. (¶) Why not take[12] a few minutes to come in and look around. Yours truly, *(130 words)*

2. Dear Mr. Banks: I have just seen the independent survey made by your committee on the poor quality to[2] be found in certain merchandise carried in various local stores. (¶) I think some of your charges are extremely[4] serious, and I strongly urge you to speak with your attorney before you do anything definite about[6] your idea to publish your findings. I feel sure that he will be inclined to agree that publication of this[8] report would probably result in legal action against you. (¶) Please let me know what you decide to do. Very[10] truly yours, *(102 words)*

3. Dear Sir: When I spoke with you on November 3, I made it quite plain that it was absolutely essential for[2] the material we ordered to be delivered no later than January 13. You said it would take[4] a period of approximately two months to make this particular shipment. (¶) It is now January[6] 6, and we are beginning to worry because we have received only partial shipment on this order. As I[8] told you, a delay of even a single day would result in a great financial loss to our firm; and we would[10] appreciate your doing whatever is necessary to speed this shipment along. (¶) We are sure you understand[12] that your ability to handle this initial order will determine our future relationship. Yours[14] truly, *(141 words)*

4. Dear Sir: This is in reply to your inquiry of August 4 in which you asked about the special courses open[2] to men who are stationed at the military hospital. (¶) In previous years, our university offered[4] a series of such courses; and

preliminary arrangements are now being made to do the same this year.[6] Although a complete summary of subjects is not yet ready, we are almost certain that we will repeat our[8] course in American history because it proved so popular last semester. Numerous men who took the[10] course made a definite point of letting us know how much they had enjoyed it. (¶) If you would like to spend some of your[12] spare time taking one of our splendid courses, you have only to fill out the application blank that is enclosed.[14] No specific requirements are necessary and no charge is made for books or materials. (¶) By the way, I[16] assume you know that permission to enroll in our school must be granted by the senior officer at the base[18] hospital; and your application must carry his signature. Sincerely yours, *(194 words)*

5. Dear Mr. Farmer: I have just come from a meeting with various officials of our company. They were obviously[2] impressed by the unusual publicity campaign that you designed for us, and they were very anxious[4] to have you join our staff. (¶) However, they feel that our company cannot afford to sign a contract with you[6] for the salary you are demanding. I am, therefore, sorry to say that, unless you are disposed toward taking[8] a slightly lower amount, we cannot reach an agreement at this time. (¶) May I remind you that, although the[10] salary we are willing to pay is not so high as you desire, you must bear in mind that you would be eligible[12] for a 10 percent bonus at Christmas time. (¶) I hope you will decide to join us. If you do, will you please call[14] me between 9:30 and 10:00 tomorrow morning. Cordially, *(151 words)*

6. Dear Mr. Hollis: Sales in this territory have been unusually high in recent months, and there has been a[2] continuous demand for the farm machinery that we manufacture. You, too, will find it financially[4] beneficial to carry our splendid line. (¶) A brief phone call to our main office will bring one of our agents to[6] visit you and explain the terms under which we will grant you the right to handle our equipment. Yours truly, *(79 words)*

Writing Assignment—Lesson 17

1. I thought you understood that it is usually customary to check the financial records before an initial order is sent on credit.

2. The officials of our hospital are desirous of thanking you for your gracious and generous help.

3. The speaker had nothing definite to say about the tremendous losses felt by various manufacturers in this territory.

4. Junior members of the American Library Club will receive a special bonus book by a world-famous author.

5. Thank you for the courteous answer to my inquiry concerning my spring supply of stationery.

6. We are sorry that you object to the manner in which we handled your previous order.

7. An inspection will probably show that the trouble with your machinery is not very serious.

8. We have had a continuous demand from numerous independent shop owners for additional display material.

Lesson 18

RULE 50 | **For the sounds of "nse" and "nsy" write a disjoined slant.**

You have learned that the final sounds of "er" and "ter' are represented by a slant that is joined to the letter or mark of punctuation that precedes it. In the present rule, however, you are instructed to write a disjoined slant – which simply means that it will not be joined to the letter or mark of punctuation that goes before it.

The word **assure,** as you know, is written *aSu* . If the sound of "nse" is added to this word to form *assurance,* you write a disjoined slant at the end of the outline: **assurance** *aSu/* . In the same way, the word **rely** is *rle* and you write **reliance** *rle/* .

Study these examples:

balance	*bl/*	**license**	*ls/*
announce	*a-/*	**allowance**	*al-/*
assistance	*ass/*	**since**	*s/*

insurance	nSu/	**correspondence**	Cs—/
convinced	kvT	**accordance**	aCd/
entrance	nT/	**expense**	xp/
remittance	rml/	**response**	rs/
convenience	kvn/	**financing**	fn/
confidence	kfd/	**experience**	xpy/
distance	ds/	**preference**	pF/

How will you form the plurals of these words? You will simply follow the rule for any outline that ends in a mark of punctuation and double the slant – as in **senses** s// ; **responses** rs// .

You write:

1. **reference** ______________ 2. **expenses** ______________

3. **attendance** ______________ 4. **conference** ______________

5. **chance** ______________ 6. **evidence** ______________

7. **difference** ______________ 8. **appearance** ______________

9. **instances** ______________ 10. **defense** ______________

11. **maintenance** ______________ 12. **influence** ______________

Confirmation:

1. rF/ 2. xp// 3. al—/ 4. kF/
5. C/ 6. evd/ 7. dF/ 8. ape/
9. ns// 10. df/ 11. mtn/ 12. nfu/

This sound of "nse" may also occur in the middle of a word. When it does, you will follow the same rule and write a disjoined slant.

Study these examples:

responsible  **principle** 

sponsored  **announcement** 

You write:

1. expensive ______________ **2. sincerely** ______________

3. compensation ______________ **4. responsibility** ______________

Confirmation:

1.  **2.**  **3.**  **4.** 

This rule also states that the disjoined slant will be used to represent the sound of "nsy"—the sound that is heard in *agency* or *fancy*. Thus: **agency**  ; **fancy**  ; **emergency**  ; **efficiency**  .

Read these sentences:

1. 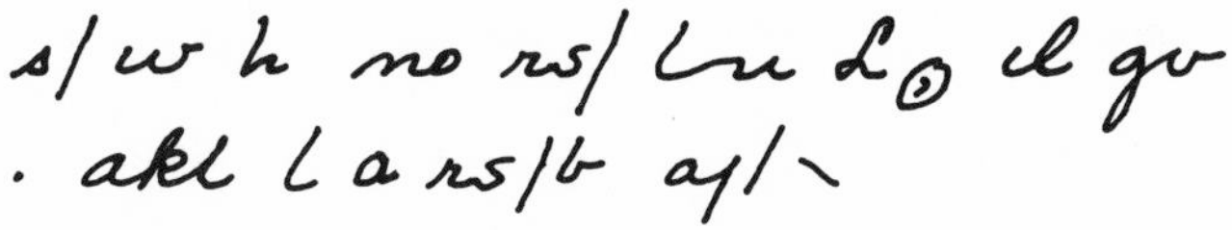

2. 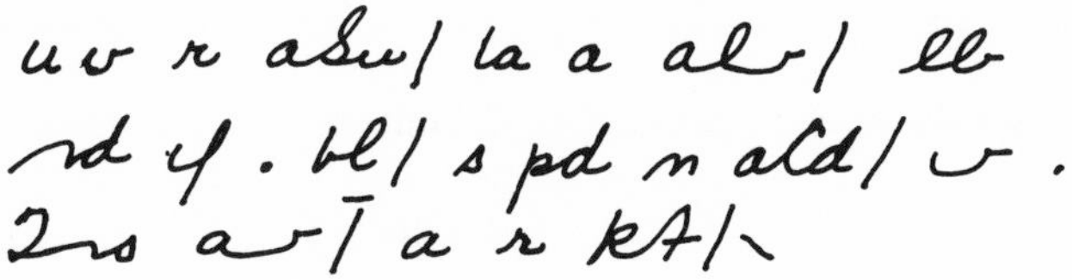

Key:

1. Since I have had no response to my letter, I will give the account to a responsible agency.

2. **You have our assurance that an allowance will be made if the balance is paid in accordance with the terms announced at our conference.**

RULE 51 | **Omit t after the sounds of "k, p, f, x"; omit pt after m.**

This rule teaches you how to handle such words as *act, instruct,* and *district* – words in which the sound of "k" is followed by *t*. Therefore, in compliance with the rule, you omit the *t* from the outline.

Study these examples:

acts	acs	**district**	dSc
instruct	nSc	**expect**	xpc
inspected	nsc̄	**factory**	fcy
project	pjc	**protect**	plc
affect	afc	**practical**	pccl
neglected	ngc̄	**practically**	pccl
respect	rsc	**conflict**	kfc
connected	kc̄	**exactly**	xcl

You write:

1. products ________ **2. contact** ________

3. fact ________ **4. effect** ________

5. practice ________ **6. selected** ________

7. exact ________ **8. conducting** ________

Confirmation:

1. pdcs 2. klc 3. fc 4. efc
5. pcs 6. slc̄ 7. xc 8. kdc

Similarly, you are instructed to eliminate *t* after the sounds of "p, f," and "x."

Study these examples:

except	xp	**left**	lf
adopt	adp	**gift**	gf
accepting	xp	**next**	nx
acceptable	xpb	**text**	tx

You write:

1. accept ______ **2. draft** ______

3. kept ______ **4. swiftly** ______

5. context ______ **6. pretext** ______

Confirmation:

1. xp 2. df 3. cp 4. sfl
5. klx 6. plx

The second part of this rule instructs you in the handling of such words as *attempt* and *prompt*. Both the *p* and *t* are omitted and the outline ends with *m*.

Study these examples:

prompt	pm	**attempt**	am
exempt	xm	**attempted**	am̄

RULE 52 | **When the nature of an outline is such that the capitalization rule cannot be applied, write r for the medial sound of a vowel + "r."**

You know that **chat** is *Cl* and **shot** is *Sl*. You also know that when the sound of a vowel plus "r" occurs in the middle of a word, you capitalize the preceding letter. But what if the letter preceding these sounds is already capitalized – for example: <u>*chart*</u> or <u>*short*</u>? The present rule says that you will simply write *r*.

Study these examples:

shortly	*Srll*	**charter**	*Cr/*
sharp	*Srp*	**church**	*CrC*
short	*Srl*	**chart**	*Crl*
shortage	*Srlj*	**natural**	*nCrl*
shorthand	*Srlh—*	**naturally**	*nCrl*

In the same way, since you cannot apply the capitalization rule to such words as *standard* or *central*, you will write **standard** *2— rd* and **central** *s- rl*.

Brief Forms

without	*wo*	**whom**	*h-*
collect	*cc*	**known**	*no*
sample	*sa-*	**conclusion**	*kclj*

once, circumstance	c/	individual, individually	ndv
describe, description	des		

Abbreviations

post office	po	memorandum	memo
figure	fg	inch	in
page	p	total	tol
parcel post	pp		

Additional Words

described	des̄	performance	pfm/
describing	des̲	individuals	ndvs
descriptive	desv	samples	sams
collection	ccj	sampled	sam̄
collected	cc̄	pages	ps
importance	ip/	figures	fgs
inches	ins	figured	fḡ

Reading Exercises

1. rd) —ān: i
s/el rGl. fc la
u S- dd n reC
u \\ n Cc r rCds
unl la. dfk
ocT cs edd nv
, Kc aD' l; fu \
aT S- as n b
s- Fr r fcy b
pp + uc xpc
l l are Srll \ ul
2. drs Gdn: a.
Kcly v r di brz
me f a nu
chns hsll er
hpe l av/ la.
rs/ l r apl z
vn g/ ln e h
hop \\ n.6 ros
s/e F, op r di
f f — — ev
rsē kT bys lol O
hfa) dl// \ lh
me n nl k
F Dy a/ll +
ogs b lso F
ndv slgns hu
obvx rcgnz .
cp/v lh Ul
pjc \\ . gf u ga
n my v u
sn l q a lq va
Ud hp l fn/
. xp/ v bld lh
—s—d hsll \
u Sd fl v
pd v. ass/
uv gv \\ lq u

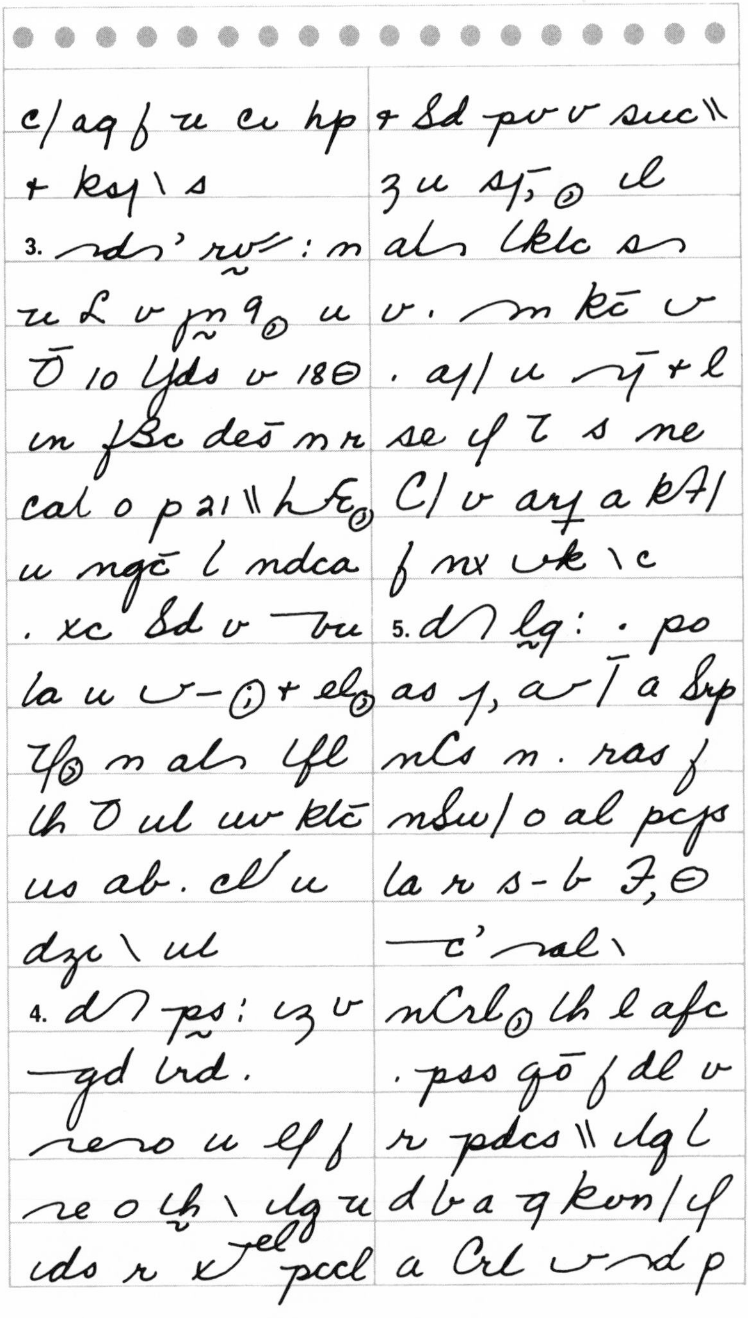

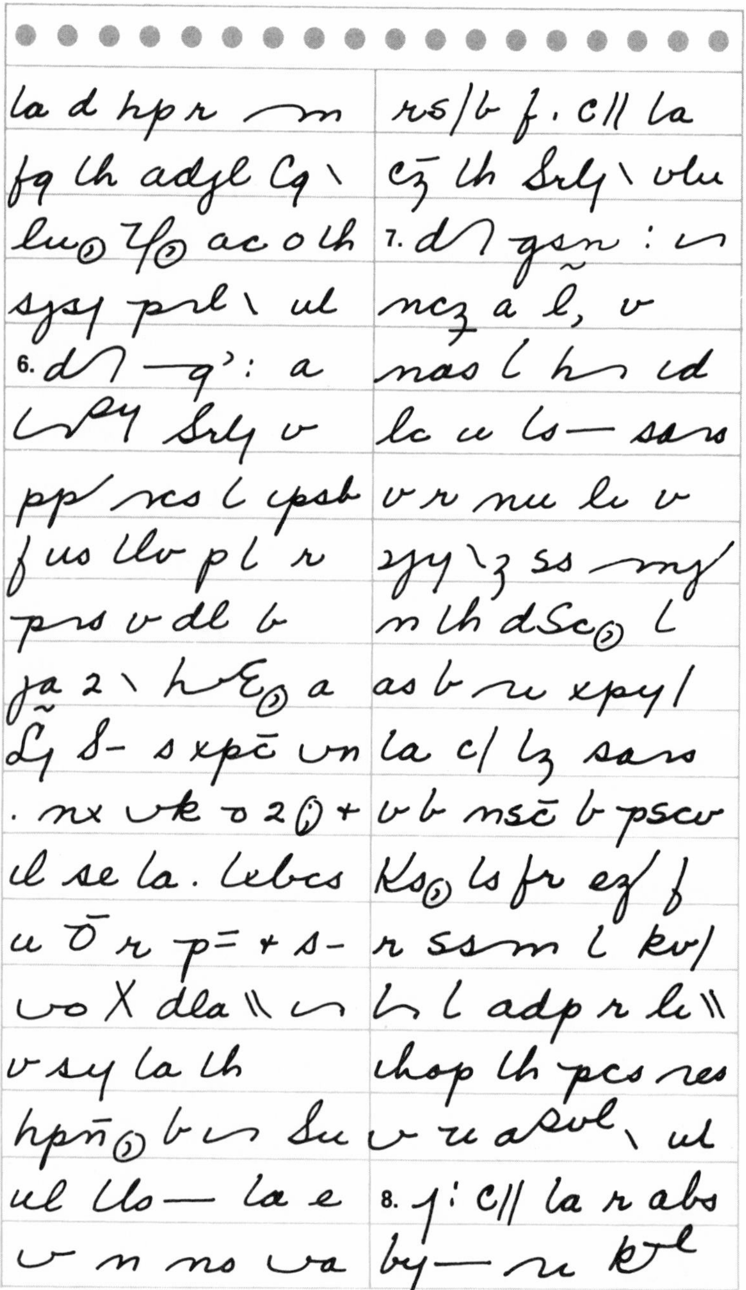

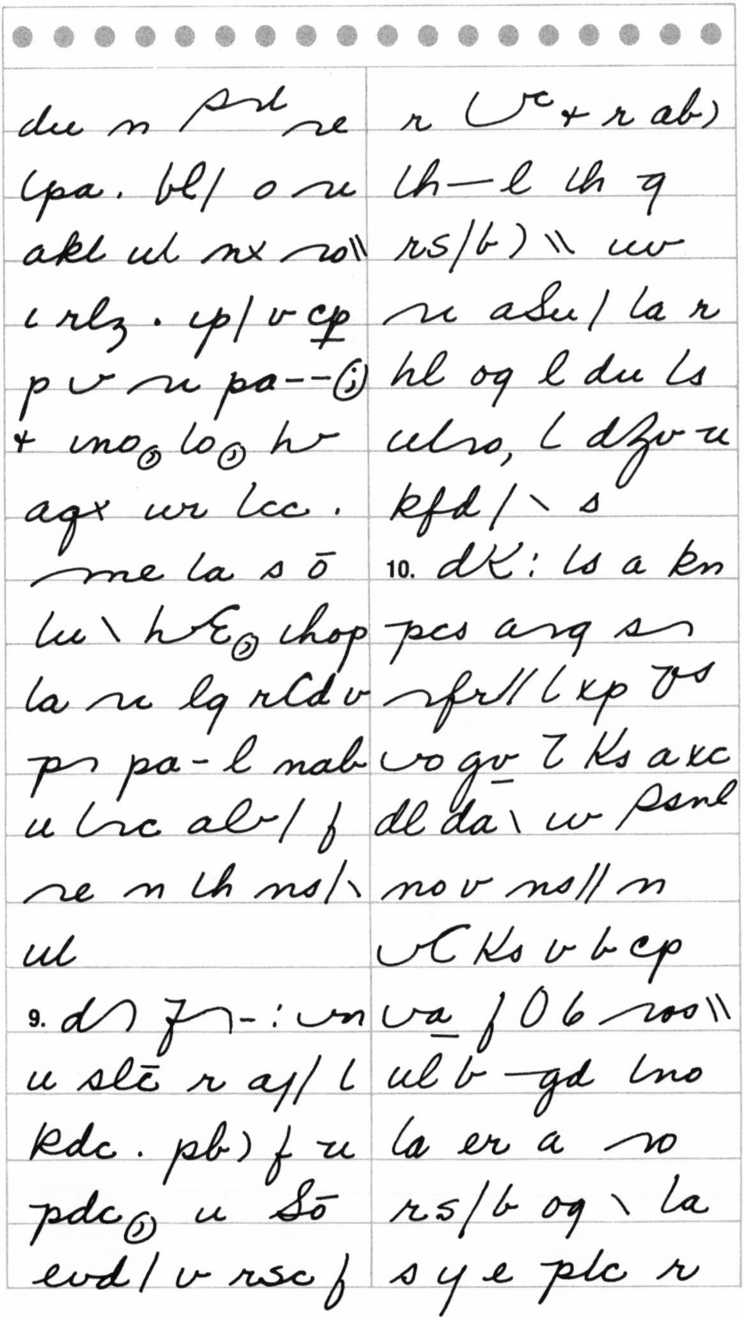

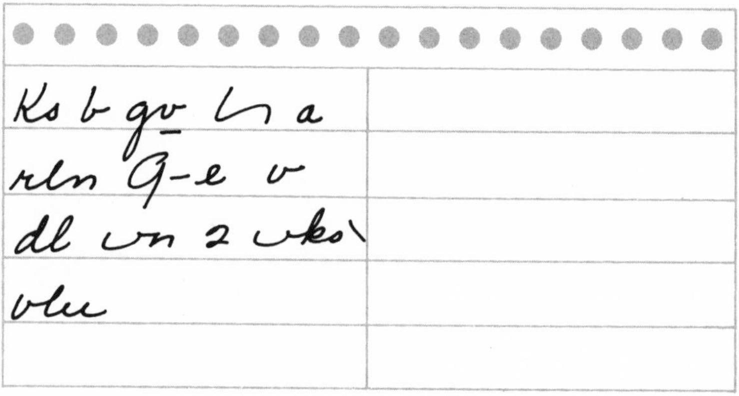

Key to Lesson 18

1. My dear Mr. Allen: I sincerely regret the fact that your shipment did not reach you. (¶) In checking our records, I note[2] that the difficulty occurred because we did not have the correct address listed for you. Another shipment[4] has now been sent from our factory by parcel post, and you can expect it to arrive shortly. Yours truly,[6] *(60 words)*

2. Dear Mrs. Gardner: At the conclusion of our drive to raise money for a new children's hospital, we are happy[2] to announce that the response to our appeal was even greater than we had hoped. (¶) In the six months since we first[4] opened our drive for funds, we have received contributions totaling over half a million dollars. This money not[6] only came from large agencies and organizations, but also from individual citizens who[8] obviously recognized the importance of this worthwhile project. (¶) The gift you gave in memory of your son will[10] go a long way toward helping to finance the expense of building this splendid hospital. You should feel very proud[12] of the assistance you have given. (¶) Thank you once again for your kind help and consideration. Sincerely, *(139 words)*

3. My dear Miss Rivers: In your letter of June 9, you ordered 10 yards of 18-inch fabric described in our[2] catalog on page 21. (¶) However, you neglected to indicate the exact shade of blue that you want; and[4] we will, therefore, not attempt to fill this order until you have contacted us about the color you desire.[6] Yours truly, *(62 words)*

4. Dear Mr. Price: I was very glad to read the memorandum you left for me on Thursday. I think your ideas[2] are extremely practical and should prove very successful. (¶) As you suggested, I will attempt to contact[4] some of the men connected with the agency you mentioned and will see if there is any chance of arranging[6] a conference for next week. Cordially, *(67 words)*

5. Dear Mr. Long: The post office has just announced a sharp increase in the rates for insurance on all packages[2] that are sent by first-class mail. Naturally, this will affect the prices quoted for delivery of our products[4]. (¶) I think it would be a great convenience if a chart were made up that would help our men figure this additional[6] charge. Will you, therefore, act on this suggestion promptly. Yours truly, *(71 words)*

6. Dear Mr. Glass: A temporary shortage of paper makes it impossible for us to live up to our promise[2] of delivery by January 2. However, a large shipment is expected within the next week[4] or two; and I will see that the textbooks you ordered are printed and sent without extra delay. (¶) I am very[6] sorry that this happened, but I am sure you will understand that we were in no way responsible for the[8] circumstances that caused this shortage. Very truly yours, *(89 words)*

7. Dear Mr. Grayson: I am enclosing a list of names to whom I would like you to send samples of our new line of[2] stationery. As sales manager in this district, it has been my experience that once these samples have been[4] inspected by prospective customers, it is far easier for our salesmen to convince them to adopt our[6] line. (¶) I

hope this practice meets with your approval. Yours truly, *(70 words)*

8. Gentlemen: Circumstances that are absolutely beyond my control do not permit me to pay the balance[2] on my account until next month. (¶) I realize the importance of keeping up with my payments; and I know, too,[4] how anxious you are to collect the money that is owed to you. However, I hope that my long record of prompt[6] payment will enable you to make allowance for me in this instance. Yours truly, *(75 words)*

9. Dear Mr. Freeman: When you selected our agency to conduct the publicity for your product, you showed[2] evidence of respect for our work and our ability to handle this great responsibility. (¶) You have my[4] assurance that our whole organization will do its utmost to deserve your confidence. Sincerely, *(58 words)*

10. Dear Customer: It is a common practice among some manufacturers to accept orders without giving[2] their customers an exact delivery date. I have personally known of instances in which customers[4] have been kept waiting for over six months. (¶) You will be glad to know that we are a more responsible organization.[6] That is why we protect our customers by giving them a written guarantee of delivery within[8] two weeks. Very truly yours, *(85 words)*

Writing Assignment – Lesson 18

1. In accordance with your memorandum, I have attempted to contact a company from whom we can charter a bus for the convenience of those individuals who attend our next conference.

2. You have my assurance that, once you have shown evidence of financial responsibility in the form of insurance, I will instruct our agency to issue your license.

3. It has been my experience that, except in unusual circumstances, compensation is paid promptly for the type of accident you describe.

4. I did not realize the importance of the announcement you made in the memorandum received by the district office.

5. In figuring my total balance, you neglected to make a correct allowance for the shortage that occurred.

6. Will you accept some free samples of our principal products?

7. This is the man without whom I could not have conducted such a successful campaign.

8. We ask your assistance in helping us collect the amount that is due.

Lesson 19

RULE 53	For the suffixes "ful and fully" and for the final sound of "fy," write *f*.

Study these examples:

careful	*caf*	respectfully	*rscf*
useful	*usf*	beautifully	*blf*
*hopeful	*hopf*	notify	*nlf*
wonderful	*⌣— rf*	qualify	*qlf̲*
carefully	*caf*	justified	*jsf̄*

*Note that the long vowel is retained in this word to avoid conflict with the outline for the word **helpful** *hpf*.

You write:

1. respectful ____________
2. colorful ____________
3. beautiful ____________
4. colorfully ____________
5. fearfully ____________
6. specify ____________
7. qualified ____________
8. simplified ____________

Confirmation:

1. rscf 2. cLf 3. blf 4. cLf
5. fef 6. ssf 7. glf̄ 8. sspf̄

In Lesson 18 you learned that *t* is omitted after the sounds of "k, p, f," and "x." Thus, **fact** fc ; **gift** gf ; **next** nx .

The following rule is similar to this and deals with the dropping of *d* when it comes before certain sounds.

RULE 54 | Omit d before "m" and "v."

Study these examples:

admit	aml	**advisory**	avzy
admittance	aml/	**advised**	avz̄
admission	ay	**advisable**	avzb
admire	amr	**advancement**	av/-
advise	avz	**advanced**	av/̄
advice	avs	**advances**	av//

RULE 55 | For the sounds of "inter" and "enter," write a capital N .

Study these examples:

enter	n	**interstate**	Nsa
entertainment	Ntn-	**interrupt**	Np
interested	N,-	**uninteresting**	uN,

You write:

1. entered ____________ **2. entered** ____________

3. internal ____________ **4. interesting** ____________

5. interests ____________ **6. international** ____________

Confirmation:

1. n̄ **2.** N **3.** Nnl **4.** N,

5. N,, **6.** Nnyl

Notice that this rule refers specifically to the sounds of "inter" and "enter"—<u>not</u> to "intra, intri," or "intro." These latter sounds, you will recall, were incorporated into the rule dealing with the writing of capital *T* for medial "tr" in such words as **intrastate** nTsa ; **intricate** nTcl ; **introduce** nTds ; **introduction** nTdc .

You have learned to write a disjoined slant to represent the sounds of "nse" and "nsy" in such words as **insurance** nSu/ and **agency** aj/ . In the following rule, you will learn that s/ also represents a certain sound.

RULE 56 | For the sounds of "self" and "selves," write s/ .

Study these examples:

self	s/	**yourself**	us/
self-interest	s/n,	**itself**	ts/
myself	ms/	**himself**	hs/
herself	Hs/	**self-addressed**	s/aD,

You are also instructed to write s/ for the sound of "selves." In other words, it is not necessary to double the mark of punctuation to indicate the formation of a plural. Thus, **themselves** ts/ and **ourselves** rs/ . The only exception to this is the word **yourselves** which is written us// to avoid conflict with **yourself** us/ . In all other examples of this rule, there can be no confusion because words in this group exist only in the singular or plural form – never both. For example, ms/ can only be read as **myself** because there is no such word *myselves*. Similarly, you will know that rs/ is **ourselves** because there is no singular form for this word.

Brief Forms

move	mv	**auto**	A
perhaps	pps	**throughout**	Tuo
entitle	ntl		

Abbreviations

mile	mi	north	N
railroad	rr	south	S
railway	ry	east	E
mortgage	mg	west	W
associate	asso	feet, foot	ft

Additional Words

grateful	gf	automotive	Av
moving	mv	automatic	Atc
moved	mv	automobile	Abl
movement	mv–	automatically	Atcl
removed	rmv	entitled	ntl
removal	rmvl	entitles	ntls
removing	rmv	associated	asso
movers	mv	association	asso
northern	Nrn	associations	assos
eastern	Ern	railroads	rrs
southern	Srn	mortgagee	mge
western	Wrn	miles	mis

Reading Exercises

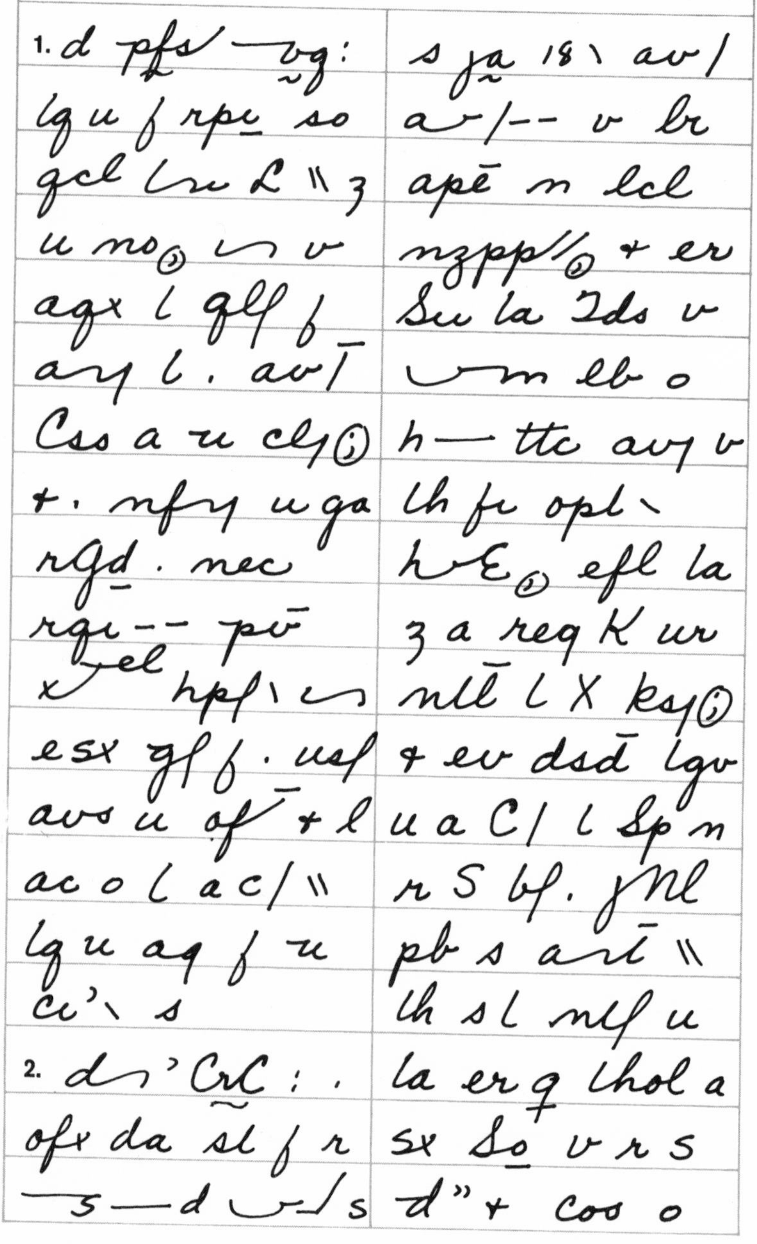

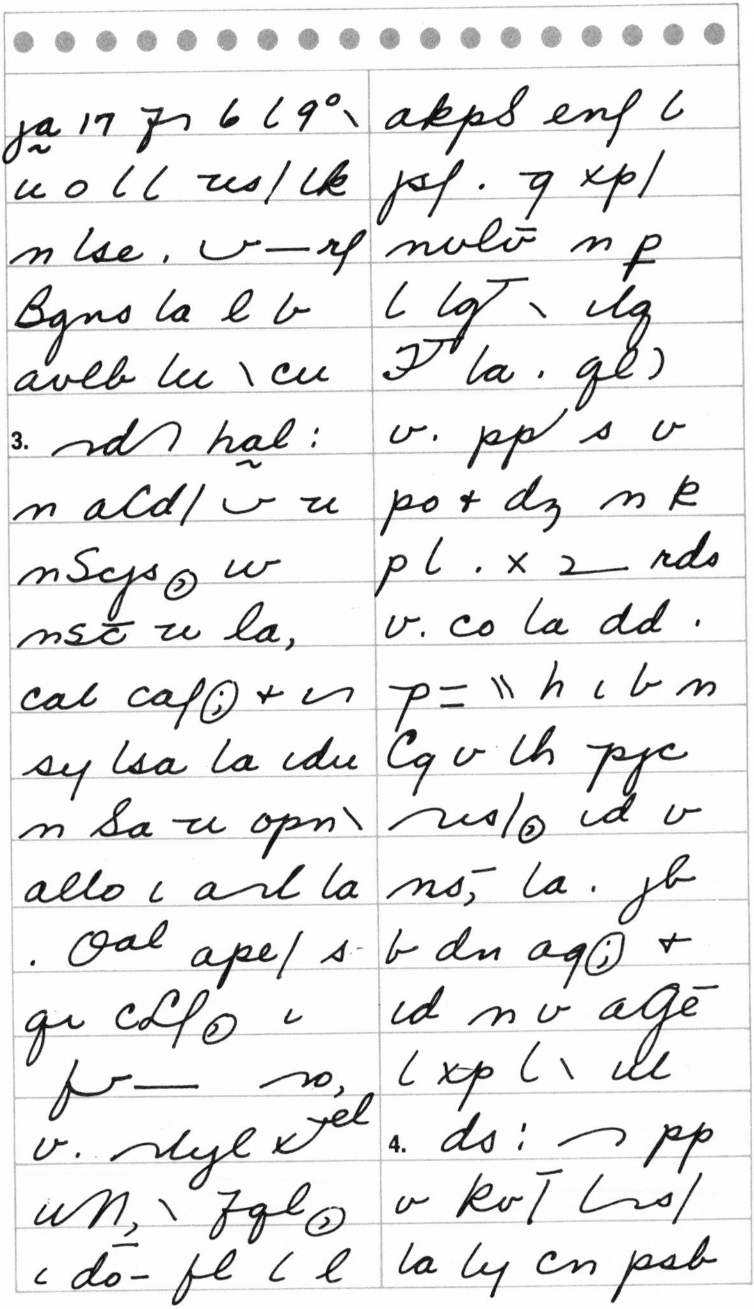

afd a nu
Arbl \ v u
dn. sa lq?
v u lol rus/
la a nu cr s
lo xp/v ?? yn
20 n a r
Sor + ll
us xpn h r
l ⊖ pa- —pn
rcol l ez lon
a bl nu cr f
rlvl ll me\
vl ur he ③
lc r a.
v—rf nu
rdls la v
7, b dē 7.
fcy \ se f

rus/ h e v
Kbin caf
KScy v bu)
v l" u ra
lso fl 7e lsc
r rep f a
d mSy rd\
af nl a fu
rus ② ul
Us— y 1s v
Arbl onl/ Tus
. c/ v b sa
la lh cr s so
ez l h—l la
l lro dis
ls/\ uvl
5. drs dS: pps
uv fgln la
pa- o u bl

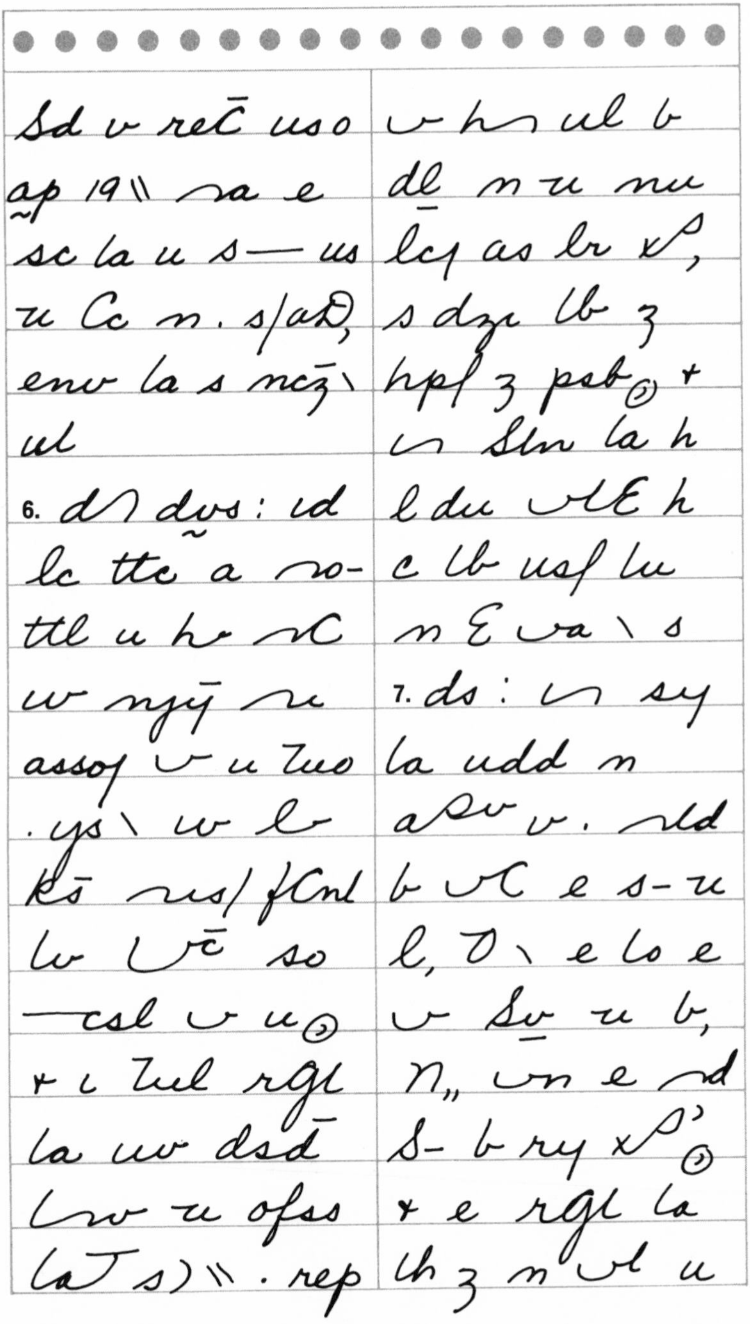

v = \\ l avyd
ne sC E/ n.
fC(3) l u caf
Ssf u pA/ n
rGd l. m/
n vC S- s
lb rd \ ul
8. d/ Ve: w
lc̄ a s p℮))
n vC u ra
b N; z a psb
sc f u nu
—p- \ / v lz
p℮)) s ab 5
rus N v. s)
+. J lus a
Srl ds/ l. U\
bo r lcā vn
a H fl v. m

hu a + vn a
fu rus v.
rr \\ c lls—
la. k) t, co
hols. rlq o
lh l— + sf,
la u Klc l
f F nfy \\
a L flos gv
dlē deso v
. p℮)) \ ul
9. f: lh s lnlf
u la w rs-l
rō F, 59 S
gl) rd l 130
E s/ sl \\
lu —p G u
rCds l ndca
ru nu aD'

so la ic b Su	
Z lb no Npj	
n. dl v ru	
sub l u	
rol raq `	
ul	

Key To Lesson 19

1. Dear Professor Blank: Thank you for replying so quickly to my letter. (¶) As you know, I am very anxious to[2] qualify for admission to the advanced courses at your college; and the information you gave regarding[4] the necessary requirements proved extremely helpful. I am especially grateful for the useful advice[6] you offered and will act on it at once. (¶) Thank you again for your kindness. Sincerely, *(75 words)*

2. Dear Miss Church: The official date set for our splendid winter sale is January 18. Advance announcements[2] have already appeared in local newspapers, and we are sure that thousands of women will be on hand to take[4] advantage of this fine opportunity. However, we feel that as a regular customer you are[6] entitled to extra consideration; and we have decided to give you a chance to shop in our store before[8] the general public is admitted. (¶) This is to notify you that we are going to hold a special showing[10] of our sale dresses and coats on January 17 from six to nine o'clock. You owe it to yourself[12] to come in to see the wonderful bargains that will be available to you. Cordially yours, *(137 words)*

3. My dear Mr. Hall: In accordance with your instructions, I have inspected your latest catalog carefully;[2] and I am sorry to say that I do not share your opinion. Although I admit that the overall appearance[4] is quite colorful, I found most of the material extremely uninteresting. Frankly, I don't feel[6] it will accomplish enough to justify the great expense involved in putting it together. I think further[8] that the quality of the paper is very poor and does not come up to the usual standards of the company[10] that did the printing. (¶) Had I been in charge of this project myself, I would have insisted that the job be done[12] again; and I would not have agreed to accept it. Yours truly, *(131 words)*

4. Dear Sir: Many people have convinced themselves that they cannot possibly afford a new automobile. Have you[2]

done the same thing? Have you told yourself that a new car is too expensive? (¶) Why not stop in at our showroom and let us explain[4] how our time-payment plan makes it easy to own a beautiful new car for relatively little[6] money. While you are here, look around at the wonderful new models that have just been delivered from the[8] factory. See for yourself how we have combined careful construction with beauty of line. (¶) You may also feel free to[10] ask our representative for a demonstration ride. After only a few miles, you will understand why millions[12] of automobile owners throughout the country have been saying that this car is so easy to handle that[14] it almost drives itself. Yours very truly, *(148 words)*

5. Dear Mrs. Dash: Perhaps you have forgotten that payment on your bill should have reached us on April 19. (¶) May we[2] ask that you send us your check in the self-addressed envelope that is enclosed. Yours truly, *(35 words)*

6. Dear Mr. Davis: I would like to take a moment to tell you how much I have enjoyed my association[2] with you throughout the years. I have always considered myself fortunate to have worked so closely with you, and I truly[4] regret that you have decided to move your offices to another city. (¶) The representative[6] with whom you will be dealing in your new location has already expressed his desire to be as helpful as[8] possible, and I am certain that he will do whatever he can to be useful to you in every way.[10] Sincerely, *(103 words)*

7. Dear Sir: I am sorry that you did not approve of the method by which we sent your last order. We thought we were[2] serving your best interests when we made shipment by railway express, and we regret that this was not what you wanted.[4] (¶) To avoid any such error in the future, will you carefully specify your preference in regard[6] to the manner in which shipment is to be made. Yours truly, *(70 words)*

8. Dear Mr. Bright: I have looked at some properties in which you may be interested as a possible site for[2] your

new plant. One of these properties is about five miles north of the city and the other lies a short distance[4] to the west. Both are located within a hundred feet of the main highway and within a few miles of the railroad.[6] (¶) I understand that the County Trust Company holds the mortgage on this land and suggest that you contact them[8] for further information. (¶) A letter follows giving detailed descriptions of the properties. Yours truly, *(97 words)*

9. Gentlemen: This is to notify you that I have recently moved from 59 South Quality Road to[2] 130 East Center Street. (¶) Will you please change your records to indicate my new address so that I can be[4] sure there will be no interruption in the delivery of my subscription to your monthly magazine. Yours[6] truly, *(61 words)*

Writing Assignment—Lesson 19

1. Membership in our automobile association will entitle you to a subscription to our interesting and useful magazine.

2. I respectfully request that you give me a chance to justify your confidence in me.

3. Our President accepted a position with an international firm on the West Coast and he will be moving there shortly.

4. I strongly advise that you carefully discuss the internal organization of the company among yourselves and notify me of your decision.

5. If you will forward your request in the self-addressed envelope that is enclosed, we will send you a colorful folder that describes our beautiful new automatic washer.

6. We would like to be helpful in this instance, but although we greatly admire the man you mentioned, we do not consider ourselves qualified to offer advice on his plan.

7. Railroads throughout the country have announced a reduction of fares for all interstate travel.

Lesson 20

Let's examine some words in which two vowels occur together but have only one sound. For example, *lease, tail, built.* In these words, the sound of only one vowel is heard. However, there are some words in which two vowels occur together – both of which are pronounced: *actual, fuel, graduate, ruin.* It is to this latter group of vowel sounds that this next rule applies.

RULE 57 | **When a word contains two medial pronounced consecutive vowels, the first vowel sound is written.**

Study these examples:

annual		**actual**	
mutual		**dual**	
fuel		**ruin**	

gradual	gdul	**trial**	tl
poet	pol	**manual**	-mul
diameter	di/	**diet**	dil

When an outline ends in a vowel, write the final vowel omitting any vowel sound that precedes it: **graduate** gda ; **create** ca ; **radio** rdo ; **area** aa .

Here is a summary of the various rules concerned with the writing and/or omission of vowels.

1. Write all initial and final vowels: **edge** ej ; **data** dla ; **value** vlu ; **item** is .
2. Omit all medial short vowels: **sell** sl ; **check** Cc .
3. Omit long vowels in words of more than one syllable unless covered by a specific rule: **music** -zc ; **prevail** pvl .
4. When "ing" or "ed" are added to a root word that contains a long vowel, retain vowel: **sailing** sal ; **reached** rec .
5. When the root word outline ends in a vowel, retain vowel when suffix is added: **reliable** rlib ; **lightly** lil ; **happiest** hpe, ; **evaluation** evlu ; **myself** -is/ ; **fairness** fa' ; **compliance** kpi/ ; **gaiety** ga) .
6. When a long vowel is followed by a sound that is represented by a mark of punctuation, retain this long

vowel in outline: **variety** vri) ; **science** si/ ; **client** ci- ; **remind** rmi- ; **acquaint** aqa-.

7. When a word contains two pronounced consecutive vowels, one long and one short, the first vowel is written: **ruin** run ; **gradual** gdul ; **poet** pol .

8. When an outline ends in a vowel, write the final vowel and omit any vowel that precedes it: **graduate** gda ; **create** ca .

There is one sound in our language that has no alphabetic representation – the sound of "zh" heard in *visual, casual, treasure*. It is to this sound that the following rule applies.

RULE 58 | For the sound of "zh," write z .

Study these examples:

casual	czul	**visual**	vzul
casualty	czul)	**treasury**	Tzy
pleasurable	pzb	**treasurer**	Tz/
leisurely	lzl	**measuring**	mz/-

You write:

1. pleasure ______ **2. enclosure** ______

3. treasure ______ **4. seizure** ______

5. enclosures ______ **6. measured** ______

7. measures ______ **8. treasured** ______

Confirmation:

1. -pz/ 2. ncz/ 3. Tz/ 4. sz/
5. ncz// 6. -z/ 7. -z// 8. Tz/

RULE 59 | For the sound of "sub," write s.

Study these examples:

submitted	smt	subsequently	ssq-l
substantial	ssx	substitute	sstu
subsistence	sss/	subtract	sTc

You write:

1. submit ____________ 2. substantially ____________

3. subsequent ____________ 4. substitution ____________

5. subway ____________ 6. submitting ____________

Confirmation:

1. smt 2. ssx 3. ssq- 4. ssty
5. swa 6. smt

And now for the final rule in *Speedwriting* Shorthand.

RULE 60 | For the sound of "trans," write T.

Study these examples:

transaction	Tacj	transferred	Tf-
transmission	Tmj	transportation	Tptj
transcription	Tcpj	transit	Tt

You write:

1. transcript ____________ 2. transfer ____________

3. transferring ____________ 4. transport ____________

Confirmation:

1. Tcp 2. Tf 3. Tf- 4. Tpt

Brief Forms

declare dec pull pu pupil pup

Abbreviations

miscellaneous	msc	bureau	Bu
pound	lb	corporation	corp
superintendent	supt	square	sq
administrate, administration	ad		

Additional Words

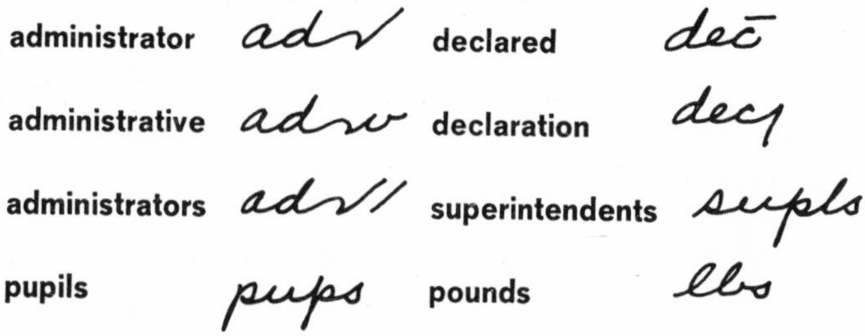

Reading Exercises

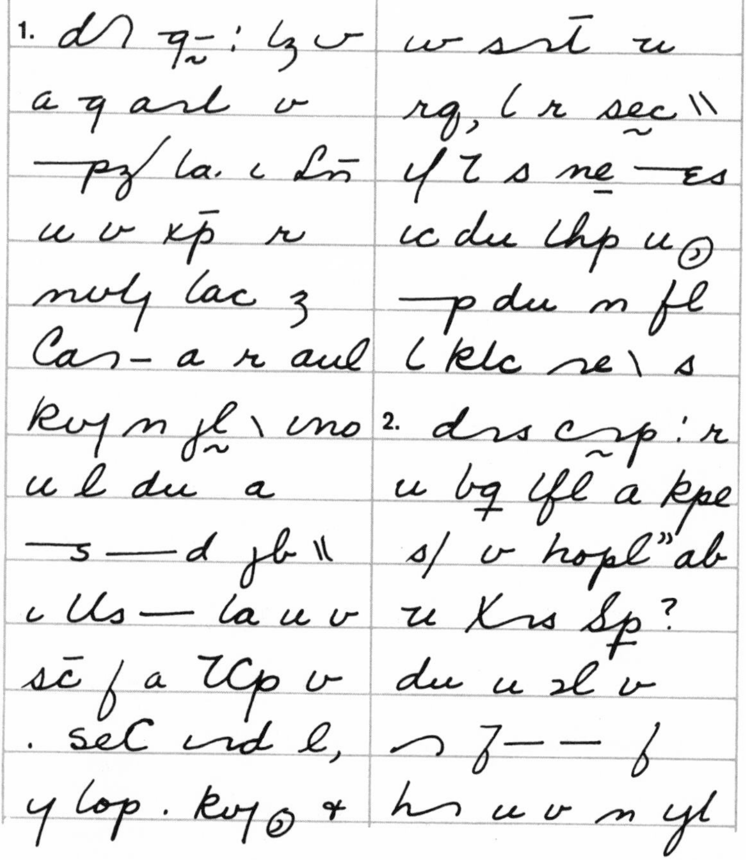

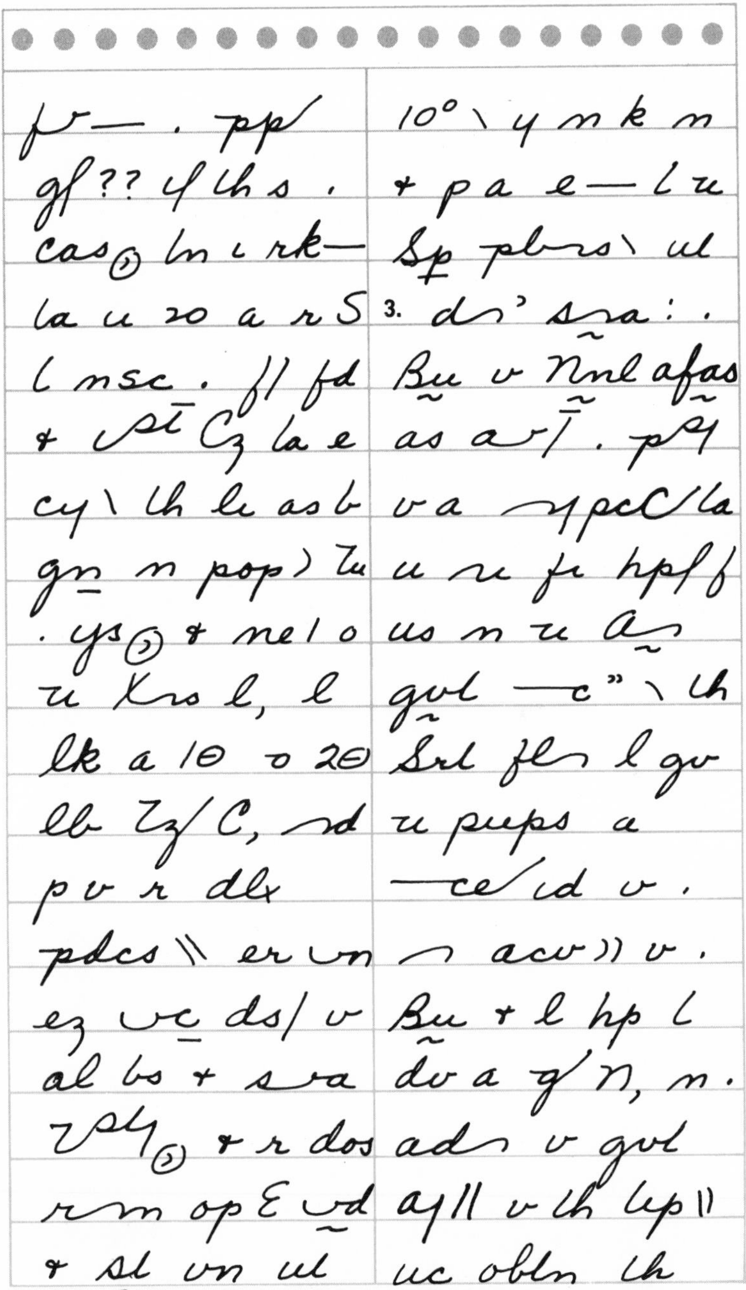
3.

fls b ssp D
u rg, l. ofs
v. supl v
scls n u aa\
cu

4. d Fq: . alC
Crl l gv u
vzul evd/ v.
fcs cga u kSn
. xcs cSu b r
corp du . p,
18 ys\ z uc se(.)
Tz nl a gdul
rz n. aul
dvd—— pd
br xchol// n.
F, 10 ys(;) b n.
pyd s/ ln(.) r
xc as db n
vlu v a ssg-
nCs n. sz v.
dvd—— dec \\
z fr z . fC s
kSn(.) er nolō
n usc Tacys
la l ca vn
no ssx pfls f
us\ f lh rzn(.)
cdu n hzla l
avz u lb r xc
z a saf nvs-f
u sv \ us

5. ds: lh s n
rs/ l. L e rsē
Fs u n vC
u d ngy
rGd r Cgs f
lpru r-ls \\

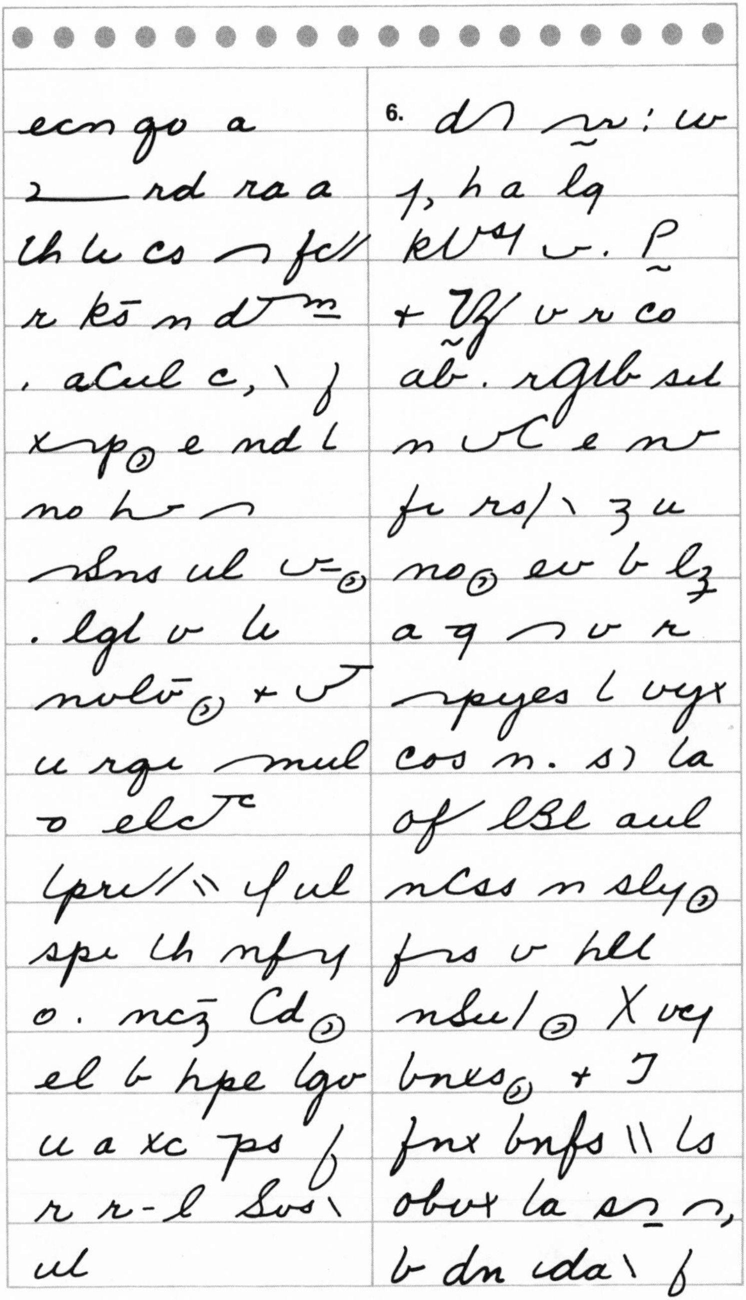

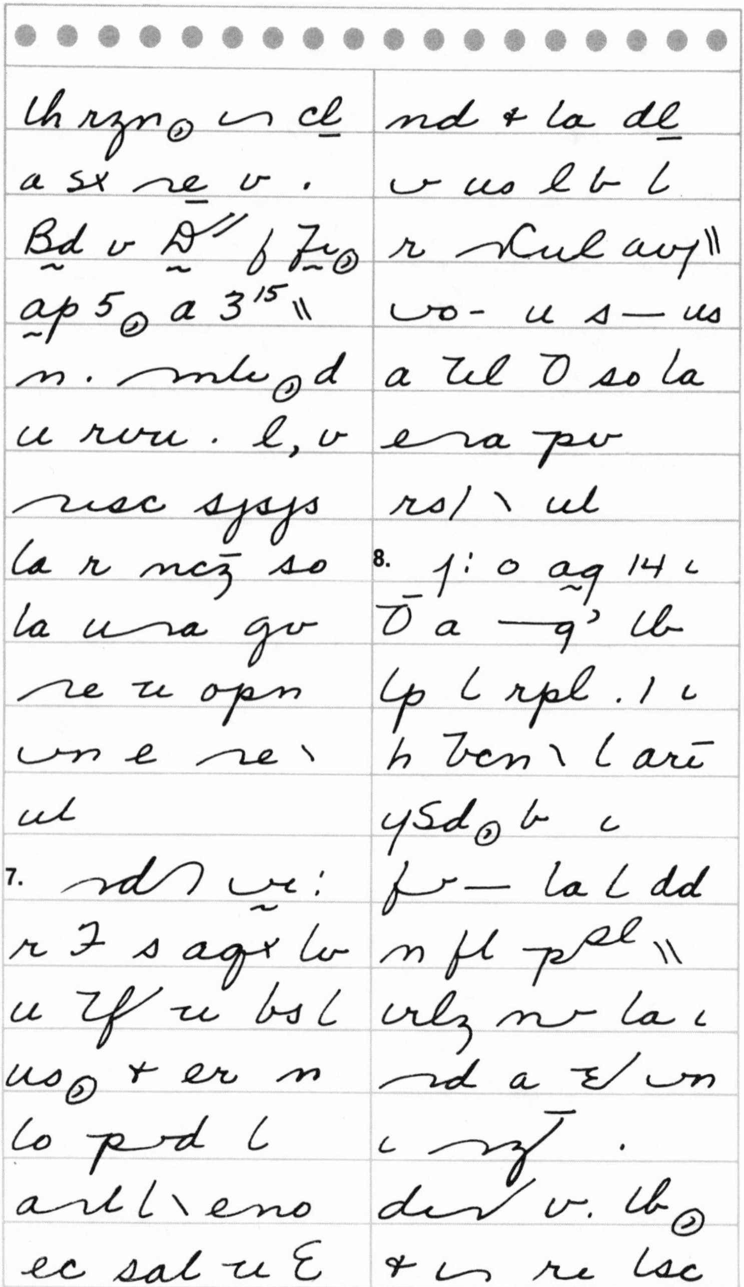
7.
8.

T sa cb
dn\ cd dpl
ap ne sjsj
uc nc la l
sv ne .
adjl xp/ v
O a nu/\
s

Key to Lesson 20

1. Dear Mr. Grant: It was with a great amount of pleasure that I learned you have accepted our invitation to[2] act as chairman at our annual convention in July. I know you will do a splendid job. (¶) I understand[4] that you have asked for a transcript of the speech I made last year to open the convention, and I have submitted[6] your request to our Secretary. (¶) If there is anything else I can do to help you, please do not fail to contact[8] me. Sincerely, *(83 words)*

2. Dear Mrs. Camp: Are you beginning to feel a complete sense of hopelessness about your Christmas shopping? Do you[2] still have many friends for whom you have not yet found the proper gift? (¶) If this is the case, then I recommend that you[4] stop at our store to inspect the fancy food and imported cheese that we carry. This line has been gaining in[6] popularity through the years, and anyone on your Christmas list will welcome a one- or two-pound treasure chest made[8] up of our delicious products. (¶) We are within easy walking distance of all bus and subway transportation,[10] and our doors remain open every Wednesday and Saturday evening until ten o'clock. Why not come in and[12] put an end to your shopping problems. Yours truly, *(128 words)*

3. Dear Miss Small: The Bureau of Internal Affairs has announced the preparation of a motion picture that you[2] might find helpful for use in your American Government classes. This short film will give your pupils a clearer[4] idea of the many activities of the Bureau and will help to develop a greater interest[6] in the administration of government agencies of this type. (¶) You can obtain this film by simply directing[8] your request to the Office of the Superintendent of Schools in your area. Cordially yours, *(98 words)*

4. Dear Frank: The attached chart will give you visual evidence of the facts I gave you concerning the stocks issued[2]

by our corporation during the past 18 years. As you can see, there was only a gradual rise in the[4] annual dividends paid to our stockholders in the first 10 years; but in the period since then, our[6] stock has doubled in value with a subsequent increase in the size of the dividends declared. (¶) As far as the[8] future is concerned, we are involved in miscellaneous transactions that will create even more substantial[10] profits for us. For this reason, I do not hesitate to advise you to buy our stock as a safe investment[12] for your savings. Yours sincerely, *(125 words)*

5. My dear Sir: This is in response to the letter we received from you in which you made inquiry regarding our[2] charges for typewriter rentals. (¶) We cannot quote a standard rate at this time because many factors are considered[4] in determining the actual cost. For example, we need to know how many machines you will want, the[6] length of time involved, and whether you require manual or electric typewriters. (¶) If you will supply this[8] information on the enclosed card, we will be happy to give you an exact price for our rental service. Yours truly,[10] *(100 words)*

6. Dear Mr. March: I have just had a long conversation with the President and Treasurer of our company[2] about the regrettable situation in which we now find ourselves. As you know, we have been losing a great[4] many of our employees to various companies in the city that offer liberal annual[6] increases in salary, forms of health insurance, extra vacation bonuses, and other financial benefits.[8] (¶) It is obvious that something must be done immediately. For this reason, I am calling a special[10] meeting of the Board of Directors for Friday, April 5, at 3:15. (¶) In the meantime, would you review the[12] list of miscellaneous suggestions that are enclosed so that you may give me your opinion when we meet. Yours[14] truly, *(141 words)*

7. My dear Mr. White: Our firm is anxious to have you transfer your business to us, and we are not too proud to admit[2] it. We know we can satisfy your every need and that

dealing with us will be to our mutual[4] advantage. (¶) Won't you send us a trial order so that we may prove ourselves. Yours truly, *(55 words)*

8. Gentlemen: On August 14 I ordered a glass table top to replace the one I had broken. It arrived[2] yesterday, but I found that it did not fit properly. (¶) I realize now that I made an error when I measured[4] the diameter of the table, and I am writing to ask whether something can be done. I would deeply[6] appreciate any suggestion you can make that will save me the additional expense of ordering a[8] new one. Sincerely, *(83 words)*

Writing Assignment – Lesson 20

1. All those who are graduating this fall should submit applications for the administrative positions open in our company.

2. The annual casualty rate has increased substantially in the past five years, and a variety of safety measures have been proposed by our bureau.

3. All transportation charges will be paid if salesmen submit expense accounts to the office of the treasurer.

4. We are confident that we can create a substantial demand for our product by sending out trial samples of merchandise.

5. Speak to the superintendent in regard to the actual amount of fuel used in the building during the winter months.

6. It is a pleasure to send you a special two-pound gift selection of our famous cheese.

7. This transaction will serve a dual purpose. It will create a great many jobs at the plant and will result in more efficient production.

BRIEF FORM and STANDARD ABBREVIATION REVIEW

Lessons 16 through 20

1. Dear Miss Rose: Several years ago an independent group of men and women, who were particularly[2] interested in the field of education, decided to organize an association of junior and[4] senior high school teachers. (¶) These individuals thought that an organization of this kind would give teachers[6] throughout America a chance to meet and learn of new methods being developed to improve the level of[8] education as a whole. The idea met with immediate success, and the organization grew from an[10] initial membership of 55 to its present total of almost three thousand. (¶) The object of this[12] letter is to tell you that the southeast division of the American Association will hold its annual[14] meeting at the conclusion of the winter term. The date will probably be during the week of January[16] 18, but more definite information will be sent as soon as available. Sincerely yours, *(178 words)*

2. Dear Sir: The superintendent of our warehouse on West Elm Street has informed me that the volume of orders being[2] shipped has increased by approximately 20 percent during the past six months. (¶) In view of these circumstances,[4] I feel we should now consider moving to larger quarters. Therefore, we are looking for a building on the[6] north side of town that will provide us with at least an additional 5,000 square feet of space and with a[8] location no more than a mile or two from the railroad. Very truly yours, *(92 words)*

3. My dear Sir: This will acknowledge receipt of your letter of June 9. (¶) I have known the young man about whom you speak[2] for a number of years. He was once a pupil at our school and was described by his teachers as being unusually[4] intelligent and hard working. I recall that his health was always rather poor, but he was able[6] to hold miscellaneous jobs around town during his summer vacations. When I last saw him, he declared his[8] intention of

applying for a job with the parcel post division of the post office; and I understand[10] that his application was approved. Sincerely yours, *(109 words)*

4. Dear Mr. West: Our organization has set up a research bureau that will collect statistics and figures[2] regarding sales in and around our city. Such information will be of particular interest to[4] manufacturers in this area and will be furnished free of charge. (¶) The signature of your corporation's[6] president on the enclosed card will entitle you to a 12-page descriptive booklet that will give you additional[8] information about this unusual service. Sincerely yours, *(92 words)*

5. Dear Mr. Long: We are sending you 3 nine-ounce samples of our latest product as well as a one-pound box of[2] various cheese we manufacture. (¶) I have also written a memorandum to my secretary to[4] remind her that you are to receive a pair of tickets to our annual food show in September. Yours truly,[6] *(60 words)*

6. Dear Mr. Mark: Our company has decided to build a railway to connect our plant with the main track of the[2] Northwest Railroad. Doing so will enable us to transport our automobiles quickly and efficiently and[4] will help to speed up delivery to all parts of the country. (¶) I understand that you hold the mortgage on the[6] property we have in mind, and I would like to meet with you to discuss the sale of this land. Yours truly, *(78 words)*

–REVIEW–

Lessons 16 through 20

1. Dear Miss Blank: A mutual friend has submitted your name as one who might be interested in a chance to make[2] some extra money in your spare time. (¶) You can do so by selling our beautiful line of Christmas cards and gift

wrappings.[4] We not only pay a liberal amount for each box sold, but we also give a generous bonus to[6] the person in each city who sends us the largest order. (¶) If you feel inclined to accept our offer, you can[8] contact us by phoning the number shown above. We hope to hear from you. Yours truly, *(95 words)*

2. My dear Mr. Able: You are undoubtedly aware of the fact that we will shortly attempt to set up a[2] training program in our factory. The main purpose of this program is to instruct our employees in the proper[4] maintenance of our machinery. We are hopeful that it will also prove useful in helping our men[6] understand the importance of adopting the safety measures you advised in your annual report. (¶) In this[8] connection, I wonder if you could spare the time to speak at one of our sessions. I think you, more than anyone else,[10] could be helpful in getting this point across to the men. (¶) May I hear from you soon? Sincerely yours, *(117 words)*

3. My dear Mrs. Ash: I am very sorry that I could not speak with you myself when you called[2] yesterday. As my secretary told you, I was attending an extremely important conference at the time and was unable[4] to interrupt the meeting to answer the phone. (¶) I did, however, receive the message you left for me[6] and will arrange to transfer your account to our central branch as soon as you notify me of your correct address. (¶)[8] If there is any other way in which I can be of help, please do not hesitate to contact me. Cordially,[10] *(100 words)*

BRIEF FORMS AND STANDARD ABBREVIATIONS

about	ab	as	z
above	bv	ask	sc
absolute, ly	abs	associate	asso
acknowledge	ak	at	a
administrate	ad	auto	A
administration	ad	avenue	ave
advantage	avj	average	av
advertise	adv	be	b
again, st	ag	because	cs
almost	lmo	been	b
already	lr	began	bg
also	lso	begin	bg
always	lw	benefit	bnf
am	⌒	between	bl
America, n	a	billion	B
amount	aml	both	bo
an	a	boulevard	blvd
and	&	bureau	Bu
appreciate	ap	business	bs
approximate, ly	apx	busy	bz
are	r	but	b
around	r	buy	b

by	b	correct	Kc
call	cl	country	c/
came	k	credit	cr
can	c	customer	K
capital	cap	day	d
catalog	cal	deal	dl
cents	c	declare	dec
certificate	cerl	definite, ly	dfn
certify	cerl	deliver	dl
charge	Cg	delivery	dl
child	ch	department	dpl
children	chn	describe	des
Christmas	Xrs	description	des
circumstance	c/	develop	dv
collect	cc	difficult	dfk
come	k	difficulty	dfk
committee	k	direct	D
company	co	discount	dis
conclusion	kclj	doctor	dr
consider	ks	dollar, s	d
continue	ku	during	du
contract	Kc	East	E
corporation	corp	easy	ez

entitle	ntl	future	fC
envelope	env	given	gv
establish	esl	go	g
even	vn	good	g
evening	vn̲	government	gvl
ever	E	great	ḡ
every	E	had	h
extra	X	has	as
extraordinary	Xo	have	v
fail	fl	he	h
federal	fed	held	hl
feel	fl	help	hp
feet	fl	him	h
field	fld	his	s
figure	fg	hole	hl
find	fi	hour	r
fine	fi	hundred	H
fire	fr	idea	id
firm	F	immediate, ly	ida
foot	fl	important	ip
for	f	in	n
full	fu	inch	in
fully	fu	independent	ind

individual, ly	ndv	merchandise	mdse
initial, ly	ix	mile	mi
intelligence	inl	million	M
intelligent, ly	inl	minimum	mn
invoice	inv	month	mo
is	s	minute	mn
it	t	miscellaneous	msc
junior	jr	mortgage	mg
keep	cp	move	mv
kind	ci	necessarily	nec
known	no	necessary	nec
letter	L	North	N
life	lf	not	n
like	lc	note	nt
line	li	number	no
little	ll	object	ob
magazine	mag	of	v
man	m-	on	o
manufacture	mfr	once	c/
many	m	only	nl
maximum	max	open	op
member	mB	opinion	opn
memorandum	memo	opportunity	opt

order	O	prove	pv
organization	og	public	pb
organize	og	publish	pb
other	T	pull	pu
ounce	oz	pupil	pup
our	r	purchase	pC
out	ou	put	p
over	O	question	q
page	p	railroad	rr
pair	pr	railway	ry
parcel post	pp	real, ly	rl
particular, ly	P	regular, ly	reg
percent	pc	regulation	reg
perhaps	pps	represent	rep
place	pl	representative	rep
please	—p	result	rsl
poor	po	room	r⌒
popular	pop	sale	S
post office	po	sample	sa⌒
pound	lb	satisfaction	sal
president	P	satisfactory	sal
price	ps	satisfy	sal
probable, ly	pb	save	sv

school	scl	the	.
second	sec	their	[illegible]
secretary	sec	there	[illegible]
senior	sr	they	ty
several	sv	this	th
shall	S	those	tos
she	S	thought	to
ship	S	thousand	Td
signature	sig	throughout	Tuo
situation	sit	to	t
small	sm	too	to
South	S	total	tol
square	sq	under	u
stop	so	until	ul
street	st	up	p
subject	sj	upon	pn
subscribe	sub	usual, ly	x
subscription	sub	very	v
success	suc	vice-president	VP
successful, ly	suc	volume	vol
superintendent	supt	warehouse	whs
telephone	tel	was	3
that	ta	we	e

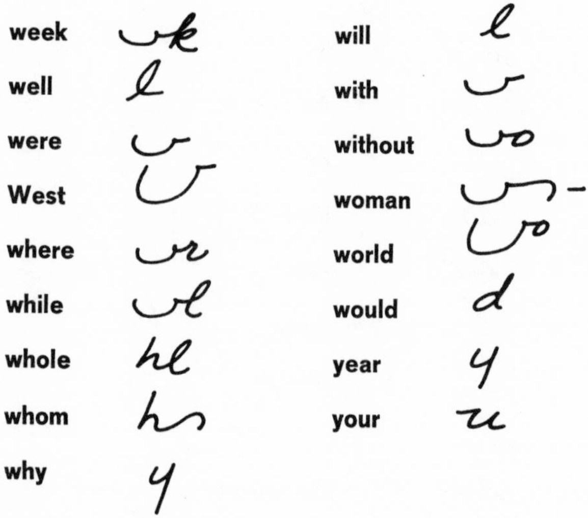

week
well
were
West
where
while
whole
whom
why
will
with
without
woman
world
would
year
your

NOW SUCCESS IS AT YOUR FINGERTIPS!

Very quickly you will have achieved your goal – a wonderfully satisfying career as a secretary. You have completed all of the theory of *Speedwriting* shorthand and have learned all the principles which make up this very efficient system. You have not only become familiar with the rules but you have had concentrated practice in writing the 3,000 words of highest frequency, which represent approximately 90 percent of everyday English. These words will form the basic framework of the dictation you will be taking on the job.

Now with confidence and enthusiasm you can move on to the final phase of your shorthand training – building speed and the automatization of an ever-increasing vocabulary. You will accomplish this by taking two types of live dictation after you have successfully passed your Final Theory Test.

The first of these methods is called *repetitive dictation* or *speed building.* As a part of this program, you will be assigned a lesson from the dictation book as homework each day. You will write each of the letters several times in *Speedwriting* shorthand; and you will, of course, check your *Speedwriting* Dictionary for any word which is unfamiliar to you. When you return to class the following day, these letters will be dictated again and again at higher and higher speeds. This repetitive process serves the purpose of making the words a part of your working vocabulary and will help you to develop a greater and more varied automatic response.

The second type of dictation to which you will be introduced is known as *unfamiliar dictation.* You will learn to take dictation from material that you have not heard before – just as you will shortly be doing from your employer. In this class, too, you will take dictation tests at various speed levels and, having passed the last of them, you will be completely confident in your ability to take dictation accurately and quickly from any employer.

Refining your dictation skill is only part of your training though. You will also learn to transcribe your notes with accuracy and speed, and you will learn to turn out a letter which is a credit to you and the company you will represent. You will master this skill too in the final stage of your dictation course.

Your *Speedwriting* shorthand course has been planned with one objective – to enable you adequately to fulfill every office dictation requirement. If you apply yourself diligently and intelligently, you will be assured of future success when you go out into the business world.

LETTER PLACEMENT CHART

The placement of a letter on a page depends upon the length of the letter. For proper balance, both the margins and the position of the inside address must be varied for letters of different lengths. Eventually, a glance at your notes will enable you to judge the placement of your letter, but this requires a good deal of practice and experience. For the present, make use of the procedure given below as a guide to proper placement. Type date 14 line spaces from top of page.

WORDS	LENGTH OF LINE	LINES FROM DATE TO INSIDE ADDRESS
50	4 inches	5
75	4 inches	5
100	4 inches	5
125	5 inches	5
150	5 inches	5
175	5 inches	5
200	6 inches	5
225	6 inches	5
250	6 inches	5
300	6 inches	5

ENVELOPES, ADDRESSING

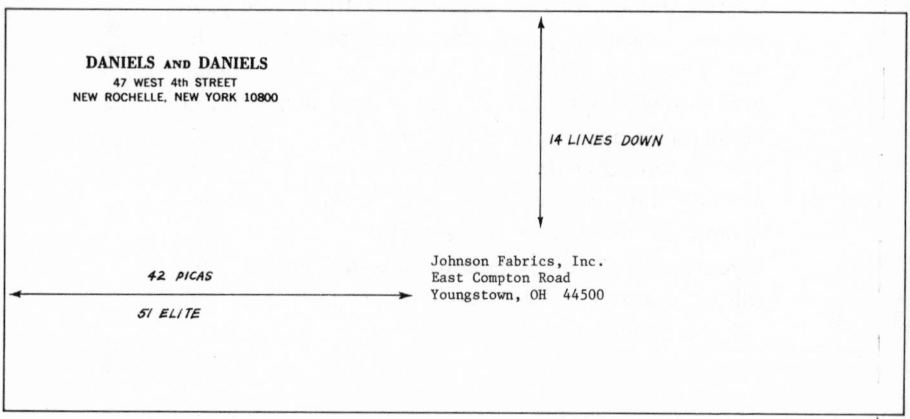

STANDARD-BLOCK STYLE LETTER

44 Years of Service

DANIELS and DANIELS

47 WEST 4th STREET • NEW ROCHELLE, NEW YORK 10800

Phone 673-7400

```
                                          x
                                          January 14, 19--

x
x
x
x
x
Johnson Fabrics, Inc.
East Compton Road
Youngstown, OH  44500
x
Gentlemen:
x
----------------------------------------------------------------------
--------------------------------------------------------------------
---------------------------------------------------------------------
----------------------------------------------------------------------
--------------------------------
x
----------------------------------------------------------------------
--------------------------------------------------------------------
-----------------------------------------------------------------------
----------------------------------------------------------------------
---------------------------------
x
---------------------------------------------------------------------
-----------------------------------------------------------------------
------------------------------------------------
                                          x
                                          Very truly yours,
                                          x
                                          DANIELS and DANIELS
                                          x
                                          x
                                          x
                                          Edward R. Jones
                                          Director
x
ERJ:jc
Enclosure
```

NOTES